THE POEMS OF CHARLES REZNIKOFF

BOOKS BY CHARLES REZNIKOFF

POETRY AND VERSE DRAMA

Rhythms (1918)
Rhythms II (1919)
Poems (1920)
Uriel Acosta: A Play & A Fourth Group of Verse (1921)
Chatterton, The Black Death & Meriwether Lewis, three plays (1922)
Coral & Captive Israel, two plays (1923)
Five Groups of Verse (1927)
Nine Plays (1927)
Jerusalem the Golden (1934)
In Memoriam: 1933 (1934)
Separate Way (1936)
Going To and Fro and Walking Up and Down (1941)
Inscriptions: 1944–1956 (1959)
By the Waters of Manhattan: Selected Verse (1962)
Testimony: The United States 1885–1890: Recitative (1965)
Testimony: The United States 1891–1900: Recitative (1968)
By the Well of Living and Seeing & The Fifth Book of the Maccabees
     (1969)
By the Well of Living and Seeing: New and Selected Poems 1918–1973
     (1974)
Holocaust (1975)
Poems 1918–1936: Volume 1 of The Complete Poems of Charles Reznikoff
     (1976)
Poems 1937–1975: Volume 2 of The Complete Poems of Charles Reznikoff
     (1977)
Poems 1918–1975: The Complete Poems of Charles Reznikoff (1989)
The Poems of Charles Reznikoff 1918–1975 (2005)

THE POEMS OF
CHARLES REZNIKOFF
1918–1975

Edited by Seamus Cooney

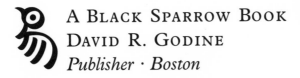
A BLACK SPARROW BOOK
DAVID R. GODINE
Publisher · Boston

This is
A Black Sparrow Book
published in 2005 by
David R. Godine, Publisher
Post Office Box 450
Jaffrey, New Hampshire 03450
www.blacksparrowbooks.com

Book design and composition by Carl W. Scarbrough
The Black Sparrow Books pressmark is by Julian Waters
www.waterslettering.com

LIBRARY OF CONGRESS CATALOGING-IN-PUBLICATION DATA
Reznikoff, Charles, 1894–1976.
The poems of Charles Reznikoff : 1918–1975 / edited by Seamus Cooney.—1st ed.
    p.   cm.
"A Black Sparrow book."
Revised ed. of: *Poems 1918–1975,* published in 1989 by Black Sparrow Press.
Includes bibliographical references and index.
ISBN-13: 978-1-57423-204-2 (hardcover : alk. paper)
ISBN-10: 1-57423-204-5 (hardcover : alk. paper)
ISBN-13: 978-1-57423-203-5 (pbk. : alk. paper)
ISBN-10: 1-57423-203-7 (pbk. : alk. paper)
I. Cooney, Seamus. II. Title.
PS3535.E98A17   2005
811'.52—dc22
              2005021218

FIRST EDITION
Printed in the United States of America

TO THE MEMORY OF
MARIE SYRKIN REZNIKOFF
1899–1989
"STILL AGLOW / THROUGH TWILIGHT AND DARKNESS"

CONTENTS

who wrote
in the great world

small for this is a way

to enter
the light on the kitchen

tables wide-

spread as the mountains'
light this is

heroic this is
the poem

to write

in the great
world small

—George Oppen

FOREWORD

The present volume is a revised edition of *Poems 1918–1975: The Complete Poems of Charles Reznikoff*, published in 1989 by Black Sparrow Press. That book reprinted both volumes of Charles Reznikoff's *Complete Poems—Poems 1918–1936* (1976) and *Poems 1937–1975* (1977)—retaining the separate pagination of each. For the present volume, the text has been reset and repaginated, the notes and index have been reorganized, and a few small corrections have been made silently. I have also added a chronology of the poet's life and, as an appendix, an essay found among Reznikoff's papers after his death that is his most comprehensive statement on the craft of poetry as he practiced it.

My chief purpose has been to establish authoritative texts of all the poems that Reznikoff collected in book form, as well as of a handful of late, uncollected items. (Poems from the various volumes of the uncompleted *Testimony: The United States 1885–1915* and the related book-length work *Holocaust* are not included here.) No attempt has been made to reconcile Reznikoff's inconsistencies in spelling (for example, "motor car," "motor-car," "motorcar") except in the few cases where inconsistencies occur within a poem or poem-sequence. The author's latest revisions have been followed in every case, with one qualification. When Reznikoff made a selection of his poems for the New Directions volume *By the Waters of Manhattan* (1962), he adopted for his early poems there reprinted the typographical style he had begun using only in his later work: that is, he dropped the convention of capital letters at the beginning of each verse line (first done in *Jerusalem the Golden*, 1934), assigned numbers to all the poems, and used arabic in preference to roman numerals. I have applied these practices consistently throughout this book. The author and I collaborated on the editing of his poems from *Rhythms* through *Separate Way*. My work on the later poems, completed after Reznikoff's death, draws on the author's corrected "working copies" of his books as sources for his final intentions, on revised version he sent me during the preparation of my edition of *By the Well of Living and Seeing: New and Selected Poems 1918–1973* (1974), and on unpublished typescript and manuscript drafts found among the Reznikoff papers (now on deposit in the Archive for New Poetry, University of California, San Diego).

For the reader interested in the process of poetic growth and revision, the Notes gives full details (I hope unobtrusively), together with the texts of poems the author omitted from later printings.

SEAMUS COONEY
Portage, Michigan
2005

Rhythms

The stars are hidden,
the lights are out;
the tall black houses
are ranked about.

I beat my fists
on the stout doors,
no answering steps
come down the floors.

I have walked until
I am faint and numb;
from one dark street
to another I come.

The comforting
winds are still.

This is a chaos
through which I stumble,
till I reach the void
and down I tumble.

The stars will then
be out forever;
the fists unclenched,
the feet walk never,

and all I say
blown by the wind
away.

The dead are walking silently.

I sank them six feet underground,
the dead are walking and no sound.

I raised on each a brown hill,
the dead are walking slow and still.

So one day, tired of the sky and host of stars,
I'll thrust the tinsel by.

I step into the fishy pool
as if into a cool
vault.
I, too, become
cold-blooded, dumb.

The dead man lies in the street.
They spread a sack over his bleeding head.
It drizzles. Gutter and walks are black.

His wife now at her window,
the supper done, the table set,
waits for his coming out of the wet.

They dug her grave so deep
no voice can creep to her.

She can feel no stir
of joy when her girl sings,

and quietly she lies
when her girl cries.

On Brooklyn Bridge I saw a man drop dead.
It meant no more than if he were a sparrow.

Above us rose Manhattan;
below, the river spread to meet sea and sky.

8

I met in a merchant's place
Diana:
lithe body and flowerlike face.

Through the woods I had looked for her
and beside the waves.

9

The shopgirls leave their work
quietly.

Machines are still, tables and chairs
darken.

The silent rounds of mice and roaches begin.

10

Hair and faces glossy with sweat in August
at night through narrow streets glaring with lights
people as if in funeral processions;
on stoops weeds in stagnant pools,
at windows waiting for a wind that never comes.
Only, a lidless eye, the sun again.

No one else in the street but a wind blowing,
store-lamps dimmed behind frosted panes,
stars, like the sun broken and scattered in bits.

11

I walked through the lonely marsh
among the white birches.

Above the birches rose
three crows,
croaking, croaking.

The trumpets blare war
and the streets are filled with the echoes.

Wringing, wringing his pierced hands,
he walks in a wood where once a flood
washed the ground into loose white sand;
and the trees stand each a twisted cross,
smooth and white with loss of leaves and bark,
together like warped yards and masts
of a fleet at anchor centuries.
No blasts come to the hollow of these dead;
long since the water has gone from the stony bed.
No fields and streets for him, his pathway runs
among these skeletons, through these white sands,
wringing, wringing his pierced hands.

13

ROMANCE

The troopers are riding, are riding by,
the troopers are riding to kill and die
that a clean flag may cleanly fly.

They touch the dust in their homes no more,
they are clean of the dirt of shop and store,
and they ride out clean to war.

14

How shall we mourn you who are killed and wasted,
sure that you would not die with your work unended,
as if the iron scythe in the grass stops for a flower?

15

Her kindliness is like the sun
toward dusk shining through a tree.

Her understanding is like the sun,
shining through mist on a width of sea.

The fingers of your thoughts
are moulding your face
ceaselessly.

The wavelets of your thoughts
are washing your face
beautiful.

17

When you sang moving your body proudly
before me wondering who you were
suddenly I remembered, Messalina.

18

The sea's white teeth
nibble the cliff;
the cliff is a man,
unafraid.

She eats his strength
little by little,
his might will be lost
in her depths.

19

My work done, I lean on the window-sill,
watching the dripping trees.
The rain is over, the wet pavement shines.
From the bare twigs
rows of drops like shining buds are hanging.

Rhythms II

I have not even been in the fields,
nor lain my fill in the soft foam,
and here you come blowing, cold wind.

2

VAUDEVILLE

I leave the theatre,
keeping step, keeping step to the music.
It sticks to my feet,
stepped into dung.

Night falls
in still flakes.

3

I knocked. A strange voice answered.
So they, too, have moved away.

We had walked up and down the block many times
until alone.

I wonder where they have moved to.

4

I look across the housetops,
through the leaves in a black pattern:
where are you hidden, moon?

Surely I saw her,
broad-bosomed and golden,
coming toward us.

5

The winter afternoon darkens.
The shoemaker bends close to the shoe,
his hammer raps faster.

An old woman waits,
rubbing the cold from her hands.

6

Stubborn flies buzzing
in the morning when she wakes.

The flat roofs, higher, lower,
chimneys, water-tanks, cornices.

7

SCRUBWOMAN

One shoulder lower,
with unsure step like a bear erect,
the smell of the wet black rags that she cleans with about her.

Scratching with four stiff fingers her half-bald head,
smiling.

8

In the shop, she, her mother, and grandmother,
thinking at times of women at windows in still streets,
or women reading, a glow on resting hands.

9

THE IDIOT

With green stagnant eyes,
arms and legs
loose ends of string in a wind,

keep smiling at your father.

10

On the kitchen shelf the dusty medicine bottles;
she in her room heaped under a sheet,
and men and women coming in with clumsy steps.

11

She who worked patiently,
her children grown,
lies in her grave patiently.

12

Beggars about the streets
pray to God between set teeth.

Up by star and star
until the outer frozen blackness,

down the earth between stones
until black rocks in ledge on ledge.

13
The Park in Winter

It rains.
The elms curve into clouds of twigs.
The lawns are empty.

14

Dark early and only the river shines
like grey ice, the ships moored fast.

15
Epidemic

Streamers of crepe idling before doors.

16

Shadows, mice whisk over the unswept floor,
tumble through rustling papers.

Squeeze into desk drawers,
biting the paper into yellowed flakes
and leaving crumbs of filth.

The sandwiches are elaborate affairs:
toast, bacon, toast, chicken, toast.

We sip our coffee watching the rouged women
walk quickly to their seats, unsmiling, contemptuous.

The imperious dawn comes
to the clink of milk bottles
and round-shouldered sparrows twittering.

We heard no step in the hall.
She came
sudden as a rainbow.

A white curtain turning in an open window.

A swan, dipping a white neck in the trees' shadow,
hardly beating the water with golden feet.

Sorrow before her
was gone like noise from a street,
snow falling.

The horses keep tossing their heads and stamp the hollow flooring,
wheel knocks into wheel
as the ferry glides out into a damp wind.

The coal-truck horses, three abreast, ponderously,
sides and rumps shaking.

With blown manes and tails
the horses fling themselves along lifting their riders.

The thin horses step beside the lawns in the park,
the small hoofs newly oiled,
heads high, their red nostrils taking the air.

22

Twilight

No stars
in the blue curve
of the heavens,
no wind.

Far off,
a white horse
in the green gloom
of the meadow.

POEMS

The sun was low over the blue morning water;
the waves of the bay were silent on the smooth beach,
where in the night the silver fish had died gasping.

Old men and boys search the wet garbage with fingers
and slip pieces in bags.

This fat old man has found the hard end of a bread
and bites it.

The girls outshout the machines
and she strains for their words, blushing.

Soon she, too, will speak
their speech glibly.

The pedlar who goes from shop to shop,
has seated himself on the stairs in the dim hallway,
and the basket of apples upon his knees, breathes the odor.

Her work was to count linings—
the day's seconds in dozens.

They have built red factories along Lake Michigan,
and the purple refuse coils like congers in the green depths.

The house-wreckers have left the door and a staircase,
now leading to the empty room of night.

Ghetto Funeral

Followed by his lodge, shabby men stumbling over the cobblestones,
and his children, faces red and ugly with tears, eyes and eyelids red,
in the black coffin in the black hearse the old man.

No longer secretly grieving
that his children are not strong enough to go the way he wanted to go
and was not strong enough.

9

Showing a torn sleeve, with stiff and shaking fingers the old man
pulls off a bit of the baked apple, shiny with sugar,
eating with reverence food, the great comforter.

10

Sleepless, breathing the black air, he heard footsteps along the street,
and click—the street-lamp was out;
darkness jumped like a black cat upon his chest.

Dawn: the window became grey,
the bed-clothes were lit up and his sleeping wife's head,
as if the darkness had melted into that heap of loose hair.

Soon her eyes would open, disks of light blue, strange in a Jewess.
He would turn away; the eyes would look curiously, the way they had
        been looking for months,
how are you getting on? still not doing well?
And her left hand would raise itself slowly and pull on the lobe of
        her left ear;
and her eyes shine with a slight pity, the way a woman looks at a mouse
        in a trap.
No longer the calm look with which she had greeted him,
when he was chief clerk in a store in that Russian town
which he now carried about like picture postal-cards in a pocket,
the town where he had shone in the light of the big store.

Day: the noise of splashing water, his children in underwear thudding
        about with bare feet,
pulling on clothes in a hurry and bending over to lace shoes.

Soon the door would close, again and again, all would be gone,
the elder to shops, the younger ones to school.
For these he had come to America that they might study and the boys
        be free from army service,
to lift and spread them as he had been doing, boughs of himself,
        the trunk.
Now the elder were going to work and could study only at night,
snipping bits for years, perhaps ten or more, to make their patched
        learning,
and pooling wages to buy food and lodging for the younger children,
        his wife, and himself.
He could only bring them food from the kitchen,
or run downstairs to the grocer's for pickles or a bottle of ketchup—
to make life tastier,
to try to stick hairs in the hide of life and make it a fur to wrap
        them snug.
Forty years in a store where business was done leisurely over glasses
        of tea,
and now to walk the streets and meet men hasty and abrupt,
between tenements and their barrels heaped with ashes and garbage.
Younger relatives now excused themselves after a few words
and hurried into the noise of their shops to some matter of their own.
If only his business were not a flower-pot into which he had spilled
        his savings
day by day carefully and had spilled loans—
and nothing came up from the black earth.

The day was the first warm day of spring.
The sunlight through the windowpanes fell in large living oblongs
        on the floor.
He opened a window; the air blew in, warm and fragrant.
The sunlight fell on his shoes, cracked and gaping, his faded trousers,
        the bottoms frayed.

In winter, when rain drummed sullen marches on pavement
        and windowpanes,
or the streets were heaped with snow turning black,
his own music was sung and his despair imaged.
Now he was forgotten—easily, like the thought of somebody else's
        sorrow.
The yards and fire-escapes were glinting with sunlight, and the
        tall fences,
dirtied by rain, their rows of nails on top bleeding rust.

Women were opening windows and shaking out clothes,
his own wife had gone to the grocer's or butcher's, his children were
        at work or school;
only he was useless, like an old pot left in the kitchen for a while.

He pulled down the window-blind and laid himself near the stove.
He folded his coat under his head, over the floor's hardness.
The pour of gas sickened him, he was half-minded to pull the rubber tube
        out of his mouth;
but he felt dizzy, too weak to move.

11

She sat by the window opening into the airshaft,
and looked across the parapet
at the new moon.

She would have taken the hairpins out of her carefully coiled hair,
and thrown herself on the bed in tears;
but he was coming and her mouth had to be pinned into a smile.
If he would have her, she would marry whatever he was.

A knock. She lit the gas and opened her door.
Her aunt and the man—skin loose under his eyes, the face slashed
        with wrinkles.
"Come in," she said as gently as she could and smiled.

12

The house was pitch-dark.
He entered his room. Books and papers were heaped over the floor.
He stuck a candle in a corner, and on his knees began to go through
        the papers.
He must finish that night: the next day the others would move in.

Yes, here was the bold handwriting, the bundle of letters tied together.
He took these into the kitchen. He did not need a light:
he ought to know the way, had walked it so often.

He crammed all into the stove and lit a match.
The fire ran over the surface and died out.
He tore the letters into bits and lit match after match,
until nothing was left but brown pieces with black, crumbled edges.

As the papers twisted and opened, tormented by fire,
Darling had stood out in the writing against the flame
for a moment before the ink was grey on black ash that fell apart.

Here was the bedroom where she had been sick.
Her teeth fell out; before the end her nose rotted off.

He uncovered a bunch of dried flowers and white gauze—
her bridal veil and bouquet left in the rubbish.
He went back to the kitchen stove. The gauze flew up in a great flame,
      but the flowers remained—blackened stalks.
Now he was through. He closed door after door softly behind him.

13

From where she lay she could see the snow crossing the darkness
      slowly,
thick about the arc-lights like moths in summer.

She could just move her head. She had been lying so for months.
Her son was growing tall and broad-shouldered, his face becoming like
      that of her father,
dead now for years.

She lay under the bed-clothes as if she, too, were covered with snow,
calm, facing the blackness of night,
through which the snow fell in the crowded movement of stars.

Dead, nailed in a box, her son was being sent to her,
through fields and cities cold and white with snow.

14

The twigs tinge the winter sky
brown.

15

A slender tree, alone in the fields,
between the roofs of the town and the woods like a low hill.

In the open
the birds are faintly overheard.

16

AUGUST

The city breaks in houses to the sea, uneasy with waves.
In the streets truck-horses, muscles sliding under the steaming hides,
pound the sparks flying about their hoofs.

17

In the streets children beneath tall houses at games greedily,
remembering clocks, the house-cats lapping time.

18

Kitten, pressed into a rude shape by cart wheels,
an end to your slinking away and trying to hide behind ash-cans.

19

The baby woke with curved, confiding fingers.
The gas had been turned down until it was only a yellow glimmer.
A rat walked slowly from under the washtub.

20

Ships dragged into the opaque green of the sea,
visible winds flinging houses apart—
and here the poplar roots lifting the pavement an inch.

21

Speaking and speaking again words like silver bubbles,
we walk at dusk through rain.

The sky has grown black with a tinge of red from the street-lamps;
triangular pools form in the square cracks of the pavement,
noisy with rain.

22

Suddenly we noticed that we were in darkness;
so we went into the house and lit the lamp.

The talk fell apart and bit by bit slid into a lake.
At last we rose and bidding each other good night went to our rooms.

In and about the house darkness lay, a black fog;
and each on his bed spoke to himself alone, making no sound.

23

Hour after hour in a rocking-chair on the porch,
hearing the wind in the shade trees.

At times a storm comes up and the dust is blown in long curves
      along the street,
over the carts driven slowly, drivers and horses nodding.

Years are thrown away as if I were immortal,
the nights spent in talking

shining words, sometimes, like fireflies in the darkness—
lighting and going out and after all no light.

24

I walked in a street, head high,
when a thug began beating a passer-by.

I gave no help with blow or cry,
but hurried on glad it wasn't I.

25
APHRODITE VRANIA

The ceaseless weaving of the uneven water.

26
MOONLIT NIGHT

The trees' shadows lie in black pools on the lawns.

27
APRIL

The stiff lines of the twigs
blurred by buds.

28

I have watched trees and the moon and walked on—
she would be beauty to go wherever I go.

29

Still much to read, but too late.
I turn out the light.

The leaves of the tree are green beside the street-lamp;
the wind hardly blows and the tree makes no noise.

Tomorrow up early,
the crowded street-car, the factory.

30

A clerk tiptoeing the office floor
in a flurry of insignificant stuff;
or with samples from store to store
to speak politely to the gruff,
entering timidly the door,
trying to bow and smile it right
with smiles seen not true enough,
a young man who was so bright.

They spoke proudly and well,
fearing and revering none,
had no longing to buy and sell
or chatter with girls half the night;
what at last have these men done,
the young men who were so bright?

A Fourth Group of Verse

1

Sunday Walks in the Suburbs

On stones mossed with hot dust, no shade but the thin, useless shadows
    of roadside grasses;
into the wood's gloom, staring back at the blue flowers on stalks thin
    as threads.

The green slime—a thicket of young trees standing in brown water;
with knobs like muscles, a naked tree stretches up,
dead; and a dead duck, head sunk in the water as if diving.

The tide is out. Only a pool is left on the creek's stinking mud.
Someone has thrown a washboiler away.
On the bank a heap of cans;
rats, covered with rust, creep in and out.
The white edges of the clouds like veining in a stone.

2

Scared dogs looking backwards with patient eyes;
at windows stooping old women, wrapped in shawls;
old men, wrinkled as knuckles, on the stoops.

A bitch, backbone and ribs showing in the sinuous back,
sniffed for food, her swollen udder nearly rubbing along the pavement.

Once a toothless woman opened her door,
chewing a slice of bacon that hung from her mouth like a tongue.

This is where I walked night after night;
this is where I walked away many years.

3

Beggar Woman

When I was four years old my mother led me to the park.
The spring sunshine was not too warm. The street was almost empty.
The witch in my fairy-book came walking along.
She stooped to fish some mouldy grapes out of the gutter.

4

RAILWAY STATION AT CLEVELAND

Under cloud on cloud the lake is black;
wheeling locomotives in the yard
pour their smoke into the crowded sky.

5

DRIZZLE

Between factories the grease coils along the river.
Tugs drag their guts of smoke, like beetles stepped on.

6

Out of the hills the trees bulge;
the sky hangs in lumps of cloud.

7

All night the wind blew.
In the morning the deck-hands
were running around to warm up.
The boat rose and fell
on the little waves.
Now and then it hit
a chopping wave.
The wind blew the white caps of the water
into spray.
Far off the wild geese
were flying over the lake.

The lake was ridged with waves,
rolling between the shores.
The northern shore was cliff,
barren of houses or trees;
on the flat southern shore
towns spread out like patches.
There was no rest from the wind:
it blew steadily colder.

The deck-hands ran about,
beating their arms over their breasts.
The wild geese far away
were flying south in squads.

8

With broad bosom and hips, her head thrown back,
she parades, her high heels clacking,
having conquered troublesome youth and not yet afraid of age.

9

Head bowed beneath her black turban, she glances up at her daughter
who eyes in the mirror herself, yellow hair and beautiful face.

10

A TAPESTRY

Isolde of the White Hands and her knights, holding their noses
    and laughing
at prisoners whose bellies soldiers open, pulling the guts into basins.

11

VISITING

I

Almost midnight. "Good night." "Good night."
I close the heavy door behind me.
The black courtyard smells of water: it has been raining.
What were we talking about?

II

He leans back along the sofa. I talk. His fingers twitch at his
    bath-robe.
I talk. I turn my pockets inside out.
In his oblique eyes a polite disdain.

This noise in the subway will sound no louder than the wind in trees;
you, too, will be used to it. After a while you will forget to care
whether you ride in subways or on horses.

13

Sparrows scream at the dawn one note:
how should they learn melody
in the street's noises?

14

EVENING

The trees in the windless field like a herd asleep.

15

INDIAN SUMMER

The men in the field are almost through stacking rows of pale
    yellow cornstalks.
On the lawn a girl is raking the leaves into a fire.

16

We children used to cross the orchard, the brown earth covered
    with little green apples,
into the field beyond;
the grass came up over our knees,
there were so many flowers we did not care to pick any—
daisies and yellow daisies, goldenrod and buttercups.
It was so hot the field smelt of cake baking.

17

After dinner, Sunday afternoons, we boys would walk slowly
to the lots between the streets and the marshes;
and seated under the pale blue sky would watch the ball game—
in a noisy, joyous crowd, lemonade men out in the fringe tinkling their
    bells beside their yellow carts.

As we walked back, the city stretched its rows of houses across
     the lots—
light after light, as the lamplighter went his way and women lit the gas
     in kitchens to make supper.

18

Swiftly the dawn became day. I went into the street.
Loudly and cheerfully the sparrows chirped.
The street-lamps were still lit, the sky pale and brightening.
Hidden in trees and on the roofs,
loudly and cheerfully the sparrows chirped.

19

He showed me the album. "But this?" I asked, surprised at such beauty.
I knew his sister, her face somewhat the picture's—coarsened.
"My mother before her marriage."
Coming in, I had met
her shrivelled face and round shoulders.
Now, after the day's work, his father at cards with friends
still outshouted the shop's wheels.
Afterwards, when I left, I had to go through their candy store
with its one showcase of candy,
in little heaps in little saucers, ever so many for a penny.
They kept no lights in the window. A single gas jet flared in the
     empty store.

20

It had long been dark, though still an hour before supper-time.
The boy stood at the window behind the curtain.
The street under the black sky was bluish white with snow.
Across the street, where the lot sloped to the pavement,
boys and girls were going down on sleds.
The boys were after him because he was a Jew.

At last his father and mother slept. He got up and dressed.
In the hall he took his sled and went out on tiptoe.
No one was in the street. The slide was worn smooth and slippery—
     just right.
He laid himself on the sled and shot away. He went down only twice.

He stood knee-deep in snow:
no one was in the street, the windows were darkened;
those near the street-lamps were ashine, but the rooms inside were dark;
on the street were long shadows of clods of snow.
He took his sled and went back into the house.

21

Grandfather was growing blind. He sat in his chair beside the window.
He went out of the house only on holy days—to synagogue.
Rosh Ha-Shonoh the boy led him to Brownsville, both afraid.
Nothing happened. But on the way back a boy, driving a grocer's wagon,
    drove near them
and leaning out, cracked his whip above their heads.

Yom Kippur Uncle went with Grandfather.
It was night and they had not come. They should have been home
    by twilight to break their fast.
The boy went down to the stoop to wait.
Grandfather was coming alone.
"Where's Uncle?" Grandfather did not answer. In his hurry upstairs
    he stumbled.
He went to his chair beside the window and sat looking into the night.
Tears rolled out of his blind eyes and fell upon his hands.
Uncle came, bare-headed, blood oozing out of his hair.

22

His sickness over, he was still abed.
He saw through the window when it was unfrosted,
clouds and a tree's branch.
Birds crossed the sky,
or a sparrow hopped from twig to twig.
He watched, becoming quiet as the branch;
it seemed to him that his blood was cool as sap.
When he moved hands or body, he moved slowly,
the branch's way at twilight.
His parents thought merely that he was still weak.

March he was well. Often when he came into his room,
he went to the window for a few minutes and stood watching the tree.
So he watched it bud and the little leaves and the leaves grown large
    and the leaves color and fall.

His parents had lost their money. They sold the house and were to
    move away.
He went up to his room for the last time.
The trunk of the tree, branches and twigs were still.
He thought, The tree is symmetrical . . . and whatever grows . . .
    in shape . . . and in change during the years. So is my life . . .
    and all lives.
He went down the stairs singing happily.
His father said, "There's so much trouble—and he sings."

23

At six o'clock it was pitch-dark. It might have been after midnight
    in the city and no lamps lit along the streets.
He would have liked to hide in the city from that sky of stars.
Beside bushes and thin, leafless trees he walked upon the frozen clods
    and ruts.
There was no wind across that blackness of fields and lakes;
only the sound of his own feet knocking on the road.
There the stars were poured, and there scattered. He thought,
The symmetry in growth and life on earth, our sense of order,
    is not controlling in the universe.

24

Their boarder had come to America before his wife and children.
He sat at the table working at a beginner's book in English.
In a moment of pity she began to teach him.
Once, when her mother was out marketing, he took hold of her hand
    and fondled it.
She snatched it away. She tried to go on with the lesson as if nothing
    had happened,
but for some time she could feel her heart pounding.
She decided to tell her mother nothing because it might worry her.
Maybe it was just a way to show his thanks. Besides, she was ashamed.
The next night he sat down to his lesson as if nothing had happened;
the lessons went on smoothly even with her mother away.

One evening she almost danced about the kitchen at her work: they had
    taken their last examination that morning,
school would soon close, and the summer vacation begin.
In the afternoon she had gone to Central Park. The girls raced over
    the meadow, noisy as birds at dawn.

After supper she and the boarder sat down to their lesson.
The color in her face and eyes had deepened. She smiled and held
     her face close to his in her eagerness to teach.
Her mother was going out to get a mouthful of fresh air after her day
     in the shop.
"It's so nice in the street, why don't you come?" "I'll be soon through,
     Mamma."
His hand was resting on the back of her chair. He pressed her to him.
     She tried to free herself
and drew her head back. He kept kissing her throat, his hands trying
     to pin down her arms.
Suddenly she was limp. He let go. She was looking at him, her mouth
     open, gasping.
She had pushed back her chair and was running out of the door.
She wondered that she was not falling she went down the stairs so fast.

25

The trees at the end of the lawn were still as cliffs.
He could see a bit of the moon, a white pebble embedded in the
     blue sky.

On the hour the bell in Switzler Hall tolled.
The strokes sank into the stillness of the afternoon.

For a while in the sunny paths that led to the colleges,
too far away to have their speech or steps on the gravel heard,
girls and men were walking.
Lying on the warm grass he rhymed:

Love, let us lie down here
on the warm grass,
glad that we are so near.

Watch on the shores of sleep
the still waves pass,
feel that sea's languid air
move in our hair,

and turn at times to trace
in quiet wise,
each other's smiling face
and sleepy eyes.

26

He woke in the dawn and saw in front of the house the treetops
        and pale sky beyond,
the darkness between the trees fading, and then the trees clear in
        the fresh blue day.

The dew lay in large drops over the grass beside the walk.
Birds were hopping about, robins large among the sparrows,
and from the bay gulls swung silently overhead.

The smell of coffee filled the screened porch. Her glance bid him
        welcome.
The sunlight edged its way along, and when she walked through it,
her yellow hair and the white flesh of her hands shone.

27

On the counter were red slabs and rolls of beef. Bolognas hung along
        the walls and from the ceiling.
He carried his sliced bologna and two cents worth of bread to a table.
She came in and flung her muff upon the table, almost upon his bread.
Waiting to be served, she stood in front of the mirror,
smoothing her dress over her hips, curving her arms to her hair,
        stretching herself.
She sat down facing him, smiled, and soon they were talking.
When she had gobbled her food, he gave her some of his.
He was through and still he sat there, warming himself at her
        quick beauty.
He had but to ask and he knew that she would come along.
He arose and went out. He walked down the street slowly, asking
        himself if he wasn't a fool.

28

His mother stepped about her kitchen, complaining in a low voice;
all day his father sat stooped at a sewing machine.
When he went to high school Webber was in his class.
Webber lived in a neighborhood where the houses are set in lawns with
        trees beside the gutters.
The boys who live there, after school, take their skates and hockey sticks
        and play in the streets until nightfall.
At twelve o'clock the boys ran out of school to a lunchroom around
        the corner.

First come, first served, and they ran as fast as they could.
Webber would run up beside him and knock him against the wall.
He tried not to mind and thought Webber would tire of it.
One day he hit Webber's side; his fist fell off Webber's overcoat. Webber
      turned with a glad shout and punched him as he cowered.
His home was in a neighborhood of workingmen where there were
      few Jews.
When he came from school he walked as quickly as he could,
his head bowed and cap pulled low over his face.
Once, a few blocks from home, a tall lad stopped him.
"Are you a Jew? I knock the block off every Jew I meet." "No,"
      he answered.
"I think you're a Jew. What's your name?" He told him,
      glad that his name was not markedly Jewish and yet foreign enough
      to answer for his looks.
"Where do you live?" He told him and added, "Come around any old
      time and ask about me." So he got away.
When he was through high school he worked in the civil service as
      a typist, taken on until a rush of business was over.
He took the test for a steady job, but his standing on the list was low,
unlikely to be reached for a long time, if ever before the new list.
Looking for work, he always came upon a group waiting for the job.
He was short and weak-looking, and looked peevish. He could not get
      work for months.
At last an old German storekeeper wanted to hire him and asked at what
      he had been working. He told him.
"It doesn't pay me to break you in, if you are going to leave me. Have
      you taken another civil service test? Are you waiting for a new
      appointment?"
"No," he answered.
In a few months a letter came to his home from the civil service board,
      asking him to report for work as a typist, a permanent
      appointment.
There was no hurry, but his father did not know and so brought
      the letter to the store.

There had been a boy in his class at school whose name was Kore.
Kore was short, too, but he had the chest of an old sailor and thick,
      bandy legs. He shouted when he spoke and was always laughing.
Kore moved into the block. With Kore he was not afraid to stand on
      the stoop after work or go walking anywhere.
Once they went to Coney Island and Kore wanted to go bathing. It was
      late at night and no one else was in.

They went along the beach until they came to the iron pier the
     steamboats dock at.
Kore boasted that he would swim around the pier and slid away
     into the black water.
At last the people were gone. The booths were long darkened.
He waited for Kore at the other side of the pier, watching the empty
     waves come in.

29

THE BURDEN

The shop in which he worked was on the tenth floor. After six o'clock
     he heard the neighboring shops closing, the windows and iron
     shutters closed.
At last there was only a light here and there.
These, too, were gone. He was alone.
He went to the stairs.
Suppose he leaned over the railing.
What was to hold him back from plunging down the stairwell?
Upon the railway platform a low railing was fencing off a drop to
     the street—a man could step over.
When the train came to the bridge and the housetops sank and sank,
     his heart began to pound and he caught his breath:
he had but to throw himself through the open window or walk to
     the train platform, no one would suspect, and jerk back
     the little gate.
He would have to ride so to and from work. His home was on the
     third floor, the shop on the tenth. He would have to pass
     windows and the stairwell always.

30

In high school she liked Latin and the balances of algebra.
Her mother had died years before and her father married again.
The new wife was solicitous for her husband. "A workingman—has he
     the means for this education of a girl?"
They took her out of school and got her a job as a bookkeeper.

A student at one of the universities whom she had met in high school,
     began to call.
She herself had been reading, but evenings are too short; besides,
     her reading was haphazard.

They talked of books that he knew and what was good in his lectures.
 Her stepmother and father said, "It will be years before he'll
 finish his studies and make a living. When he'll be ready to
 marry, you'll be too old. He's wasting your time."
It was useless talking to her, but they spoke to him and he stopped
 calling.

A salesman, professionally good-humored, introduced himself to
 her father. A good match, they all said. Besides, home was
 uncomfortable with a nagging stepmother.

31

THE BELLY

When the boys next door practiced on the 'cello, he would draw up
 a chair and listen, pressing his palms against the wall as if to
 gather the sounds.
His mother would drive him away. "Do your lessons, you'll be left back
 again in school!"
But in the evening she would speak to her husband in Russian, so that
 the boy might not understand. "He is longing for it, let him take
 music lessons."
"Don't put such ideas into his head. Do I want my son to grow up
 a fiddler? Let him do his school work, why don't you see he's
 neglecting that?"

They thought that his father might make a man of him in business.
Gabriel liked to open and help lift the cases of cotton goods, to hammer
 nails into the cases they shipped and carry bundles to customers.
His father spoke kindly to him and told his mother, "He'll be all right
 after all."
He began to ask again for 'cello lessons. Spittle dripped from his
 father's lips. "What does he want of me?
If he wants to study, let him go to night school and take up bookkeeping,
 for instance.
I always wanted to study algebra, but what chance was there in Russia?
 Here the world is open for a young man.
But he has taken a notion to scratch on a fiddle into his head and
 I can't hammer it out.
If he had a great talent—but where will he end up, a fiddler at weddings
 or in a theatre?"

A rich uncle came on a visit when Gabriel was twenty. They were out
    walking and Gabriel spoke to him.
His uncle answered kindly, "Do you know what I advise you: stay with
    your father and do your best in the business; your father wants
    to do the best for you.
If he sees you're willing and capable, he'll take you into the firm. Then,
    when you're established and make a comfortable living, take up
    whatever side-line you want to, music or anything else;
as long as you're dependent on your father, you must obey." "At that
    time, Uncle, I'll be too old to begin my music." "One is never
    too old to learn."

He saved some money from his allowance and left home. He priced
    'cellos.
He did not want to work for any of the cotton merchants and meet
    his father.
He had found no job and all his money was spent.
He had not eaten that day and could not sleep at night. When day came
    he fell asleep and woke at noon.
Holding on to the banisters, he walked down the stairs of the lodging
    house. He began to walk along the street, his head light as if it
    were a balloon.
Each step was a distance. He sat on stoops to rest. If no stoop was near,
    he sat down on the curb-stone.
When he reached home, he tried to walk upstairs, but afraid of fainting,
    he went up on hands and knees.

32

He was afraid to go through their grocery store, where his father was
    still talking to customers. He went through the tenement hallway
    into the room where they ate and slept, in back of the store.
His little brothers and sisters were asleep along the big bed. He took
    the book which he had bought at a pushcart, to read just a page
    or two more by the dimmed gaslight.
His father stood over him and punched his head twice,
whispering in Yiddish, "Where have you been lost all day, you louse
    that feeds on me? I needed you to deliver orders."
In the dawn he carried milk and rolls to the doors of customers. At seven
    he was in his chum's room. "I'll stay here with you till I get a job."

He worked for a printer. When he was twenty-one he set up a press in
    a basement. It was harder to pay off than he had thought.

He fell behind in his installments. If they took the press away, he would
    have to work for someone else all over again.
Rosh Ha-Shonoh he went to his father's house. They had been speaking
    to each other again for years.
Once a friend had turned a poem of his into Hebrew. It was printed in
    a Hebrew magazine. He showed it to his father, and his father
    showed it around to the neighbors.
After dinner his father said, "Business has been good, thank God.
    I have saved over a thousand dollars this year. How have you
    been doing?"
"Well." "But I hear that you need money, that you're trying to borrow
    some?" "Yes." His father paused.
"I hope you get it."

33

Passing the shop after school, he would look up at the sign and go on,
    glad that his own life had to do with books.
Now at night when he saw the grey in his parents' hair and heard their
    talk of that day's worries and the next:
lack of orders, if orders, lack of workers, if workers, lack of goods,
    if there were workers and goods, lack of orders again,
for the tenth time he said, "I'm going in with you: there's more money
    in business."
His father answered, "Since when do you care about money? You don't
    know what kind of a life you're going into—but you have always
    had your own way."

He went out selling: in the morning he read the *Arrival of Buyers* in
    The Times; he packed half a dozen samples into a box and went
    from office to office.
Others like himself, sometimes a crowd, were waiting to thrust their
    cards through a partition opening.

When he ate, vexations were forgotten for a while. A quarter past eleven
    was the time to go down the steps to Holz's lunch counter.
He would mount one of the stools. The food, steaming fragrance,
    just brought from the kitchen, would be dumped into the trays
    of the steam-table.
Hamburger steak, mashed potatoes, onions and gravy, or a knackwurst
    and sauerkraut; after that, a pudding with a square of sugar and
    butter sliding from the top and red fruit juice dripping over
    the saucer.
He was growing fat.

34
PROVIDED FOR

Her father and mother were anxious to see her married and provided for
  as soon as possible.
Squat and ugly, her face pimpled, she was stupid and had just managed
  to get through grammar-school, two years older than
  her companions.
Her father wanted her to marry his clerk. He had a good-looking,
  womanish face.
She used to say, "He's marrying me for money, he hates me!"

Her father bought him a store in the Italian quarter.
The man who sold the store had it for years and had made money.
Her husband despised Italians. When they would not buy, he lost
  his patience, glared or shouted.
He sniffed at the men when they came in after a day's ditching,
  cheated when he could and still could not make the store pay.

His father-in-law bought him a store in another neighborhood. He could
  not make a living and was always borrowing.
Once his father-in-law refused him more money.
He came home. The two elder children were in bed. His wife was
  suckling the baby. She stared out of the window,
  tears in her eyes.
He slapped her face. "Tell your father! And if he doesn't help me out—!"

35
A SON WITH A FUTURE

When he was four years old, he stood at the window during a thunder-
  storm. His father, a tailor, sat on the table sewing. He came up to
  his father and said, "I know what makes thunder: two clouds
  knock together."
When he was older, he recited well-known rants at parties. They all said
  that he would be a lawyer.
At law school he won a prize for an essay. Afterwards, he became
  the chum of an only son of rich people. They were said to think
  the world of the young lawyer.
The Appellate Division considered the matter of his disbarment.
  His relatives heard rumours of embezzlement.

When a boy, to keep himself at school, he had worked in a drug store.
Now he turned to this half-forgotten work, among perfumes and
      pungent drugs, quiet after the hubble-bubble of the courts and
      the search in law books.
He had just enough money to buy a drug store in a side street.
Influenza broke out. The old tailor was still keeping his shop and sitting
      cross-legged on the table sewing, but he was half-blind.
He, too, was taken sick. As he lay in bed he thought, "What a lot of
      money doctors and druggists must be making; now is my
      son's chance."
They did not tell him that his son was dead of influenza.

36

In a month they would be married.
He sang a song to himself in which her name was the only word.
His mother was waiting up for him. She said, "I was told today that her
      mother died an epileptic,
and her brother is an idiot in a home somewhere. Why didn't she
      tell you?"
He thought of hugging her narrow shoulders, comforting her;
of noting their children's quirks and screeches fearfully—
how the moonlight had been glittering in her eyes.

37
A DESERTER

Their new landlord was a handsome man. On his rounds to collect
      rent she became friendly.
Finally, she asked him in to have a cup of tea. After that he came often.

Once his mouth jerked, and turning, she saw her husband in
      the doorway.
She thought, One of the neighbors must have told him.
She smiled and opened her mouth to speak, but could say nothing.
Her husband stood looking at the floor. He turned and went away.

She lay awake all night waiting for him.
In the morning she went to his store. It was closed.
She sent for his brothers and told them he had not been home.
      They went to the police. Hospitals and morgues were searched.
      For weeks they were called to identify drowned men.

His business had been prosperous; bank account and all were
untouched. She and their baby girl were provided for.
In a few years they heard of him. He was dead.
He had been making a poor living in a far off city. One day he stepped
in front of a street-car and was killed.

She married again. Her daughter married and had children.
She named none after her father.

38

At night, after the day's work, he wrote. Year after year he had written,
but the right words were still not all there, the right rhythms
not always used. He corrected the old and added new.
While away on a business trip he died. His children playing about
the house, left home by the widow out at work, found
the manuscript so carefully written and rewritten.
The paper was good to scribble on. Then they tore it into bits. At night
the mother came home and swept it out.

39

When at forty he went to America, the family was glad to be rid of him,
envious and quarrelsome. All but him had married and were
well-to-do.
The smallpox when a child had left him ugly. Because it had also left him
sickly, he had been humored in not going to school, and so could
not read or cypher.
To strengthen him he had been apprenticed to a blacksmith.
When he walked he kept hitching up his shoulders and throwing out
his hands.
He spoke indistinctly and so foolishly that when understood, his hearers
could not help smiling. Sure that they did not understand,
he would repeat what he had said until tears were in his eyes.

In New York he stayed with a pushcart pedlar. The pedlar had a daughter
who had worked her way through high school and was in college.
The blacksmith's arm became infected and he could not work.
He stayed at home waiting for his arm to heal, silently watching as she
moved about the house or did her lessons. She tried not to mind
his eyes always on her.
At last she insisted that he move away. So he had to take lodgings
elsewhere.

After supper he would stand in front of the house in which she lived,
    hoping that she would come out on an errand.
The boys playing in the street, discovered him, and searched the gutters
    for peach pits and apple cores
to throw over their shoulders at him as they passed, intent upon the sky.
He would chase them in his jerky way.

                                40

As he read, his mother sat down beside him. "Read me a little."
"You wouldn't understand, Ma." "What do you care? Read me a little.
When I was a girl I wanted to study so much, but who could?
My father used to cry when I talked to him about it,
but he cried because he couldn't afford to educate the boys—even."
As he read, she listened gravely; then went back to her ironing.
The gaslight shone on her round, ruddy face and the white cotton sheets
    that she spread and ironed;
from the shelf the alarm-clock ticked and ticked rapidly.

                                41

He had a rich uncle who sent him to a university and would have taken
    him into the firm; but he went off and married a girl, the men
    of whose family were truckmen.
His uncle would have nothing to do with him, and he became a cigar
    pedlar; but his wife was beautiful.
Even after she had borne children and had had to drudge and scrimp
    all her married life, whenever she came to his lodge ball,
    men and women turned to look at her.

His uncle died and left him a little money. And just in time, because
    he was growing too old to walk around at his business the way
    he had to.
He bought a formula for making an oil, rented a loft in which to
    manufacture, hired a salesman.
Perhaps the formula was a swindle, perhaps it was lack of experience in
    the business, but in a year or two he lost his money.
He went back to cigar peddling. His wife's hair had become white,
    but it gave her new beauty.

His father carved umbrella handles, but when umbrella handles were
    made by machinery, there was only one man for whom his father
    could work.
The pay was small, though it had once been a good trade.
They lived in the poorest part of the ghetto, near the lots where people
    dump ashes.
His father was anxious that his son should stay at school and get out of
    the mess he himself was in. "Learning is the best merchandise,"
    he would say.
His father died; there was his mother to be taken care of. He taught in
    a school in the ghetto.
Some pupils came at nine and stayed until three; others came after
    public school and stayed until evening; most of the pupils came
    in the evening.
The courses were crammed, lasting a few months, pupils and teachers
    anxious to be rid of the matter as soon as possible.
So he worked day and night, week-days and Sunday.

His mother was dead. It was cold in the street and windy. A dry snow
    had fallen and the feet of the walkers were turning it into
    brown sand.
He was forty.
Now he was free. To do what? He knew no one whom he cared to marry.
    And who would go into his poverty?
If he were to give up this work he knew so well, to what else could
    he turn?
He would just keep on. He had lost this world and knew there was
    no other.

43
THE LAWYER

A man made cloaks of material furnished. The man for whom the cloaks
    were made refused them: defects in the material. But the material
    was yours. But the defects were shown by white strings in the
    selvage; your cutter should have avoided them.
A woman fell downstairs; no light in the hallway. There was! but boys
    stole the electric bulbs. The janitor was told; he should have lit
    the gas.
Water from the chop-suey joint upstairs came through the ceiling upon
    our silk. The water fell on a table where it damaged nothing;

they took their silk, gone out of style, and dabbled it in the water.
The silks were on the table to be cut.
Our union takes steam-shovel engineers only, but their union takes all
kinds; they want to put us out of business. One of our men was on
a job; they call out the locomotive engineers and make the boss—
Why was he spending his life in such squabbles?

44

Both daughters had married well; their husbands earned enough,
and more each year.
Her husband's business was good and they had as much as two elderly
people wanted.

Her younger daughter died in childbed.

Her husband had gone to his store long before.
She wrapped her head and shoulders in her shawl, knitting her thoughts.
She got up at last and poured herself some brandy.
When she went out she took a brandy flask in her bag to nip in lavatories.

Her other daughter died in childbed.
Her son-in-law married again. The new wife took the elder children
from school and sent them to work.
They became coarse; their house was full of quarreling.

Their grandmother was now in an asylum.
Her husband came to see her. Once he saw the lunatic children playing
in the yard.
"Why do you cry?" she asked. "You cry for them, but not for me . . .
I am sharpening a knife to kill my grandchildren, but not you: you must
pay for my board here."

45

He had a house of his own and a store. His wife took care of the store,
and he at home studied Torah and Talmud.
His store was burned down. In those days they were not insured,
but still he had the house.
He rented all of it but a room where he stayed and studied.
Once, when he was saying the morning prayer, Mendel, one of his
tenants, came to him and said, "My son, the lawyer, has been
arrested; won't you sign his bond here?"

It was not a bail bond but a deed; and in a few months Mendel made
      him move out of the house.
He went to a lawyer. The lawyer told him, "We can get the house
      back easily."
"What will they do to Mendel?" "Send him to Siberia." "Would it be
      right for me to put a Jew into the hands of *goyim*?"
He had to give children lessons in Hebrew. His son became a glazier.
      While working in another town his son died.
His daughter-in-law baked *begel* and his grandchildren sold them in
      the streets.

One day Mendel came to ask forgiveness.
He, too, had lost his money, and his son, too, the lawyer, had died.
He turned his face from Mendel; and so they stood, two old men.

46

When the club met in her home, embarrassed, she asked them not
      to begin: her father wanted to speak to them.
The members whispered to each other, "Who is her father?"
"I thank you, young men and women," he said, "for the honor of your
      visit. I suppose you would like to hear some of my poems."
      And he began to chant.

47

THE DOCTOR'S WIFE

The neighbors called her *die Schiesterka*—the shoemaker's wife.
She was squat, her speech coarse as their own.
People are always moving in and out of tenements;
the newcomers learnt the name and passed it on to others
who moved in afterwards, and all liked to use it.

She and the children were going to the country.
She had on a new waist, starched white and stiff,
and kept rubbing her red, sweating face with a handkerchief.
The doctor waved his hand from the stoop, and turned back to
      the office, now still and empty.

The conductor raised a hullabaloo about Minnie,
and she and Minnie raised such a hullabaloo back
that when full fare for Minnie was paid,
the conductor was too tired to argue about the others.

The ride became tiresome, babies cried, the windows had to be closed
    to keep out the cinders—
and opened because it became hot.
They reached their station at last. The boarding-house keeper had
    a buggy waiting.
"Drink the fresh air, children," she shouted,
"drink, drink, *ach gut!* If only Papa was here!"

48

The shoemaker sat in the cellar's dusk beside his bench and sewing-
    machine, his large, blackened hands, finger tips flattened and
    broad, busy.
Through the grating in the sidewalk over his window, paper and dust
    were falling year by year.

At evening Passover would begin. The sunny street was crowded.
    The shoemaker could see the feet of those who walked over
    the grating.
He had one pair of shoes to finish and he would be through.
His friend came in, a man with a long, black beard, in shabby, dirty
    clothes, but with shoes newly cobbled and blacked.
"Beautiful outside, really the world is beautiful."
A pot of fish was boiling on the stove. Sometimes the water bubbled
    over and hissed. The smell of the fish filled the cellar.
"It must be beautiful in the park now. After our fish we'll take a walk
    in the park." The shoemaker nodded.
The shoemaker hurried his work on the last shoe. The pot on the stove
    bubbled and hissed. His friend walked up and down the cellar
    in shoes newly cobbled and blacked.

A Fifth Group of Verse

I charge you, lips and teeth,
keep watch upon my tongue:
silence is legal tender everywhere.

I have a quarrel with the clock.
Quick, quick!
These inconsiderable seconds fill
the basins of our lives to overflowing,
and we are emptied
into the sink and pipes of death.
How furiously it ticks this fine morning.
Sun, of all that lived God has only listened to Joshua,
how shall I hope that He will listen to me?

FARQUHAR

I

> *Margaret.* I have never regretted that my father gamed away
>   his fortune
> as much as I do, now that I have met George Farquhar.
> I am convinced that were I wealthy he would marry me.
> *Her Friend.* How is he to know that you are not?
> *Margaret.* Not know the town's tattle?
> *Her Friend.* If there is tattle that you are penniless,
> there may be tattle that you are rich
> as a daughter of Hesperus—
> *Margaret.* What a subtle and ingenious mind you have, darling!—
> *Her Friend.* In whose estate
> are quiet rooms where white Apollo smiles,
> and penniless George Farquhar
> may write comedies to outshine Congreve.
> *Margaret.* Excellent!
> *Her Friend.* You silly, should he bite and you two marry?
> What are you to live by;
> for Adam cannot delve nor this Eve spin?
> *Margaret.* Dearest, what *do* I live by?
> The gratuities of friends.

If we marry, I am sure
of some happiness; for the rest,
I'll chance it—
I am my father's daughter.
Gossip until I have him caught
and my own, my very own.
>   *Her Friend.* I'll talk your wealth, I'll make you rich—in lies.
>   *Margaret.* In love!

II

>   *Margaret to Farquhar who has become consumptive.*
>   O my dear, my dear, you were so dear to me
that I threw my arms about your neck
and pulled you down.
Darling, it is I who have done this to you:
my kisses have sucked away your breath.
What friends we had among the rich and great!
But when we married and had most need of friends,
they left us to befriend each other . . .
I am unlucky;
my father was unlucky, too.
I know there is no meeting of the dead:
that we should be together once again—
oh, that would be too lucky for the like of me!

4

ESTABLISHED

I

The music within the house is loud, the dancing swift. Outside
>   *A Woman.* This one still peddling, this one's son—a thief!
This one dead and that one dead,
but she's done well.
>   *Another Woman.* She worked hard.
>   *A Third Woman.* What's going on?
>   *The First Woman.* She's marrying off her younger daughter.
Now both children are married—
married well.
The elder daughter has two children and soon—a third.
The grandchildren will not have to start where she did.
>   *The Second Woman.* She worked hard; now she eats the fruit of it.

II

A Woman. Who's dead?
Another. I don't know.
The First Woman. Do you live on this block? Who's dead?
A Third Woman. A woman died in childbed.
The First Woman. What a heavy tread on the stairs! . . .
They are bringing down the coffin.

III

A Woman. He is marrying again.
Another. So soon?
The First Woman. Why not?
Her children—
these need a mother.
    The Second Woman. But their grandmother?
    The First Woman. If in a drawer
she finds a trinket that her daughter used to wear,
or in a grandchild's face
sees her dead daughter and begins to cry—
the children have had enough of sorrow.

IV

A Woman. Who's dead?
Another. I don't know.
The First Woman. Do you live on this block? Who's dead?
Another. A young woman. She died in childbed.

V

    The Mother of the Dead Women. I had this lump of lead before
when my father died,
but I was younger and my blood warm enough
to melt it away;
now it will weigh me down into the grave.
This lump of ice was here before,
but my blood when younger
could warm it into tears.

VI

A Woman to Another. If their mother lived,
would they be sent to work?
What else can children become in shops and offices?
If at least home—
but their home!

5
Autumn Night

The asphalt winds in and out
about the trees, the lawns, the lake;
a thousand lights shine among the trees,
and in the circles underneath
the grass is brightly green;
but all these lights do not warm the wind.

6
Dawn

No one is on the lawn so early but the birds,
sparrows and robins pecking at the seeds
the wind has blown here; the wind itself is gone.

7

How miserly this bush is:
why do you crouch behind a fence,
holding on to your little copper leaves?
Have you no faith in spring?

8

From the fog a gull flies slowly
and is lost in fog. The buildings are only clouds.

9

DAVID

The shadow that does not leave my feet,
how shrunken now it lies;
with sunshine I am anointed king,
I leap before the ark, I sing;
I seem to walk but I dance about,
you think me silent but I shout.

10

A CITIZEN

I know little about bushes and trees,
I have met them in backyards and streets;
I shall become disreputable if I hang about them.
Yet to see them comforts me,
when I think of my life as snarled.
Was not knowledge first on trees?

11

A star rides the twilight now,
all heaven to itself.

12

A SUNNY DAY

The curved leaves of the little tree are shining;
the bushes across the street are purple with flowers.
A man with a red beard talks to a woman with yellow hair;
she laughs like the clash of brass cymbals.

Two Negresses are coming down the street;
they munch lettuce
and pull the leaves slowly out of a bag.

The pigeons wheel in the bright air,
now white, now the grey backs showing.
They settle down upon a roof;
the children shout, the owner swings his bamboo.

13

BUILDING BOOM

The avenue of willows leads nowhere:
it begins at the blank wall of a new apartment house
and ends in the middle of a lot for sale.
Papers and cans are thrown about the trees.
The disorder does not touch the flowing branches;
but the trees have become small among the new houses,
and will be cut down;
their beauty cannot save them.

14

How difficult for me is Hebrew:
even the Hebrew for *mother*, for *bread*, for *sun*
is foreign. How far have I been exiled, Zion.

15

I have learnt the Hebrew blessing before eating bread;
is there no blessing before reading Hebrew?

16

My thoughts have become like the ancient Hebrew
in two tenses only, past and future—
I was and I shall be with you.

17

God saw Adam in a town
without flowers and trees and fields to look upon,
and so gave him Eve
to be all these.
There is no furniture for a room
like a beautiful woman.

18

The sun shone into the bare, wet tree;
it became a pyramid of criss-cross lights,
and in each corner the light nested.

After I had worked all day at what I earn my living,
I was tired. Now my own work has lost another day,
I thought, but began slowly,
and slowly my strength came back to me.
Surely, the tide comes in twice a day.

SAMUEL

All day I am before the altar
and at night sleep beside it;
I think in psalms, my mind a psalter.
I sit in the temple. From inside it
I see the smoke eddy in the wind;
now and then a leaf will ride it
upward and when the leaf has spinned
its moment, the winds hide it.
Against their hurly-burly
I shut the window of my mind,
and the world at the winds' will,
find myself calm and still.

The days in this room become precious to others also,
as the seed hidden in the earth becomes a tree,
as the secret joy of the bride and her husband becomes a man.

Whatever unfriendly stars and comets do,
whatever stormy heavens are unfurled,
my spirit be like fire in this, too,
that all the straws and rubbish of the world
only feed its flame.

The seasons change.
That is change enough.
Chance planted me beside a stream of water;
content, I serve the land,
whoever lives here and whoever passes.

ISRAEL

ISRAEL

I

Our eldest son is like Ishmael, Jacob is like you;
therefore, you like Esau better:
because he is a hunter, a man of the fields,
can bring you venison from distant cliffs,
is strong, and covered with hair like a ram;
but Jacob who is like you, a quiet man, dwelling in tents, is the better.
Esau is like a club, Jacob a knife,
Esau is stupid, Jacob shrewd,
Jacob is like my brother Laban.
My father, sit and eat of my venison.
How is it that you have found it so quickly?
God helped me.
Come near that I may feel you, my son,
whether you are my very son Esau or not;
the voice is Jacob's voice, but the hands are Esau's.
Are you my son Esau?
I am.
Come near now and kiss me, my son.

How dreadful are these cliffs!
I who have always lived in booths,
seldom far from the song of women at the doors,
or at the farthest, near the shepherd's flute—.
When Abraham's servant came to us,
he brought gifts of clothing, jewels of silver and gold;
you came with empty hands, it seemed;
but my cattle have been well cared for.
(Can Jacob match himself against Laban,
a young man who has nothing among strangers,
against a man grown grizzled among strong and crafty men?)

The seven years that I served for you, Rachel,
were but a few days.

Why have you cheated me?
In our place the younger is not given before the first-born.
Had Rachel been married first, the tears of Leah
would have made your marriage bitter.

When this beauty of which you keep telling me is gone,
as the petals are shaken from a tree—
surely, although they are so many, at last they have all fallen—
Leah now hires you of me with the mandrakes
her eldest finds in the field,
but who will find me anything in those days?

My companions so many nights,
physicians to whom I told my secrets,
I touch you:
you are wood;
so is the staff that helps us on our way,
the spoon that feeds us, and at last our coffin.
Does Laban among sons and brothers need you?
We need you,
a shepherd, women, children, and a flock of sheep,
among the mountains in the wilderness. *(She steals the idols.)*

Why have you stolen away,
and carried away my daughters as if they were captives of the sword?
Why did you not tell me,
that I might have sent you away with mirth and songs,
with drum and harp?
Why did you not let me kiss my sons and daughters?
The daughters are my daughters, the children are my children, and
　　　the flocks my flocks,
all that you see is mine;
but what can I do to these, my daughters,
or to the children whom they have borne?

How unworthy I am of the kindness which you have shown me,
God of Abraham and Isaac,
for with my staff I crossed the Jordan,
and am now two companies.
Deliver me now from the hand of Esau!
And whose are the children?
My children.
And what meant the company I met?
To find favor in your sight.
I have enough. Let that which you have be yours.

Look, Joseph is coming, the master of dreams.
What do the camels carry?

Spicery and balm and myrrh to Egypt.
What profit shall we have in the death of our brother?
Lift him out of the pit and sell him to these for pieces of silver;
and dip his coat in a goat's blood,
and send it to our father,
and say, we have found this and do not know whether it is your
     son's coat or not;
and he will think a beast tore Joseph to pieces.

II

Since Potiphar made you his overseer,
he has been blessed in house and field;
all that he has is in your hand,
and he knows of nothing but the bread that he eats.
And you in our house have become comely—
you were nothing but a bag of bones.
Come here!
Your cheeks were sunken so,
your eyes staring and your hair
dishevelled like this, like this.
Are not my hands soft?
You stepped as lightly as a deer,
as slim and graceful as a deer,
and held your head as proudly.
Sit here.
Kiss me.
Not so.
Oh, you don't know how to kiss.
Kiss me so.
Wet your lips and kiss me so.
Kiss my eyes, my throat,
now my mouth—
oh, you fool! You fool!

You are magicians and wise men at my feasts;
now, what is the meaning of my dreams?
"Have me in mind when it shall be well with you,
     make mention of me to Pharaoh, and bring me out of this house;
     for I was stolen from the land of the Hebrews;
     and here also I have done nothing that they should put me into
          the dungeon."
Since then, two full years have passed, and until this day I have forgotten
     Joseph.

Therefore, let Pharaoh set a man, discreet and wise,
to appoint overseers, and these gather in the cities from the fields
        about them
grain in the good years against the years of famine.
Where can we find such a man?
I have no one discreet and wise as you.
You shall be over my house, and according to your word shall my people
        be ruled;
only I, on the throne, will be greater.
Clothe him in fine linen and put a gold chain about his neck,
he shall ride in the second chariot and all cry out before him,
        Bend the knee!

You are spies, you come to see the nakedness of the land.
No, my lord, we are not spies, we have come to buy food.
We are brothers, the sons of one man in Canaan.
And is your father yet alive?
He is.
Have you another brother?
We have.
We were twelve,
the youngest is with our father,
and one is no more.

My lord, we have brought you a present of the fruit of our land:
A little balm, a little honey, spicery and myrrh, pistachios and almonds.
Is your father well, the old man of whom you spoke? Is he yet alive?
Is this your youngest brother of whom you spoke?

Why have you rewarded evil for good? Where is the cup from which
        my lord drinks?
The man in whose hand the cup was found shall be my bondsman.
Now when I come to the servant your father and the lad is not
        with us—
his brother is dead, and he alone is left of his mother, and his father
        loves him—
let me remain instead of the lad, a bondsman to my lord.

Let every man go out but these.
I am Joseph.
Come nearer.
I am Joseph, your brother, whom you sold into Egypt.
And now be not grieved, nor angry with yourselves,

for I was sent before you to save us all alive;
you meant evil against me, but it was meant for good.
Go up to our father and say to him,
your son Joseph has become head of all Egypt;
without Joseph no man, except Pharaoh on the throne, lifts hand or foot
        throughout Egypt.
You have not thought to see his face and you shall see his sons also.
Come to him and you shall dwell in the land of Goshen—
and he shall be near me and his children and his children's children,
and bring all your flocks and herds and all that you have;
for there are yet five years of famine.
You shall tell my father of all my glory in Egypt;
you shall take wagons out of Egypt for your little ones and your wives,
        and bring our father and come;
and I will give you all the good of the land of Egypt.
I will establish my people like a pyramid,
no longer to be blown along like sand.

III

Our lives are bitter with service in mortar and brick,
we whose fathers watched the flock of stars,
and had no Pharaoh but the sun. When he came,
they led their sheep to pasture at the pace of the lambs—
few and evil are the days of our lives.
We have built Pithom and Raamses. What are two
cities to Pharaoh?
We must build him many as the stars.

Why do you complain? The more you are afflicted,
the more you multiply, the more you spread abroad.
What have you become?
A shepherd in a wilderness.
Your hair is grey;
how much longer
before you attempt the dreams of your heart?
Deliver my people out of Egypt,
bring them out of that land to a good land,
a land of milk and honey, the land of your fathers.

What is this you have done? Who sent for you?
Before Pharaoh and his court come two shabby Hebrews and say,
Let our people go, we pray you, three days' journey into the wilderness,

to hold a feast to God.
Who asked you to speak for us?
No wonder Pharaoh's court burst into laughter;
we have heard how Pharaoh smiled, leaned forward and said,
Who is your God that I should listen to Him?
I know Him not.
Then you should have known enough to be silent,
but you must speak on;
until Pharaoh answered in anger,
Why do you loose the people from their work? Get to your burdens.
And he commanded his officer, Give the people no more straw to
      make brick,
let them gather straw for themselves;
and the number of bricks they did make, you shall lay upon them,
you shall not make it less,
for they are idle, therefore they cry, Let us go and sacrifice to our God.

We are scattered throughout Egypt to gather stubble for straw,
and the taskmasters are urgent,
fulfill your work, your daily tasks, as when there was straw.
We are beaten and the taskmasters demand of us,
Why have you not fulfilled your task both yesterday and today?
You are idle, you are idle, therefore you say, Let us go and sacrifice to
      our God.
Who asked you to speak for us? God judge you,
because you made us hateful in the eyes of Pharaoh and his servants,
and put a sword in their hand to kill us.

The God of the Hebrews sent us to say,
Let my people go to serve Me in the wilderness,
and Pharaoh did not listen.
In the morning, when Pharaoh came to his barge,
was not the river foul? Pharaoh turned and went into his house.
The fish in the river died, the Egyptians loathed to drink from the river,
the water was foul in vessels of wood and vessels of stone;
and they dug for water—they could not drink the water of the river.
Still Pharaoh would not let us go.
And the dust became lice throughout Egypt,
there were lice upon man and beast;
and the river swarmed with frogs.
The frogs came up into the houses and into the bedrooms and upon
      the beds,
and into the ovens and into the kneading troughs.

Still Pharaoh would not let us go.
The frogs gathered themselves into heaps and the land stank;
and swarms of flies came into the houses
upon Pharaoh and his servants and his people—
the air was black with flies.
Still Pharaoh would not let us go.
Then a murrain was upon the cattle in the field,
upon the horses, upon the asses, upon the camels, upon the herds, and
      upon the flocks,
and the cattle died; boils broke out upon men;
it thundered and rained hail and fire ran down into the earth,
and the hail struck every man and beast in the field,
every herb of the field, and broke every tree;
the flax and barley were struck down,
for the barley was in the ear and the flax was in bloom.
And still Pharaoh would not let us go.
And an east wind blew all day and all night,
and in the morning brought the locusts;
they covered the earth so that the land was darkened
and ate what had escaped the hail,
every herb of the land and all the fruit of the trees—
not a blade or a leaf or anything green was left.
Still Pharaoh would not let us go.
Now there has been darkness throughout Egypt for three days
so that men grope in the darkness.
Let us go,
with our young and old, with our sons and daughters,
with our flocks and herds to hold a feast to our God, as He
      commanded us.

The water of the river has been foul before.
Then there were lice and frogs, flies, and a murrain upon the cattle,
and boils upon men. What have these to do with it—or their God?
It has hailed in Egypt before the Hebrews were here;
we have known locusts often enough and darkness.
Why do you come before me as magicians and charmers?
Are we Hebrews to believe this?
See my face no more. The day you see my face again,
you die. Drive them from me.

The first-born of the Egyptians die,
from the son of the Pharaoh upon the throne
to the son of the servant behind the mill,

to the son of the prisoner in the dungeon;
not a house among them is now without its dead!
You hear the cry throughout Egypt;
now take your flocks and herds, the jewels of silver and the jewels of gold,
the fine clothing you have borrowed from the Egyptians,
your young and old, your sons and daughters,
take the dough before it is leavened,
the kneading-troughs upon your shoulders,
and hurry out of this land!

Why did you take us away to die in the wilderness;
were there no graves in Egypt?
Did we not say to you, Let us alone;
was it not better for us to serve in Egypt than to die in the wilderness?

The Egyptians turn, they turn, they cannot drive!
Their chariot wheels are bound with sand!
The waters return, return upon the Egyptians,
upon the horses and the chariots;
Pharaoh's host and his captains are sunk in the sea!

The water is bitter, we cannot drink it. The water is bitter.
Is there only the bitter for us from which to choose?
The water is bitter, we cannot drink it.
The water is bitter. The water is bitter, we cannot drink it.

That we had died in Egypt,
when we sat by the fleshpots, when we ate bread to the full.
I remember the fish we did eat for nothing in Egypt.
The cucumbers and the melons, the onions, the leeks, and the garlic—
our soul is dried away;
there is nothing except this manna to look upon.

You are not to be like other nations;
you are to be a kingdom of priests, a holy nation.
You shall have no other gods besides Him;
you shall make no image,
or the likeness of anything in the heavens,
on the earth, or in the water,
to bow down to it and serve it.
By righteousness shall you serve God:
you shall not swear by his name falsely;
six days shall you do your work and on the seventh, rest,

in ploughing time and harvest you shall rest
that your ox and ass may rest and your servants;
honor your father and mother; you shall not kill;
you shall not whore; you shall not steal;
you shall not deal falsely with each other;
you shall not covet your neighbor's house,
your neighbor's wife, nor his manservant, his maidservant,
his ox, his ass, nor anything your neighbor's.
In righteousness shall you judge your neighbor:
you shall not respect the person of the poor nor honor the person of
    the mighty,
neither shall you favor a poor man in his cause.
If a witness has testified falsely,
as he thought to do to his brother, you shall do to him.
You shall put away evil from among you and your eyes shall not pity:
life for life, eye for eye, tooth for tooth, hand for hand, foot for foot,
burning for burning, wound for wound, stripe for stripe;
as a man does to his neighbor it shall be done to him.
You shall not follow a multitude to do evil,
you shall not go up and down, a talebearer,
you shall not hate your brother in your heart:
rebuke your neighbor,
but you shall not take vengeance, nor bear a grudge;
you shall love your neighbor as yourself.
If you meet your enemy's ox or his ass astray,
you shall surely bring it back;
if you see the ass of him who hates you lying under his burden,
you shall surely set it free.
You shall be holy men before God;
you shall make a distinction between the unclean and clean.
These you may eat: the ox, the sheep, the goat, the hart,
the gazelle, the roebuck, the wild goat, the antelope, and the chamois,
but not the camel, the coney, the hare, and the swine,
nor whatever beasts go upon paws,
nor whatever dies of itself,
nor of all that move in the waters,
whatever has not fins and scales;
and of those that fly, the flesh of these is an abomination:
the eagle, the vulture, the kite, the falcon, and every raven,
the ostrich, the sea-mew, the night hawk and the little hawk,
the cormorant, the great owl, the horned owl,
the pelican, the stork, the heron, the hoopoe and the bat;
and all creeping things,

whatever goes upon its belly or has many feet,
the weasel and the mouse, the great lizard, the gecko, the crocodile,
      the sand lizard and the chameleon.
When you come into the land that shall be yours,
and reap your harvest,
you shall not reap the corners of the field,
neither shall you gather the gleanings:
you shall not glean your vineyard,
neither shall you gather the fallen fruit;
you shall leave them for the poor and the wanderer.
The wages of a hired servant shall not remain with you all night until
      the morning;
you shall not muzzle the ox when he treads out the corn.
If a stranger comes among you, you shall not do him wrong;
the stranger shall be as the home-born among you,
you shall love him as yourself;
for you know the heart of a stranger, you were strangers in Egypt.
You shall do no unrighteousness in measures of length, of weight, or
      of quantity:
you shall have just balances, just weights, a just ephah, and a just hin.
When you go out to battle and see horses and chariots and a people
      more than you,
the officers shall say,
What man has built a house and has not dedicated it?
Let him return lest he die in the battle and another dedicate it.
What man has planted a vineyard and has not used the fruit?
Let him return lest he die in the battle and another use the fruit.
And what man has betrothed a wife and has not taken her?
Let him return lest he die in the battle and another take her.
What man is faint-hearted?
Let him return lest his brother's heart melt as his.
Six years you shall sow and reap;
the seventh year you shall let the land lie fallow
that the poor may eat and what they leave the beast of the field shall eat.
The poor will never cease:
therefore, I command you,
you shall open your hand to your brother—enough for his need.
If your brother be sold to you and serve you seven years,
at the end of the seventh year you shall set him free,
and you shall not let him go empty-handed:
you shall furnish him out of your flock and out of your threshing-floor
      and your wine-press,
as you have been blessed you shall give,

you shall remember that you were a bondsman in Egypt.
At the end of every seven years,
the creditor shall release that which he has lent:
he shall not exact it of his neighbor.
And you shall number seven sabbaths of years, seven times seven years,
then you shall sound the trumpet throughout the land
and shall hallow the fiftieth year and proclaim liberty to all
      the inhabitants:
it shall be a year of jubilee.
The land shall not be sold forever: the land is God's,
you are strangers and sojourners before Him;
you shall grant a redemption for the land;
but if the land is not redeemed,
it shall stay with him who bought it until the jubilee,
and in the jubilee he who sold it shall return to his possession.

You are not to do each what is right in his own eyes:
the words of this day shall be upon your heart,
teach them diligently to your children,
talk of them when you sit in your house,
along the way, when you lie down, and when you rise up,
bind them upon your hand,
they shall be frontlets between your eyes,
you shall write them upon the door-posts of your house and upon
      your gates.

King David

"And David said to Solomon, 'My son, as for me, it was in my mind to
build an house unto the name of the Lord my God:
But the word of the Lord came to me, saying, Thou has shed blood abun-
dantly, and hast made great wars: thou shall not build an house unto my
name, because thou hast shed much blood upon the earth in my sight.'"

—I Chronicles XXII: 7,8.

I

     His height was six cubits and a span;
his helmet brass,
the weight of his coat-of-mail is five thousand shekels of brass,
he had greaves of brass upon his legs,
and a target of brass upon his shoulders;
the staff of his spear is like a weaver's beam,
the weight of his spearhead is five hundred shekels of iron.
He stood before our camp and shouted,
Am I not a Philistine and you servants of Saul?
Choose a man to fight with me;
if he is able to kill me, we are your servants,
if not, you are ours.
And we stood there, dismayed—
even Jonathan.
Now there had come to the camp a lad from Bethlehem,
whose three eldest brothers had followed Saul to battle:
the lad brought them parched corn, and loaves and cheese for
        their captain.
And he asked of the soldiers, Who is this Philistine that he should
        challenge the armies of the living God?
They told him how the king had said that he would enrich the man who
        killed the Philistine,
and give the man Michal—the king's daughter—for a wife;
and then the soldiers jeered at him and said, Do you think to kill him?
His eldest brother pushed through the soldiers and said,
What are you doing here?
With whom have you left our few sheep in the wilderness?
I know your naughtiness: you have come to see the battle.
The lad answered them all, I will go and fight with this Philistine,
and they reasoned with him: What are you thinking of?
You are only a lad
and he has been a man of war since his youth.
I will go with my staff and sling and the stones in my scrip.

Goliath called out, Am I a dog that you come against me with a stick?
Come on, and I will give your flesh to the birds of heaven and the beasts
of the field,
but as he lifted his spear,
the lad took a stone and slung it, and it sank into Goliath's forehead.
At this we rushed upon the Philistines.
Jonathan
has given the lad his own robe, girdle, sword and bow;
now David shall stay among the men of war,
and be Michal's husband.

II
The Feast in Saul's House

Tell us how Ehud stabbed the king of Moab,
or of Deborah,
of Gideon, Jephthah, or Samson.
Tell us of Jonathan!
Tell us again how the city of Dan was taken.

The kings came and fought,
they took no spoil;
the river Kishon swept them away.
The stars fought from heaven,
from their courses they fought against Sisera.
Tell of it you that ride on white asses,
that sit on rich carpets,
or walk, far from the noise of archers, by the pools of water.
Sisera's mother is looking from her window.
She cries through the lattice,
Why is his chariot so long in coming?
Her women answer her,
yes, she answers herself,
Have they not found, are they not sharing the spoil?
A woman, two women to every man!

Micah said to his mother,
The silver taken from you, about which you did utter a curse—
I took it.
She said, Blessed be my son, and gave two hundred pieces of the silver
to the moulder to cast an image of God to stand in Micah's house.
Now there came to the hill country a young man,
a Levite looking for a place,

and Micah said to him, Stay with me, be my priest,
I will give you ten pieces of silver a year, a suit of clothes and your food;
the young man was content.
And Micah said, Now I know that God will be good to me,
for I have a Levite as my priest.
The Danites had sent five men to spy out the land and they lodged in
           Micah's house,
went on and came to a city, Laish,
and saw how the people lived there—quietly, far from other Sidonians.
And their spies told the Danites of Laish.
Six hundred of them set out with weapons of war and on the way
           passed Micah's house.
The five who had been there went in and took the image and said to
           its priest,
Be still!
But why not come with us and be our priest?
Is it better for you to be a priest in the house of one man or to a tribe
         of Israel?
And the Levite went along gladly.
Micah and his neighbors ran after them shouting,
and the Danites said, What is the matter with you?
He answered, You have taken away my God and my priest, and you
           ask me what is the matter?
A Danite answered him then, Let us hear no more from you; there are
           angry fellows among us,
and they may fall upon you and sweep you away and the lives of
           your household.
The Danites went on and came to Laish and killed all who lived there
           and set it on fire:
there was no one to save it, for it was far from Sidon,
and they had dealings with no one, but had lived—a quiet people—
           in their valley.
The Danites rebuilt the city and called it Dan.

    Then Abner said, Tell us of Saul,
tell us how he went looking for his father's asses
and met Samuel and was anointed king;
how Saul saved the people of Jabesh-gilead from the Ammonites;
how he fought the Philistines,
not a sword or a spear in the hand of any of us—
did they leave us a smith in all Israel?—
our people had hidden themselves in caves and in thickets and in rocks
           and in pits,

the Philistines in three companies were pillaging the land,
and not a city was without its garrison of Philistines;
tell us about ourselves, for we are heroes too!

Now Jonathan, the son of Saul, said to the young man who
            carried his armour,
Come, let us go over to the Philistines' garrison.
The passes by which Jonathan went
were between crags on one side and crags on the other,
and the Philistines said, Look, the Hebrews are coming out of their holes.
And the men of the garrison called to Jonathan,
Come up to us and we will show you a thing or two;
he climbed up on his hands and feet—and they fell before him!
That first slaughter was of about twenty men
within as it were half a furrow's length in an acre of land;
there was a trembling in the camp, in the field, and among all the people,
the garrison and those going out to pillage trembled.
The watchmen of Saul looked and saw the multitude going this way
            and that,
and Saul said to his priest, Bring the ark of God;
but while Saul talked to the priest the tumult in the Philistines' camp
            went on and grew—
and we hurried to the battle!
The Hebrews who had come with the Philistines into their camp from
            the country about,
they, too, fought with Saul and Jonathan against the Philistines;
and those who had hidden themselves in the hills of Ephraim,
when they heard that the Philistines fled, followed them hard.

The evil spirit is in the king: he neither sees nor hears.
Let David play;
when David used to play,
the king would wipe his eyes upon his sleeves,
and be himself again.

When the women came out of the cities,
to meet us from the slaughter of the Philistines,
did you not hear them answer each other,
as they played upon the timbrels,
Saul has slain his thousands,
and David his ten thousands?
They said of David ten thousands
and of me only thousands;
can he have more except the kingdom?

What has he done? What is his wickedness?
He has done nothing that you should want his life!
　　　You lie, you rebel! you son of a rebellious woman!
Do I not know that you have chosen the son of Jesse to your
　　　　　own confusion
and to the confusion of your mother's nakedness?
As long as the son of Jesse lives upon the ground,
you will not be established nor your kingdom;
bring him to me at once for he shall die!
Why should he die? What has he done?

　　　III
　　　Michal

　　　The grave men who will write
the history of the kings of Israel and of the wars of God,
will not trouble to write of our happiness:
I had never hoped for a husband brave as Jonathan,
and handsomer than my father—
there is none like David among the young men.

　　　What have I done that your father seeks my life?
　　　God forbid! It is not so!
　　　There is only a step between me and death:
as I sat before your father at meat—
in all that I have done have I not served him only?
Where is David?
He is sick.
Then we will bring him in his bed to the king. Let us in!
I cannot. He is sick.
Why have you fooled me and let my enemy escape?

　　　IV

　　　His brothers and all his father's house have come to David,
and every one in distress and in debt,
every one discontented:
he is their captain;
and he and his band are now in the land of Judah—in the forest
　　　　　of Hareth.

　　　If he is in the land at all,
I will search him out among all the thousands of Judah.

We heard that David is in the land of Ziph;
and that he was lurking in the wilderness of Maon,
and from there that he has slipped away to the strongholds of En-gedi—
on the rocks of the wild goats.

My lord, he and his band have escaped to the Philistines,
and found favor in the eyes of the king of Gath;
the king has given them a town in which to live.
They raid the Amalekites,
and leave not a man or woman alive to tell on them in Gath;
when the king asks, Where have you made a raid today?
David answers, In the south of Judah,
and so the king believes of him, He has made his people hate him.
    Hear, you Benjaminites,
will the son of Jesse give every one of you fields and vineyards,
and make you all captains of hundreds and of thousands,
that all of you have conspired against me,
and no one shows me that my son has made a league with the son
        of Jesse,
and none of you is sorry for me?

I saw the son of Jesse coming to Ahimelech the priest,
and Ahimelech inquired of the Lord for him
and gave him food and Goliath's sword.
    He came to me and I asked, Why are you alone?
And he answered, The king commanded me, Let no one know anything
        of the business about which I send you.
Now what have you?
Give me five loaves of bread or what there is.
I had only the hallowed bread;
and he answered, Let me have it,
and is there not a sword or a spear here?
I brought neither:
the king's business required haste.
And I gave him the sword of Goliath whom he had killed,
which had been wrapped in a cloth among the vestments.
Who seemed so faithful among all your servants as David,
the king's son-in-law?
And did I begin to inquire of God for him?
Let not the king impute anything to his servant nor to any of my
        father's house;
for your servant knew nothing of all this.

You shall die, you and all your father's house!
Kill him!
Because his hand also is with David
and he helped him when he fled.
Here, you Edomite,
kill the priest!
And take his city,
kill his men and women, their children and sucklings,
their oxen, asses, and sheep!
You!
Paltiel,
you shall marry my daughter Michal,
whom I have given to David,
for you are a good man, a quiet man.
And listen, all of you, and you, Jonathan,
let me hear no more of this David—
except to hear that he is dead.

V

So the leader of the Philistines said to the king of Gath,
what are these Hebrews doing in the rear of your company,
in an army we have gathered against Saul?
The king of Gath answered, This is David who was Saul's servant:
he has been with me many years and I have found no fault in him.
But the leader of the Philistines said, Make the fellow go back to the
           place you have given him;
let him not go with us to battle,
that in the battle he should not turn against us;
for with what should he reconcile himself to his master
if not with our heads?
And another Philistine said, Is not this the David of whom the Hebrews
           sang to one another in their dances,
Saul slew his thousands and David his ten thousands?
Then the king of Gath sent for David and said to him,
Surely you have been upright;
I have found no evil in you since the day you came to me,
but the lords will not have you.
Go in peace, then, not to displease the lords of the Philistines.
And David answered, What have I done?
Have you not promised me, Surely you shall go out with me to battle,
           you and your men?
What evil have you found in me

that I may not fight the enemies of my lord the king
to show what I can do?
But the king of Gath said, You are good in my sight as an angel of God,
but the princes have said, You shall not go with us to battle;
now then, early in the morning with those of Saul's servants that have
          come with you,
as soon as you have light, return.

          Now when Saul saw that the Philistines had come by hundreds
                    and by thousands,
and God did not answer him,
neither by prophets nor by dreams,
he disguised himself and came to a woman at En-dor
that could bring up the dead, to speak to Samuel;
and said, I was a lad of the smallest of the tribes,
and my family the least of all the tribe of Benjamin
and you met me in the gate of your city,
as I came to ask about my father's asses that had wandered away and
          were lost,
to ask where they were for a fourth part of a shekel of silver—
and you anointed me king of Israel.
And we spent the night in talk upon your roof;
you showed me all the work before my hand;
though I hid among the wagons when the tribes were called together,
you searched me out and anointed me;
though I followed my oxen, ploughing my fields year after year,
the messengers of Jabesh-gilead came to me.
And all that I did since you know:
how I freed Jabesh-gilead from the Ammonites,
how I fought the Philistines and the Amalekites and ruled our people,
and had no rest, neither by day nor by night.
Now the Philistines come against Israel by hundreds and by thousands—
and Samuel answered, Why have you disquieted me and brought me up
          from the dead?
Why do you ask me, if God has gone from you and has become your foe?
He has torn the kingdom from your hand and given you to
          the Philistines;
tomorrow you and your sons shall be with me.

The seer was against him
and all the witches:
Saul and Jonathan are dead
on the field of battle,

on the field of defeat.
Accursed,
nevertheless
they went into battle,
Saul and Jonathan,
and died bravely.

The men ran and fell dead on Mount Gilboa,
and the Philistines followed hard upon Saul and his sons
and killed Jonathan.
The archers overtook Saul.
His head and armour are in the house of their idols,
his body is fastened to the wall of Beth-shan.
An Amalekite who was near the field of battle
to see what he could find
ran to tell David,
and brought him the crown that was on Saul's head,
and the bracelet that was on his arm.
David has taken the spoil that his band has gathered
and is sending it to the elders,
as presents to his friends in the cities,
that he and his may live again in Judah.

        For he saved us from the Ammonites—
let us steal away Saul's body and the bodies of his sons
and bury them here in Jabesh-gilead.

        VI
        Ish-bosheth and Abner

        Why have you taken my father's concubine?
Do you mean to be king in my stead?

        Who made you king of Israel and Benjamin, if not I?
I am kind to your house not to give you up to the king of Judah.

        Have I not heard how you sent a messenger to David
to make a league with him:
to bring him all Israel,
to say to the elders,
You have looked for David to be your king;
now do it,
for by him God will save Israel?

You have betrayed me, Abner!
But take care, you will meet a sudden death one of these days:
have you forgotten how you killed Joab's brother
when David's men and yours were playing by the pool of Gideon,
when they fought each other and caught each other by the head and
        sent their swords into each other's sides,
and you struck Joab's brother with the staff of your spear
so that the end of it came out behind his body and he fell down
        and died?
Do you think Joab has forgotten?
Do you think David's captain will let you become as great in David's
        court as here?

      Joab knows that I called to the lad to turn away,
to catch one of the young men and take his armour;
that he would not, but turned neither to the right nor left but
        followed me—
but never fear for me, you unworthy son of Saul,
but for yourself,
that none of your captains
comes into your house as you lie upon your bed
and sticks his knife into the fat of your belly until the dirt comes out,
and cuts off your head to bring it as a gift to David.

      Have you this in mind?

      Not I.
I have no need to steal upon a man asleep or unawares.
But I have come not to quarrel, but with a piece of news:
David sends me word that I should bring him Michal, whom Saul gave
        him as his wife.
Now send for her that I may bring her to David;
we must humour the king of Judah—
and your father was unjust to take her away and give her to another.
Look at Paltiel,
whom Saul chose for a son-in-law;
look at the tears in his eyes.
What, are you afraid to draw your sword at the Lion of Judah?
Well, well,
we shall let you run beside Michal,
weeping all the way,
as we bring her to David.
But do not go a step beyond the border of Israel,

or David's sword may take a swift dislike to you
at the thought of the five sons she has borne you.

VII

While I was away on this foray to bring spoil for my lord
the king,
you feasted Abner and sent him away in peace!
And now I am told the king mourns for Abner!

And you sent messengers in my name after Abner;
and as he came back to Hebron, met him in the gate,
and took him aside as if to speak with him—and stabbed him!
The guilt fall upon you!
May your house never be without a leper or one that leans on a staff or
one dead by the sword or one that lacks bread!
Put on sackcloth and mourn for Abner;
a prince and a great man has fallen today in Israel!

You know Abner brought Michal to deceive you,
to find out all you do—.
In the heat of the day we came to Ish-bosheth's house—
we were captains of his—
Ish-bosheth lay on his bed,
we came into the house as if to take wheat,
and cut off his head!
Here is the head of Ish-bosheth, the son of your enemy, Saul;
God has avenged my lord the king today!
When one told me among the Philistines, Saul is dead,
thinking to have brought me good news,
I killed him:
that was his reward for his news.
How much more should I do
to wicked men who have murdered a righteous man
in his own house and upon his bed?
Cut off their hands and feet,
and hang them up beside the pool in the garden;
bury Ish-bosheth's head in Abner's grave.

Now, my lord, the elders of the tribes of Israel will come to you
and say—
for they have neither captain left nor king—
they will say, We are your bone and flesh;

when Saul was king,
you led us out to battle and brought us back;
be our king.
See, my lord, God was with me when I struck Abner;
the enemies of my lord the king and all that rise against you
be as he is!

And yet the Michal that I knew
with all the airs that suited Saul's daughter
and pleased me, newly from the sheepfold.
The sweat and fingerprints of another man upon her.

VIII

I should like to see the mighty men David has:
I hear that they can use both the right hand and the left in
            slinging stones
and in shooting arrows from the bow;
that their faces are like the faces of lions,
and they are swift as the roes upon the mountains.

I should like to see Joab and Joab's brother, Abishai—
I have heard that when the Philistines were in Bethlehem,
David said, That I had a drink of the water of Bethlehem from the well
            by the gate;
and Abishai and two others broke through the Philistines' garrison,
and drew water out of the well and brought it to David;
but he would not drink of it and poured it out to the Lord,
for he said, Is not this the blood of those who risked their lives to
            bring it?

We have heard that Rizpah who was Saul's woman,
is under the tree on which the Gibeonites have hanged her sons and
            the five sons of Michal,
that she is there night and day
to drive away the birds of the air and the beasts of the field
that the birds do not rest on the dead by day nor the beasts tear them
            by night.
            Did not David himself say that the famine in the land was because
                of Saul and his bloody house,
because he massacred us, broke the covenant we have with Israel?
We want neither Saul's gold nor silver for atonement;

David himself gave us Saul's two sons by Rizpah and the five sons
          of Michal
to hang up to the Lord in Gibeah.

      We are an embassy from the king of Hamath:
we have heard how you fought the Philistines
and have taken the bridle out of their hands;
how you have put garrisons in Syria and Moab and Edom and they
          have become your servants and brought you gifts;
and how you have fought the king of the Ammonites
and taken to Jerusalem their shields of gold;
my father, the king of Hamath, sends me to greet you and bless you,
and bring you vessels of gold, of silver, and of brass.

      The Lord took me from following the sheep
to be ruler of Israel,
and now He has given me rest from all my enemies.
Who am I, my God, and what is my house
that You have brought me so far?
I was surrounded
by the sorrows of death,
and the flood of ungodly men
frightened me;
I cried to my God!
He shot out His lightnings;
He took me
and drew me out of the deep waters.
By Him
I have run through a troop,
and jumped over a wall;
He teaches my hands war,
to bend the bow
He has given me my enemies:
I made them as dust before the wind;
I threw them away as dirt in the street.

      IX
      David and Michal

      God—
Who chose me rather than your father and all his house
to be king of Israel;
but you shall die childless.

After you have hanged my sons,
from the eldest who was as tall as I
to the youngest who had not yet learned to walk:
this was my payment.
How much wiser was my father than his daughter or his son Jonathan!
What did you want now with me,
an aging woman who has had five children?
Only the tarnished glory that still is Saul's,
that you should have Saul's daughter for a wife.
Did you expect the girlish body,
the young and cheerful face I had?—
I knew you would not care for me,
that I should never bear a child of yours,
that you had had a hundred women, a thousand women,
and had sent for me,
perhaps because the name of Saul was something still to you and
        your Jerusalem.
Now I see when they say
you found Saul in a cave asleep and caught your servant's hand
that would have killed him—
it was no kindness—
you knew Saul's time would come;
if you had killed the Lord's Anointed,
there would have been war between you and Israel until your death.
And when you killed those who killed my brother Ish-bosheth,
you were the righteous man,
but you had all the profit of their wrong.
Joab you have not killed—who killed Abner—
Joab you need, you are afraid of Joab, he is your captain;
but Joab, too, will find you out some day, as I have found you out—
when his grey hairs go bloody to the grave.
Your scribes will write you down a great king,
and of me—if they say anything at all—
but I belong to that doomed house of Saul
not even Jonathan could save.
I shall not weep before you again;
these tears are the last:
now I have wept them all away.
And I can speak of all my dead
without a tear.
Your scribes will write me down a cold, proud woman,
wandering about the garden of the king,
and you a glorious king, a glorious king.

JERUSALEM THE GOLDEN

1

The Hebrew of your poets, Zion,
is like oil upon a burn,
cool as oil;
after work,
the smell in the street at night
of the hedge in flower.
Like Solomon,
I have married and married the speech of strangers;
none are like you, Shulamite.

2

HELLENIST

As I, barbarian, at last, although slowly, could read Greek,
at "blue-eyed Athena"
I greeted her picture that had long been on the wall:
the head slightly bent forward under the heavy helmet,
as if to listen; the beautiful lips slightly scornful.

3

The moon shines in the summer night;
now I begin to understand the Hebrews
who could forget the Lord, throw kisses at the moon,
until the archers came against Israel
and bronze chariots from the north
rolled into the cities of Judah and the streets of Jerusalem.
What then must happen, you Jeremiahs,
to me who look at moon and stars and trees?

4

Shameless moon, naked upon the cloudless sky,
showing your rosy and silver bosom
to all the city,

King Davids, we meditate business, and you
must now be bathing on a housetop in the pool of evening,
Bathsheba.

5

In a strange street, among strangers,
I looked about: above the houses
you were there, sole companion many a night—
the moon.

6

From my window I could not see the moon,
and yet it was shining:

the yard among the houses—
snow upon it,
an oblong in the darkness.

7

In the dark woods
the dark birds fly:
do you
with your single star, new moon,
come to light this darkness?

8

The wind blows the rain into our faces
as we go down the hillside
upon rusted cans and old newspapers,
past the tree on whose bare branches
the boys have hung iron hoops,
until we reach at last the crushed earthworms
stretched and stretching on the wet sidewalk.

9

On the hillside
facing the morning sun
how clear and straight each weed is.
On our way to the subway this morning
the wind blows handfuls of white petals upon us
from the blossoming tree on the hillside;

how like confetti—
but, of course,
this is the festival of spring.

10

These days the papers in the street
leap into the air or burst across the lawns—
not a scrap but has the breath of life:
these in a gust of wind
play about,
those for a moment lie still and sun themselves.

11

The river is like a lake this morning
for quiet—image of houses and green bank.

A barge is lying at a dock;
nothing moves but the crane
emptying the cargo.

The dark green hill,
the sunset, staining the river—
quiet as a lake;
the tree beside me
covered with white blossoms
that cover but cannot hide
the black gnarled branches.

12

At night walking along the streets, the darker because of trees,
we came to a tree, white with flowers,
and the pavement under the branches was white with flowers too.

13

On this beach the waves are never high:
broken on the sand bars, when they reach the shore—
a stranger might think the sea a bay
so gently do the waters splash and draw away.

The air is sweet, the hedge is in flower;
at such an hour, near such water, lawn, and wood,
the sage writing of our beginnings must have been:
lifting his eyes from the page he chanted,
"And God saw the earth and seas—that it was good."

14

This tree in the twilit street—
the pods hang from its bare symmetrical branches
motionless—
but if, like God, a century were to us
the twinkling of an eye,
we should see the frenzy of growth.

15

In the street I have just left
the small leaves of the trees along the gutter
were steadfast
in the blue heavens.
Now the subway
express
picks up speed
and a wind
blows through the car,
blows dust
on the passengers,
and along the floor
bits of paper—
wrappers of candy,
of gum, tinfoil,
pieces of newspaper. . . .

16

Going to work in the subway
this bright May morning
you have put on red slippers;
do they dance behind the counters
in the store, or about the machines
in the shop where you work?

Rails in the subway,
what did you know of happiness,
when you were ore in the earth;
now the electric lights shine upon you.

Walk about the subway station
in a grove of steel pillars;
how their knobs, the rivet-heads—
unlike those of oaks—
are regularly placed;
how barren the ground is
except here and there on the platform
a flat black fungus
that was chewing-gum.

FOR AN INSCRIPTION OVER THE ENTRANCE TO A SUBWAY STATION

This is the gift of Hephæstus, the artificer,
the god men say is lame.

In steel clouds
to the sound of thunder
like the ancient gods:
our sky, cement;
the earth, cement;
our trees, steel;
instead of sunshine,
a light that has no twilight,
neither morning nor evening,
only noon.

Coming up the subway stairs, I thought the moon
only another street-light—
a little crooked.

SUBURBAN RIVER: SUMMER

In the clear morning
the gulls float
on the blue water,
white birds on the blue water,
on the rosy glitter of dawn.

The white gulls
hover
above the glistening river
where the sewers empty
their slow ripples.

22

The pigeon on the rocks has an anklet about each foot;
the feet slip a little on the granite.
The pigeon shrinks from the
spray
and peers into the
holes
between the rocks.

23

Upon a warm sunny afternoon in June,
where the water overflows the marble basins of the fountain,
the blue-black pigeons walk along the edges,
wading, and the spray ruffles their feathers.

24

JULY

No one is in the street but a sparrow;
it hops on the glittering sidewalk,
and at last flies—into a dusty tree.

25

About an excavation
a flock of bright red lanterns
has settled.

26

The twigs of our neighbor's bush are so thin,
I can hardly see the black lines;
the green leaves seem to float in the air.

27

The bush with gaudy purple flowers is in the back yard—
seen only by its mistress, cats, and the white butterflies.

28

The cat in our neighbor's yard has convulsions:
from her mouth a green jet on the pavement—
she has added a leaf to their garden.

29
AUGUST

The trees have worn their leaves shabby.

30
RHETORIC

These streets, crowded an hour ago, are empty—
what crows that followed the armies of old
will be the scavengers?
The winds of night.

31

All day the street has been quiet.
Not a branch sways,
only the leaves of the corner tree twinkle.

32

The branches about the street-lamp
are so thick with leaves, it shines
only on a flag of pavement;
leaf behind leaf the night rings.

33
SEPTEMBER

The blue luminous sky furrowed into clouds; the clear air
crowded with rain—the dark harvest.

34
AFTER RAIN

The motor-cars on the shining street move in semicircles of spray,
    semicircles of spray.

35

The morning light
is dim and blue—
the silent light
of woods;
but now begins
the slight yet multitudinous
noise of rain.

36

Along the flat roofs beneath our window
in the morning sunshine,
I read the signature of last night's rain.

37

See, your armor of scales, snake,
has not been good against this jagged rock,
and now you are coiled beside the walk,
pink flesh of your body showing,
and the sharp teeth of your open mouth.

Of our visitors—I do not know which I dislike most:
the silent beetles or these noisy flies.

What are you doing in our street among the automobiles,
horse?
How are your cousins, the centaur and the unicorn?

Rooted among roofs, their smoke among the clouds,
factory chimneys—our cedars of Lebanon.

SUBURB

If a naturalist came to this hillside,
he'd find many old newspapers among the weeds
to study.

Permit me to warn you
against this automobile rushing to embrace you
with outstretched fender.

From the middle of the pool
in the concrete pavement a fountain
in neat jets; the wind scatters it
upon the water. The untidy trees
drop their leaves upon the pavement.

44
LAMENT OF THE JEWISH WOMEN FOR TAMMUZ
EZEK.VIII:14

Now the white roses, wilted and yellowing fast,
hang in the leaves and briers.
Now the maple trees squander their yellow leaves;
and the brown leaves of the oak have left Ur and become wanderers.

Now they are scattered over the pavements—
the delicate skeletons of the leaves.

45
HUNTING SEASON

In the light of the street-lamp a dozen leaves
cling to the twigs of our tree for dear life;

an eager star is dogging the moon.

46

Feast, you who cross the bridge
this cold twilight
on these honeycombs of light, the buildings of Manhattan.

47

I thought for a moment, The bush in the backyard has blossomed:
it was only some of the old leaves covered with snow.

48

This smoky winter morning—
do not despise the green jewel shining among the twigs
because it is a traffic light.

49
A Garden

About the railway station as the taxicabs leave,
the smoke from their exhaust pipes is murky blue—
stinking flowers, budding, unfolding, over the ruts in the snow.

50

A black horse and a white horse, pulling a truck this winter day,
as the smoke of their nostrils reaches to the ground,
seem fabulous.

51

The dead tree at the corner
from the gray boughs of which the bark has fallen
in places and all the twigs—
be thankful, you other trees,
that, bare and brown, are only leafless
in a winter of your lives.

52

Now that black ground and bushes—
saplings, trees,
each twig and limb—are suddenly white with snow,
and earth becomes brighter than the sky,

that intricate shrub
of nerves, veins, arteries—
myself—uncurls
its knotted leaves
to the shining air.

Upon this wooded hillside,
pied with snow, I hear
only the melting snow
drop from the twigs.

53

SUBURBAN RIVER: WINTER

The street lights
begin to shine
on the snow;
the river is
flowing
in cakes of ice;
from the luminous twilight
falls
a handful of snowflakes.

54

The days are long again, the skies are blue;
the hedges are green again, the trees are green;
only the twigs of the elms are dark.
At night the wind is cold again;
but by day the snow of your absence is melting:
soon May will be here and you the queen of the May.

55

You tell me that you write only a little now.
I wrote this a year or two ago
about a girl whose stories I had read and wished to meet:
The traveller
whom a bird's notes surprise—
his eyes
search the trees.
And when I met her she was plain enough.
So is the nightingale, they say—
and I am glad that you do not belong
to those whose beauty is all song.

56

Meeting often, we find we cannot meet enough,
and words are counterfeit, silence only golden,
and streets at night are beautiful.
I find the valentines are true, the hearts and arrows—

sighs and misty eyes; and the old poems—
I find them true.

57

It was in my heart to give her wine and dainties,
silken gowns, furs against the wind;
a woolen scarf,
coffee and bread was all that I could buy:
It is enough, she said.

It was in my heart to show her foreign lands,
at least the fields beyond the city:
I could not pay our way;
when she would see a row of street-lamps shining,
How beautiful, she would say.

58

You think yourself a woman,
because you have children and lovers;
but in a street
with only Orion and the Pleiades to see us,
you begin to sing, you begin to skip.

59

All day the pavement has been black
with rain, but in our warm brightly-lit
room, Praise God,
I kept saying to myself,
and saying not a word,
Amen, you answered.

60

Though our thoughts often, we ourselves
are seldom together.
We have told each other
all that has happened; it seems to me—
for want of a better word—that we are both unlucky.
Even our meetings have been so brief

we should call them partings, and of our words
I remember most "good-by".

61

Our nightingale, the clock,
our lark,
perched on the mantel,
sings so steadily:
O bird of prey!

62

The clock
on the bookcase ticks,
the watch on the table ticks—
these busy insects
are eating away my world.

63

My hair was caught in the wheels of a clock
and torn from my head: see, I am bald!

64

If you ask me about the plans that I made last night
of steel and granite—
I think the sun must have melted them,
or this gentle wind blown them away.

65

I once tore up a sapling to make myself a stick:
it clung to the earth, but I cut away its roots,
stripped off its twigs and bark;
a woman passing nodded her head as if to say, What a pity,
and I had no joy of the stick and threw it away.

If there is a scheme,
perhaps this too is in the scheme,
as when a subway car turns on a switch,
the wheels screeching against the rails,
and the lights go out—
but are on again in a moment.

The sun shining on the little waves of the bay, the little leaves of
        the hedge—
with these I school myself to be content.

The house is warm in winter, cool in summer;
but the cloth of the awning ripples and flutters,
the leaves of the shade tree are uneasy,
the twigs of the bushes keep nodding together.

Among the heaps of brick and plaster lies
a girder, still itself among the rubbish.

Out of the inexhaustible sea
the waves curve under the weight of their foam,
and the water rushes up to us;
the wind blowing out of the night,
out of the endless darkness,
blowing star after star upon the sky
out of the inexhaustible night;
wave after wave
rising out of the sea.

When the sky is blue, the water over the sandy bottom is green.
They have dropped newspapers on it, cans, a bedspring, sticks
    and stones;
but these the patient waters corrode, those a patient moss covers.

72
THE EVIL DAYS

The sun lights up
each mote upon the table,
but the old man
finds the page blurred
and lights the lamp.

73
ASYLUM PRODUCT

Brown and black felt, unevenly stitched with purple thread;
what unhappiness is perpetuated in the brown and black of
    this pincushion,
lunatic?

74
THE ENGLISH IN VIRGINIA, APRIL 1607[*]

They landed and could
    see nothing but
    meadows and tall
    trees—
cypress, nearly three
    fathoms about at the
    roots,
rising straight for
    sixty or eighty feet
    without a branch.
In the woods were
    cedars, oaks, and
    walnut trees;

---

* Based upon the *Works of Captain John Smith*, edited by Edward Arber.

some beech, some elm,
  black walnut, ash,
  and sassafras; mul-
  berry trees in
  groves;
honey-suckle and
  other vines hanging
  in clusters on
  many trees.
They stepped on
  violets and other
  sweet flowers,
many kinds in many
  colors; straw-
  berries and rasp-
  berries were on
  the ground.
Blackbirds with red
  shoulders were
  flying about
and many small birds,
  some red, some blue;
the woods were full of deer;
and running
  everywhere
  fresh water—
  brooks, rundles,
  springs and creeks.
In the twilight,
  through the thickets
  and tall grass,
creeping upon all
  fours—the
  savages, their
  bows in their
  mouths.

Jeremiah in the Stocks
An Arrangement of the Prophecies

Jeremiah, in the stocks in the gate of Benjamin, cried to the princes of
   Judah, I have been born a man of quarrels—O that I had a lodging-
   place in the wilderness that I might go from my people! I sat alone
   because of the Lord; I found his word and did eat it—it was to me
   joy and rejoicing. But I was derided, all were sided against me, since
   I cried out—cried violence and spoil! Then I said, I will not mention
   Him any more, but bore His word like a fire shut up in my bones—
   and could not keep still.
Then Pash-hur, the chief officer in the Lord's house, who had placed
   Jeremiah in the stocks, faced the princes of Judah sitting in the gate,
   and cried, This man should die because he has lied and prophesied
   against this city, and has prophesied in the name of the Lord for the
   house of the Lord the same end as Shiloh's! and, pushing aside
   those in the muck about the stocks, struck Jeremiah.
And one of the princes said, Jeremiah, you Benjaminite, even your brothers,
   the priests in Anatoth, have said to you, Do not prophesy or you die
   by our hands; what then do you look for at the hands of others? If
   you have raced with the footmen and they outpaced you, how will
   you run beside horses? And if in the land of your dwelling in which
   you trusted—what will you do in the swelling of Jordan? And at this
   Pash-hur began to cry, This man should die! He must die!
One of the elders that stood beside the princes said, Micah prophesied in
   the days of King Hezekiah and spoke to all Judah, The pride of Zion
   shall be plowed like a field and proud Jerusalem become heaps. Did
   the king put him to death? King Hezekiah weeps, hears the Lord
   and fears the Lord and does justice before the Lord—until the Lord
   repented of what he was to do against Judah. Jeremiah shall not be
   given to the people to be put to death! And all the elders began to
   cry, He shall not die!
Pash-hur answered them, Uriah who prophesied against this city and
   against this land, according to all that Jeremiah had said, when he
   heard that the king was about to put him to the sword and fled into
   Egypt, did not the king send a band even into Egypt who brought
   out Uriah to his death? And is Jeremiah himself to live? The man
   must die!
And Jeremiah said, Blow the trumpets throughout the land, gather
   together, go into the walled cities, set up the standards; for the Lord
   has sent a fierce nation, a scowling people, against you—lament and
   howl! The king and the princes are afraid, the heart of the king shall
   sink and the hearts of the princes, the priests and prophets are dis-

mayed because of the fierce anger of the Lord. Run through the streets of Jerusalem, search in its broad places for a just man, and I, said the Lord, will pardon the city. And I answered, Surely these must be the poor—they are the foolish; I will go to the great, for those know the way of the Lord, to the chambers painted in vermilion, with ceilings of cedar, smelling of incense of Sheba and the burning of sweet cane—as a cage is full of birds, so their houses of deceit; they have grown fat, the folds and collops of their faces shine. Take away the battlements; they are not Mine! says the Lord. From the least of them to the greatest they are covetous; from the priest to the prophet —every one is false. I will take from them, the Lord says, their mirth and gladness, the voice of the bridegroom and the voice of the bride, the sound the millstones make and the light of the candle.

I looked about
and there was no one; all the birds of heaven were fled;
the fruitful place was a wilderness,
and the cities of Judah were broken down.
A great people, whose language you do not know, is coming from
        the north; they grasp bow and spear, their voice is like the sea,
        and they ride upon horses
to mar the pride of Judah, the great pride of Jerusalem;
we shall not go into the fields
for fear of them—
Daughter of Zion,
comely and delicate woman,
the Lord has called Zion a green olive tree;
with the crash of thunder
He has kindled a fire upon it
and the branches of it are broken.
If one goes into the fields, he sees them thick with slain;
if he enters the city, he sees those that are sick with famine.
Because of the sword, because of the famine and of the pestilence,
Jerusalem is given to the Chaldeans that fight against it!
At this Pash-hur shouts again, Should not men like this die?
But the elders reply, He prophesies in the name of the Lord—he shall
        not die!

76

Because of their abominations under every tree,
on every hill, let them die;
because they did not care for poor or weak,
but ate the fatted steer from out the stall,

and on their couches in the ivory houses
early in the morning were drinking wine,
let them die.

Because the lot of some was death, the lot of some, the sword,
the lot of others, famine, and of the rest, exile;
but these wept beside the waters of Babylon and Rome,
and did not forget Jerusalem nor the citadel of the Lord,
let them live, let them live.

77

JOSHUA AT SHECHEM

JOSHUA XXIV: 13

You Hebrews are too snug in Ur,
said God; wander about waste places,
north and south leave your dead;
let kings fight against you,
and the heavens rain fire and brimstone
on you. And it was so.
And God looked again and saw
the Hebrews with their sons and daughters
rich in flocks and herds,
with jewels of silver
and jewels of gold.
And God said, Be slaves
to Pharaoh. And it was so.
And God looked again and saw
the Hebrews at the fleshpots,
with fish to eat,
cucumbers and melons.
And God said, Be gone
into the wilderness by the Red Sea
and the wilderness of Shur and the wilderness
of Shin; let Amalek come upon you,
and fiery serpents bite you. And it was so.
And God looked again and saw in a land of brooks and springs and
fountains,
wheat and barley,
the Hebrews, in a land on which they did not labor,
in cities which they did not build,
eating of vineyards and olive trees which they did not plant.

And God scattered them—
through the cities of the Medes, beside the waters of Babylon;
they fled before Him into Egypt and went down to the sea in ships;
the whales swallowed them,
the birds brought word of them to the king;
the young men met them with weapons of war,
the old men with proverbs—
and God looked and saw the Hebrews
citizens of the great cities,
talking Hebrew in every language under the sun.

78

LUZZATO

PADUA 1727

The sentences we studied are rungs upon the ladder Jacob saw;
the law itself is nothing but the road;
I have become impatient of what the rabbis said,
and try to listen to what the angels say.
I have left Padua and am in Jerusalem at last, my friend;
for, as our God was never of wood or bone,
our land is not of stones or earth.

79

JERUSALEM THE GOLDEN

I

The Lion of Judah

The men of war spoke: Your hand against mine.
Mine against yours. The field is mine! The water is mine!
If the city is taken, kill the men of war,
kill every male; rip up the women with child!
The prophet has said, Let not their cattle live,
not even calf nor lamb before the Lord;
and Samuel, the old man, so feeble he leaned against his staff,
cried to Saul, Give me their king,
give me their smiling king to cut into pieces before the Lord.
But Nathan said to the king, even David, the great king,
You have dealt deceitfully with the Hittite, your faithful servant;
and you shall not build the Lord's house,
because your hands have shed much blood.

II
The Shield of David

Then spoke the prophets: Our God is not of clay,
to be carried in our saddle-bags;
nor to be molten of silver or fine gold,
a calf to stand in our houses with unseeing eyes, unbending knees;
Who is the King of Glory?
He is from everlasting to everlasting;
we go down to the darkness of the grave,
but all the lights of heaven are His.

The smoke of your sacrifices is hateful, says the Lord,
I hate your festivals, your feasts, and your fasts;
worship Me in righteousness;
worship Me in kindness to the poor and weak,
in justice to the orphan, the widow, the stranger among you,
and in justice to him who takes his hire from your hand;
for I am the God of Justice, I am the God of Righteousness.

III
Spinoza

He is the stars,
multitudinous as the drops of rain,
and the worm at our feet,
leaving only a blot on the stone;
except God there is nothing.

God neither hates nor loves, has neither pleasure nor pain;
were God to hate or love, He would not be God;
He is not a hero to fight our enemies,
nor like a king to be angry or pleased at us,
nor even a father to give us our daily bread, forgive us our trespasses;
nothing is but as He wishes,
nothing was but as He willed it;
as He wills it, so it will be.

IV
Karl Marx

We shall arise while the stars are still shining,
while the street-lights burn brightly in the dawn,
to begin the work we delight in,

and no one shall tell us, Go,
you must go now
to the shop or office you work in
to waste your life for your living.
There shall be no more war, no more hatred;
none of us shall die of sickness;
there shall be bread and no one hunger for bread—
and fruit better than any a wild tree grew.
Wheels of steel and pistons of steel
shall fetch us water and hew us wood;
we shall call nothing mine—nothing for ourselves only.
Proclaim to the seed of man
throughout the length and breadth of the continents,
From each according to his strength,
to each according to his need.

In Memoriam: 1933

1. Samaria Fallen: 722 b.c.e.

The Sentry. Samaria is fallen, king and princes of Judah!
From the roof see now for yourselves
how hidden in fourfold wings of smoke
the Assyrian bull gores
and stamps the loveliest city of Israel
into pebbles and ashes.
  The King. Why do you all,
priests and captains, prophets and princes, servants, serfs and slaves,
delight in bringing me news
worse and still worse, as if speaking the fear of your cowardly hearts
were enchantment against it—
is there never a hamlet in all Israel to go up in smoke,
never a grove,
but you must hurry here to tell me Samaria itself is fallen?
  The Sentry. Have we not counted the cities of Israel
as a poor man counts the coins that must last him or he starves;
have I not notched the losses of Israel
upon my breastbone, that I am not to know when Samaria falls,
where Samaria burns? If it has been the guilt of my feet
to hurry here with bad news, how swiftly would they have run
to bring you cause for joy and rejoicing!
  One of the Guard. An Israelite is come:
he can talk as yet no more than a gasping fish,
but leans against our wall, breathing deep and quickly
the sweet air of Judah, as if he had nearly lost the trick of breathing.
  The Israelite. The mounds their captives, Israelites among them,
had been building higher and higher
overtopped us—
the swarm of us
who had hurried behind the stout walls, into the rooms of stone,
from the fields, the vineyards, and the pastures;
and they looked down upon Samaria,
as a boy coming upon a habitation of ants
leans over it—
streets and store-rooms, galleries and walls—
the little heap
sand beneath his foot and the lives of its multitude
his.
Then from our lurking places we saw a commotion
in the Assyrian camp and thought it perhaps
such as Saul had once seen among the Philistines

when Jonathan and his armor-bearer climbed among them;
and in broad daylight the Assyrians marched away,
king and captains, soldiers and captives,
and we thought,
Perhaps the Lord has interceded for us at last;
but the host marched towards Egypt,
and left only a single captain and his men to storm the city—
so little was Samaria of the marble palaces for Nineveh,
so small a mouthful Israel and his ten tribes!
The strength of the ants is their multitude,
but Israel is few
and *these* captives,
to be taken a thousand miles,
beyond the great rivers,
among the cities of the Medes, into the outermost provinces,
lost among multitudes.
As for me, what god was in me—
but as I saw troop after troop of captives,
knotted to each other with rope, whipped along,
marched off in clouds of dust,
I who was among those still untied,
sprang away through the files of bowmen,
among the wheeling chariots and prancing horses,
spears and arrows kicking up dust about me,
hearing the shouts and thinking only,
Let it be death if it must be death,
but if it is life, I am free.

    One of the Princes. An unlucky day it was for you, Joseph,
when your sons shouted, To your tents, Israel,
what share have we in Judah?
when you forsook the holy kingdom of the sons of David,
and, worshipping the golden calves of Jeroboam,
came no more to the temple of our God;
then, as one who goes from his city
and meets in a path a band of thieves
and his throat is cut for his cloak,
as an animal is taken for its hide;
as a child, wandering in its play
beyond the street of its father's house,
caught and trussed and shipped for a silver penny
over leagues of desert or the pathless sea—
so you are lost, Israel.

    Another of the Princes. Let the king command those who are
        skilled in words,

to make a lament for the tribes of Israel
that shall outlast the monuments of the Assyrians:
let them tell of the glory of Joseph in Egypt;
how Zebulun and Naphtali under Barak and Deborah
fought the kings of Canaan beside the river Kishon
until the river swept them away;
how Menasseh, Naphtali and Asher followed Gideon;
how Japhtah of Gilead fought the Ammonites,
and of Samson the Danite who fought the Philistines;
let them tell of the prophets of Israel:
of Samuel who anointed Saul of Benjamin king,
of Elijah the Tishbite who prophesied against the priests of Baal,
and of Hosea who pleaded with Ephraim.
The wisdom of Deborah and Hosea,
the bravery of Barak and Gideon,
the strength of Samson,
the zeal of Samuel and the saintliness of Elijah
are gone from us to be lost among the cities of the Medes;
Israel and Judah were small among the nations,
small and afraid, but they were brothers,
quarreling and striking at each other,
and holding each other by the hand;
now Israel, the stronger,
whose land was fertile and whose cities numerous,
whose tribes were ten and ours are only two—
lament for Israel, poets of Judah,
as David lamented for his brother Jonathan.
        The King. Let those of you who are magicians and sorcerers
whisper your incantations and answer me;
answer me, you who are priests
and sacrifice the doves, the lambs and rams of our people
upon the altars of our God,
bright with undying fires of perfumed wood;
answer, you who are learned in the wisdom of Egypt,
and you who are wise with the learning of the Chaldeans;
you prophets and you sons of prophets, answer me;
answer, you who are skilled in war,
who are captains of my bands,
tell me what Judah and Jerusalem are to do,
what I am to do now, the anointed of the Lord,
the son of David,
before the Assyrians shout their taunts at our walls
and at our God,
while their captives are building the siege-works above our towers.

The Chief of the Captains. It is an old saying of our people
that the battle is not always to the strong;
were it otherwise there would be no beasts but the young lions,
no birds but eagles, no fish but Leviathan—
God has given each his life and his strength.
If the Assyrian, like the very locusts for number,
come against us, his horses and his chariots
will ride us down,
and he will take our fenced cities, even Jerusalem.
Now I say to the king, Let us choose men,
even as Gideon when he fought the Midianites
and took the gold moons of their camels,
and make ourselves places in the hills,
even as David on the rocks of En-gedi,
as Moses when he fled into the desert,
where no riders can follow and no chariot come;
if the citizens live, what matter that the cities are broken down.
Let the weak die, but the hardy need not fear;
in our strongholds we shall outstay the Assyrians
until, as a wind blows and is still,
their empire is like that of Egypt now,
as the might of the Philistines;
for if the righteous die, so do the wicked;
if death is a tyrant, he also frees.
We must become what we were—soldiers,
no longer watching herds for others to harry,
gathering the summer fruits for others to rob.

     A Prince. Your captain, my lord, has spoken like a soldier,
and cautiously, as a captain should;
but, before a siege, I have heard the herald's speech,
and, I think, we need not fight at the citadel
before the walls are lost.
Because on the hills and in caves,
as our father Jacob became Israel,
we shall become Esaus,
rather than to give up cities and fields,
our vineyards and our olive trees,
let us pay his tribute to the Assyrian.
Let us cut the gold from the pillars of the temple
and take the cups and basins from its treasury,
the candlesticks and shields of gold, of silver, and of brass,
and send them as a present to the Assyrian;
for it is better that we lose this than all,
or even that we lose all than our lives.

The Prophet. The strength of soldiers, the skill of the captain,
and the wisdom of councillors, cannot save us;
neither arms nor craft will save us
from the multitude of Assyria or the multitudes of Egypt;
the Lord our God alone can save us.
Who is the Lord our God? The God of Righteousness.
The God of Justice will not let the just perish utterly;
the God of Judah hates the wrongdoer:
though he seem to touch the stars with the plume of his helmet,
he shall leave no footprint on the rock
and the wind of morning
shall sweep his tracks from the sand.
Even though your grey hairs go bloody to the grave,
and the chariots press their ruts
across the bodies of your children in the dust,
fear not, you who believe in the Lord:
whether a remnant is hidden in the caves of Judah
or are slaves in the cities of those who speak a language unknown to you,
so long as Jacob remembers his God,
and binds the ordinances of the Lord upon his hand and brow,
hammers them upon the doorpost,
and thinks of them when he rises to work and when he lies down to rest,
Jerusalem is not taken, nor has Judah perished,
neither has the God of Judah become like the idol of a captured city,
that lies, blackened with smoke and blood, fallen from his throne.

2. BABYLON: 539 B.C.E.

An Elder. Our fathers were saved from the deaths
others died by hunger, plague, or sword,
when the cities of Judah and Jerusalem itself were taken,
and from the deaths so many died
along the journey that left our fathers
—the hills of Judah and the sea
out of sight many months and years—
exiles by the quiet waters and willows of Babylon;
but for us the noise of battle, not the battle itself,
is over; there is no shouting of soldiers
to warn us; no arrows; no shrieks
of the wounded;
only the suction
of this city
to pull us off our feet
until the remnant of Judah—Jerusalem and our God forgotten—
are particles in the dust of Babylon,
like other thousands and tens of thousands
Babylon has taken.
    Another Elder. Did the Lord, whom our fathers served,
come from the sky to stand beside them,
or even from the safety of the clouds with His lightnings
save His citadel?—
an aloof God, saving a few alive
of all Judah's thousands and tens of thousands.
Is there another people who, their cities taken,
the temple of their God become the stones it had been,
and they themselves scattered from the land,
are still worshippers of its God?
Nor, as it might have happened, are we captives among a savage people,
a brutish people, living in tents or caves:
these Babylonians are a great people,
living in palaces and gardens—
but we were only shepherds and herdsmen,
tenders of vineyards and of trees, ploughmen;
this is a nation of merchants and warriors,
priests of triumphant gods.
It was meant for ill to us,
but it has been for good, as to Joseph
who was brought to Egypt among slaves
to be second in his master's and in the king's house.

Messenger. To all you Jews,
captives of Babylon,
Cyrus the Persian, worshipper of one god and hater of idols,
proclaims,
Joy and rejoicing!
Your enemy is about to fall
and Babylon become a proverb among the nations!
Return to Judah,
rebuild Jerusalem
and the temple of your God;
your captivity is ended!
    The First Elder. Surely the sun rises in the east!
Let it not be said that God has forgotten Judah,
or that the Lord was aloof
when puddles of blood stood in the streets of Jerusalem;
we looked for one of us—
and our deliverer is a stranger;
now let us hear no more of the God of Judah,
but tell us of the Lord of the Universe and of Eternity,
before whom the multitudes of Babylonia
are as powerless
as when their cities,
the great angels of granite before their palaces,
the great gods and the lesser gods,
will be looked for with spoons in the desert
and remembered
only because Judah has remembered them for evil.
    An Elder. It was hard for our fathers when they were slaves
        in Egypt,
building a mountain range of granite
along the flat banks of the Nile,
under the quick fists and staffs of taskmasters,
to leave the pots of fish that were theirs for the taking
and the plentiful sweet water
for the wilderness
and the knives of its tribes;
how much harder will it be for you, Judah,
to leave the gardens of Babylon,
the suits of linen and the cloaks of wool,
the meats and the cool fruits and wine
to become again dusty shepherds and herdsmen
on your barren hills, Judah;
to toil in your fields

eating only of what they shall plant,
if locusts and grasshoppers
leave what is saved from drouth and the storm,
and thieves and armed bands
what is spared by the locusts and worms.
Now shall the longings of your heart
and the words of your mouth, Jacob,
the sighs and groans, the cries and outcries of fifty years,
be put to the proof;
for the time is come of choosing and refusing:
your deliverer
calls upon Judah with the crash of thunder,
speaking your name with the voice of the earthquake.
      The Prince of the Captivity. Servant of Cyrus,
who hates even as we do,
the vanity of idols,
in a world where their worshippers are like the sands for number,
those who love the truth are drawn to each other
like particles of iron that have known the loadstone;
build on each other like coral in the sea
against the waves, the tides and spring tides, tempests and typhoons,
that would sweep us all away!
The Jews are few; Judah is small among the nations,
without cities and land,
and you Persians have become a mighty people;
but in the battle we have known a pebble in a sling
to do as much
as a spear weighing many shekels of brass,
and Judah will not forget the friendliness of Cyrus.
Now let the young men who are ill at ease
where all the ground is field and garden, street and square,
and all the water is canals,
or the smooth river flowing between steps,
men who like the taste of salt better than that of honey,
try their strength against the hills
and from the rubbish heaps that are Jerusalem
rebuild the city;
replant the land
with olive trees and fig trees, with vineyards and fields of barley, fields
        of wheat;
so shall Judah like a tree that has seen many tribes—
many cities become mounds and heaps—
flourish and renew itself;

for here we are only so much timber,
although smoothed and polished.
And there is other work to do in Babylon—
in courtyards, where flowers and leaves are brilliant
against a white-washed wall, the only noise
that of the fountain and the long leaves of the palms;
in cool rooms
where one need only put out his hand
to take food from the dish
or lift the cup to his lips
while the noise of the street
touches the listener no more than rain;
here others have their work,
like the stars in their orbits, seemingly
motionless,
but shining, not without influence,
upon the action of the world.
Let hands build the walls
hands more numerous
may pull down again,
but we must build in Babylon
another Zion
of precepts, laws, ordinances and commandments
to outlast stone or metal,
between every Jew and the fury or blandishment of any land—
that shall keep up a man as much as bread
and swallows of water in his belly, strengthen him
like links of armor on his body.
Let other people come as streams
that overflow a valley
and leave dead bodies, uprooted trees and fields of sand;
we Jews are as the dew,
on every blade of grass,
trodden under foot today
and here tomorrow morning.

A Rabbi. When I was a boy, sent a captive to Rome,
the ship was dashed, stern foremost, upon a rock,
and other rocks, smooth with weeds, across which the waves were sliding,
stretched beyond, as far as we could see;
when I heard the crash
and saw the steep deck sloping
to the dark water, into which Romans and slaves were spilled,
their hands and feet
finding no hold or step,
and no cry from all those mouths
sound
in the howling wind,
yet there was no such terror in my heart
as now.
    Another Rabbi. In the Galilean hills,
a troop of Romans and Idumeans hunting us,
I hid in a cave
that led I knew not where, but knew it safe,
for the mouth was low,
in a thicket and covered well with vines,
known only to our band and the serpents;
and there was an earthquake—
so slight a shock that, seated as I was,
it rocked me gently,
but enough to start
the ledge
under which we crept
crashing,
and I in the dusty blackness
bruising my hands against the rock
where the twilight of the opening
had been shining.
To stay there was to die;
through vents
I could not stand in,
too low
for walking
and at last
for crawling,
vaults so large,

I hardly heard the
waterfall,
upon a shore
without wave or ripple,
leaning away from
chasms—
cliff below cliff,
down which the falling
stone would strike and
fall, strike
ever fainter,
until it fell in silence,
my hands, antennae,
around stalagmites and rocks, through dung
of bats, touching
cold rock, cold flesh of shuddering
things, bats flying
against my face, squeezing
their mouselike faces
between my lips—
now
to stay here is to die.
      Johanan. Times like these
may strengthen us, as water becomes steam
and climbs to the clouds, or ice
and for a time iron;
our anger at the legions
that camp about Jerusalem,
sure of their eagles that have flown
at a thousand victories,
until the world is become only the suburbs
of their city
and the idols
sergeants of their emperor;
the stench from our heaps of slain
in the fields about the city
and from those that lie
singly in the gutters,
dead of hunger or the plague or a stray arrow,
heat our bodies
to swiftness
and strength muscles never had,

freeze our breasts
hard as breastplates,
and our hands
as their blades;
and yet,
as our quarreling captains know,
and those schismatics who stab each other—
Jerusalem will fall,
this month or next,
this year or this decade,
and Vespasian or his son
and the meanest follower
walk, smiling at the bronze signs
that forbid the foreigner, into the temple,
looking about in the
empty gloom for the
God who has escaped them,
even into the holy of holies,
where only the high priest goes
only on the holiest day.
Here we are
like a pool that the rains have left
in a hollow of the street,
drying slowly in the shade,
and every day it lasts, it stinks the more.
    Another Rabbi. Saul, never doubting Samuel,
knew that he would die on Mount Gilboa
in the morning,
he and Jonathan,
yet they went into battle;
and we, knowing Jerusalem is lost,
our temple to be open not only to Romans and Idumeans,
Greeks and Syrians, but the dogs of the street
will run about its stones,
the birds of the ditches nest there,
and the glory of Judah
darken as a stream darkens at twilight,
may well do no less than Saul and Jonathan.
    Johanan. You have seen a bush beside the road
whose leaves the passing beasts pluck at
and whose twigs are sometimes broken
by a wheel, and yet it flourishes,
because the roots are sound—

such a heavy wheel is Rome;
these Romans,
all the legions of the East
from Egypt and Syria,
the islands of the sea and the rivers of Parthia,
gathered here
to trample down Jerusalem,
when they have become a legend
and Rome a fable,
that old men will tell of in the city's gate,
the tellers will be Jews and their speech Hebrew.
The hurricane, leaving its dead or dying,
leaves also the healing and the hale,
but the sunshine and the stars,
the air we breathe,
the daily bread,
the words we listen to,
and the thoughts of our hearts
become ourselves and our sons.
We who have outlived the empires
of the ancients—Egypt, Assyria, and Babylon,
withstood their conquests or been conquered
and, captives or fugitives, slaves or strangers,
still were Jews,
have nothing to fear from Rome;
I fear
the teachings of the stranger
and the renegade:
it was not because of the captains of Assyria
but because of the priests of Baal
that the ten tribes were lost among the Medes.
Now, instead of the calves
of the rustic Canaanites,
the gods of Olympus—
Aphrodite and Artemis, Zeus and Apollo:
gods of those
who have slaves
and spend their days in gymnasiums,
or in groves talking of wisdom,
and their nights at banquets—
Sodomites;
but our God is the God of Adam,
who must earn his bread,

and yet not the God of the fishermen,
of slaves
and the silly women of Rome,
the followers of Jesus,
who have scraps of the psalms
and the teachings of the Essenes
and of Hillel,
who talk of love and hell-fire,
who are witty about the Torah but believe
in a God who has a Son,
in the Virgin who gives birth,
and the God Who is slain and rises from the dead.
Jerusalem will sink and we must
escape the whirlpool
of its sinking
and save, not ourselves—
its books
in the cupboards of our minds—
but the city
of which these streets and walls,
even citadel and temple,
are only body;
if Judah
shall ride the flood
which rolls down upon the world
to bring all living under its cold waters,
come,
brothers in learning as in arms,
when battlements and fortresses,
strongholds and castles sink,
only a school
will float our cargo.

4. The Synagogue Defeated: Anno 1096

The Monk. A thousand, yes, more than a thousand, years ago
God sent His only Son
to bring peace on earth,
good will to all mankind,
and the Jews took Him
and bound Him
and brought Him before the governor of their land
shouting that He called Himself the Messiah,
that is, their king,
and they scourged the Christ
and put a crown of thorns upon His head
and crucified Him,
as daily they crucify Him still
by their malice towards all Christians
and by their usury which holds in bondage
the bravest.
Many of you have often thought, no doubt,
your fingers itching
for the hilt of your sword or closing tightly
upon your staff, if only you were there
when they led the Lord
through the streets of Jerusalem
or when they nailed Him
to the cross,
how you would have burst through the crowds
to stand beside Him
and have a thrust at that circle of dark faces,
those jeering mouths.
The glory of such a death,
the bliss of it,
were you only there in the muck,
trampled upon by the Jews,
even if no cherubim and seraphim,
angels and archangels
were streaming through the firmament
to greet you,
shouting hosannahs
and singing psalms of praise!
No,
I think you would have denied Him,
as Peter did;

even as He was hanging by His bleeding hands,
you would have denied Him twice or thrice
to the maidservants and the grooms,
before the cocks had crowed;
for is there a town of yours
in which there is not a Jew's stone house,
while many and many a Christian is glad of a hut,
a street along which Jews do not walk, yes, ride,
jingling their spurs,
and none, for all your paternosters, orisons, and masses,
lifts his hand,
and only a child, perhaps,
throws a stone at them
or calls out an unfriendly word.
But your knights
speak softly and pledge them the land of God
for the devil's little coins;
yes, many acres are now in the Jews' chests,
while they go up and down
unashamed before the crucifixes,
sowing a little heresy here,
a little blasphemy there—
brothers in Christ, shall it be said
that the Jew's stone walls and oak door
are stronger than the hands of Christians?
If oak is stronger than flame
and iron than fire,
and a cluster of toadstools
than the step of a man!
Burn and blaze,
step and stamp;
the Jews and their parchments
to the flames,
their children to the font!
    The Painter. Priests and monks
and the preaching friars
may mouth as much as they like
in Latin, or your language,
of Jesus
talking to the fishermen
as they pull in the nets
full of dark seaweed and shining fish;
the blood trickling down His face

in twenty little streams
from the crown of thorns,
and His fingers twisted
about the spikes driven through His hands;
or the ranks of saints
moving before Him in Heaven
as the waves of a stream in sunlight—
you understand their speech because we paint it
on the white-washed walls of churches;
hating whatever is ugly,
preachers,
we paint the knights with lean faces
and smooth yellow hair,
sunburnt and windburnt,
who are not afraid to kill or die for lord or lady,
and the ladies with hollow cheeks,
bodies big with child,
who look proudly out of grey eyes
and give to beggars
with a sidelong glance;
the healing trees
in flower beside the street,
sending their petals to drift upon the stones;
the night
bringing man and beast
smarting in the glare and sweat of day
darkness—
quiet fields and streets;
the day itself
beating with innumerable rays
the night into shadows
and shaping out of chaos
the loveliness
of lifeless and of living things,
washing their colors clean of darkness.
In a field,
feeling the sunshine
as if your flesh were glass—
twigs and leaves in order
on every bush and tree,
bright flowers below,
bright birds about and above—
should you see

the fat body of a snake
and the flat head lifted, eyes watching,
would you not spring away
to catch up a stick and stones;
or, along a road
at dead of night,
toads thumping
about your feet,
would you not step upon the lumps
but for disgust?
The hairy insects
on your table,
the Jews—
brush to the floor
and stamp into the rushes!
The leaves of your city are become
green skeletons
from which hang worms and the white threads
of worms; citizens,
like the rain for number,
splash and dash
against walls and cobblestones—
wash away the Jews!
Set the beauty of flames
to their ugliness;
pick and pluck,
rake and sweep,
kindle;
let not the hair
of a Jew's beard
escape in the wind!
       The Crowd. The burgomaster!
       The Burgomaster. I know you—
shoemakers, makers of hoods or jerkins,
herdsmen, shepherds, and farmers,
merchants of cheese and wool,
priests and soldiers;
so were your fathers,
so your sons,
by sunlight and starlight in our places—
in fields and streets,
in houses, church or castle,
with love and charity

to those below us, in obedience and love
to those above,
from sacrament to sacrament,
from baptism to extreme unction.
But what are you in the city,
one of the synagogue?
A Jew,
come from the east or west,
and going north or south;
no trade but buyer and seller,
no merchandise but money;
every man's servant
and the liege of none;
pulling off his cap to the peasants
and saying, my lords, but in his heart calling the lords louts.
We have no need of you
and no place for you;
we did not bid you come
and will not let you go—
what you have gathered
here and in all Christendom
shall be the harvest
your blood shall grow for us
between the cobblestones of our streets.

5. Spain: Anno 1492

Torquemada. Now that Castile and Aragon in holy wedlock
are Spain,
and the last city of the Moors in Spain is Spanish
except for Moor and Jew—
about every crucifix in every market-place
and in the court itself the Jews!—
as seven centuries of Christian valor, Christian piety
triumph
stay not your hand;
Spain of the knights,
one in fealty to your majesties,
become one in faith,
Spain of the saints!
Like the sun,
rising as our Savior from His tomb into the brilliant sky
blaze
until the clouds that still obscure the light
are drawn into His brightness
and earth is brilliant as the sky is bright.
Spain newly united
still divided—
as the season of cold is the season of darkness
in the spring of our rejoicing that the Moor is gone from Spain,
the Jew go too!
But if the Spaniard speaks,
I speak no less a Christian:
throw away the curse, you Jews,
of fifteen hundred years;
stay and prosper
and Church and Heaven prosper,
in our nets a goodly catch.
Think not that we want aught of you
but your souls;
your money and your jewels—
all your trash—
keep if you stay and are Christian,
take if you are Jews and go;
we ask of you nothing but your Judaism
which has brought you so much misery
and will bring each of you—
the youngest and the gentlest—

to the flames of Hell
and the worm that dies not.
We give you,
miserable sinners,
the waters of
Paradise;
we give you the blessings of the saints,
the blessings of Mary, the blessed mother of Christ,
and the blessings of our Lord Jesus.

     Isabella. There is a sweet reasonableness in the words of our prior;
it is Saint Dominic who speaks to us
through his Dominican or Saint James himself.

     Abrabanel. No noble in your court, your majesties,
proud of his forefather, conquering Goth or Visigoth or Vandal,
is of an older Spanish line than we—
Jews in Iberia before the Romans came.
No noble boasting his service
boasts of more than that Jew who through a thousand shoals and reefs
piloted Aragon to Castile—your marriage and Spain's glory.
The rest of us, many tens of thousands,
serve you humbly
in smithy, field or vineyard, soldiers or physicians,
as we have served in Spain two thousand years,
Spaniards, true to your majesties
as we are to the God of Israel—and of Spain,
unlike the others only in our faith
for which, if we must answer,
we shall answer to our God.

     Torquemada. Since all we do,
and each word spoken, if only in our hearts,
must be in worship—
not a leaf falls slowly but in His service—
to be unlike us in our faith
is to be unlike in everything.
True, you Jews must answer to your God,
and in the flames and burning ice of Hell forever
you shall answer;
but we too, priests, bishops, queen and king,
must answer for you:
farmer or captain answers;
shall we be less answerable for souls?

     Abrabanel. You do not honor your God
by bringing Him captives,

like a mere emperor
who must have retainers and retinue,
serfs and forced labor;
the loadstone
without visible motion
draws to itself every particle of iron;
the sword—even though a winged angel swings it—
served only
to drive Adam from his paradise.
Your fingers stiff with rings and jewels,
you dishonor your faith, your majesties, by cruelty,
give it whatever noble name you will
as princes make a rogue knight or lord.
Will thieves and pirates be gentler with us
than your constables and soldiers?—
your majesties will hear of many
ripped up for the jewels it will be said they swallowed;
many left by sailors to die on reefs and sandbars
for a smock or a pair of hose; many dead of plague
or found like birds in winter
dead in the fields about towns or like fish upon a beach;
many will die as slaves at work
beasts would be fitter for but costlier,
who have written a page of Castilian
or handled a Toledo blade with the best.
And yet the weak has each his strength,
Spain of Spaniard, Basque, and Catalonian, Moor and Gypsy,
else all beasts were tigers,
all fish sharks,
and only giants left;
the stricken remember—
as wounds and scars last longer than the blow—
and if drops of water wear channels in the rock
on which the earth itself is,
in the action of centuries
how powerful are tears.
Would you have our religion
like our clothes—for comfort and the eyes of men,
put off at night,
and we left lying naked in the darkness?
The body is like roots stretching down into the earth—
forcing still a way over stones and under rock, through sand,
sucking nourishment in darkness,

bearing the tread of man and beast,
and of the earth forever;
but the spirit—
twigs and leaves
spreading
through sunshine
or the luminous darkness
of twilight, evening, night, and dawn,
moving
in every wind of heaven
and turning
to whatever corner of the sky is brightest,
compelled by nothing stronger than the light;
the body is like earth,
the spirit like water
without which earth is sand
and which must be free or stagnant;
or if the body is as water,
the spirit is like air
that must have doors and windows
or else is stuffy and unbreathable—
or like the fire
of which sun and stars have been compounded,
which Joshua could command but for an hour.

     Isabella. If our eye offends us,
pluck it out!
Even so, we will sweep away the Jews
from every town and hamlet, field and corner of our dominion,
though they are the sands for number.
Go and begone—but stay as Christians;
come and be dear to us,
as the Prodigal!

     Abrabanel. We Jews have been accused of love of wealth,
but not for all our wealth in Spain,
fields and vineyards, houses of timber and houses of stone
that we must leave,
and all the wealth that will be stolen from us,
will we stay;
we Jews have been accused of arrogance,
but not for all the dignities that we must leave,
our offices and honors
in this, the proudest court of Christendom,
will we stay;

we Jews have been accused of love of life,
delighting in the flesh,
but though we shall die along a thousand roads
we will not stay—
striking roots
somewhere
to flourish
as we flourished,
giving shade and fruit.

6. POLAND: *ANNO 1700*

An Old Jew. There we were throughout Poland,
a Jew or two in each hamlet, a dozen in each village,
and a thousand or so in every town—
who knows how many thousands and tens of thousands—
going about in the dust of summer
or against the cold wind with noses deep in our collars,
hands pushed into our sleeves,
selling and buying—
this lord's cow and that lord's sack of wheat,
scheming as hard to earn our bread
as a minister might to rule a kingdom,
when, crash!
as a dish slips from a woman's hands
and lies in pieces on the ground,
our bustling ended,
and we were scurrying from the Cossacks
straight for the towns—
their bands trotting along the roads,
booty hanging about their saddles,
lances tall as the chimneys;
many a Jew and Pole were skewered together
on those lances, or hanged
side by side with a pig between them—
boughs were heavy with that harvest;
and still the Cossacks came
breeding in the plunder,
until cannon no longer stopped them,
and gates of towns could not keep them out—
Kiev was taken;
the dead along highway and byway,
pools of blood in streets and houses
drew the troops of them on their swift horses out of the steppes,
many and as pitiless as insects.
    A Young Jew. How tiresome these old stories are—
Assyrians and Syrians,
now Germans and now the Cossacks;
how the Cossacks plundered and killed the Jews of Poland
or that the glory of the Jews in Spain
was muddied
as sunshine on a pool by cattle.
Tell us of the Jews along the Rhine

before the crusades; before the Inquisition,
upon the plains from which the snowy Pyrenees are seen;
tell us of our glory in Babylon,
of our glory in Egypt,
that we who in the alleys and the byways
of these Polish cities
have only synagogues of wood,
who in the fairs and market-places sweat or freeze beside our booths
        and wagons
from dawn to darkness,
may hide that splendor
in our hearts.
      The Old Jew. As soldiers in their drill
charge and beat back the charge
of a foe they may never meet,
so we strengthen ourselves
in struggling with our fathers' foes, long harmless
and merely the people of our thoughts—
but some day ready again to act in flesh and blood,
surely as a hard winter brings the wolves howling
along the forest roads and even to the streets.
      Another Jew. These are the pools
where the market-place is sunken,
but the ground is wet
and the rain is falling everywhere.
The wind is blowing in every street—
only banging a shutter
or whirling up dust
in a corner;
but it will blow a storm again.
Unravel this world
with your nervous fingers
and reweave the knotted thread
on the loom of the Talmud;
sort the dirty rags of the world,
buyers of old clothes, ragpickers;
gather the bits
and refine it in the fire of the Torah,
buyers of bottles and rusty metal,
dealers in junk;
peddlers and keepers of stands and booths,
and even you who have stores on streets,
you great merchants who buy flax in Russia

and ship furs to Germany,
I have heard it said there is no goods like the Talmud,
no goods like the Torah.
The sun was heavy on my head,
the earth was hot beneath my shoes
in the alley
that led to other alleys
and other alleys,
but I stepped into the garden,
into the cool palace of the Torah.
    A Young Jew. You look at the world through printed pages—
dirty panes of glass;
and even if the pages are the Talmud
and those who have written wrote with diamonds,
the more they scratched, less clearly we can see.
I see neither rag nor bark,
flesh nor leaf,
I feel neither sticks nor stones,
cloth nor pillow,
neither rain nor snow nor wind nor sunshine;
I see God only and my spirit brightens
like a mirror;
I touch Him touching all I touch;
on earth I am as close to Him as those in Heaven.
Could I teach myself to want nothing,
nothing could be taken from me;
I should be unafraid of today or tomorrow,
and live in eternity like God.
Cold and hunger, pain and grief
do not last,
are mortal like myself;
only the joy in God has no end—
this it is that in the wind
showers the petals upon the grass,
whirls up the glistening snow,
or sweeps the dust along the streets before the storm;
it shines into me
as the sun upon a tree in winter
after rain.
Light becomes colors,
colors
light and shadows—
dusk and dawn;

tasting God in the salt water
and the sweet rain,
I sink and my feet have nothing to rest on,
I rise and my hands find nothing to hold,
and am carried slowly,
now swiftly,
towards night and towards noon.

7. RUSSIA: ANNO 1905

A Young Jew. The weed of their hatred
which has grown so tall
now turns towards us
many heads,
many pointed petals and leaves;
what did they whisper to each other before the ikons,
and smile at over the glasses of vodka,
the spies and gendarmes, Cossacks and police,
that a crowd of ragged strangers burst into the street
leaving crooked shields of David in every pane of glass
and a Jew here and there in the gutter
clubbed to death for his coat like an animal for its skin,
the open mouth toothless, the beard stiffened with blood—
away, Jew, away!
obey the ancient summons, hurry out of this land!

Republic,
garrisoned by the waves;
every man welcome if distressed by lord or king;
and learning free to all as the streets and highways,
free as the light of street lamps,
piped into every house as the sweet water;
nation whose founders were not leaders of legions or regiments,
or masters of the long ships of war, of bowmen or artillery,
but farmers, who spoke of liberty and justice for all
and planted these abstractions in the soil
to send their seed
by every current of wind and water
to the despotisms of the earth;
your name
is like the cool wind
in a summer day
under the tyranny of the sun;
like a warm room
when, against the tyranny of the wind,
one has come a long way
on frozen ruts and clods;
the oblongs of your buildings in the west—
smooth brightness of electric light
on the white stone
and the motorcars gliding along your crowded streets—

are as the triangles of Egypt were,
and the semicircles of the arches of Rome;
how great you have become, United States!

Or to the land of rock and sand, mountain and marsh,
where the sun still woos Delilah
and the night entraps Samson,
Palestine—
and your speech shall be Hebrew;
what the mother has spun,
the daughter shall weave;
where the father has cleared away the stones,
the son shall sow and reap;
and lives will not burn singly
in single candlesticks—
how much better to live
where his fathers have lived,
than to be going about from land to land—
wasting one's life in beginnings;
how pleasant it is
for the body to sweat in the sun,
to be cool in the wind,
from dawn until twilight,
starlight to starlight;
how much better to live in the tip of the flame,
the blue blaze of sunshine,
than creep about in corners,
safe in cracks—
dribble away your days in pennies.
In that air
salty with the deeds of heroes and the speech of prophets,
as when one has left the streets and come to the
plunging and orderly sea, the green water
tumbling into yellow sand and rushing foam,
and rising in incessant waves—
upon your hills, Judah,
in your streets and narrow places
upon your cobblestones, Jerusalem!

Yet like the worm in horseradish
for whom there is no sweeter root,
should I, setting my wits against this icy circumstance,
make, like the Eskimo, my home of it?

The dust of this Russia,
breathed these many years,
is stored in my bones,
stains the skull and cortex of my brain—
the chameleon in us
that willy-nilly
takes the color where we lie.
Should I, like Abraham, become the Hebrew,
leave Ur of the Chaldees, the accident of place,
and go to other pastures, from well to well;
or, the Jew, stay,
others buzzing on the windowpanes of heaven,
flatten myself
against the ground
at the sound of a boot;
as others choose the thistle or the edelweiss,
take the reed, knowing that the grey hairs of murderers
sometimes go bloody to the grave,
that the wicked die even as the good.
Or, a Russian,
the heat by day, the same frost at night,
the same enemies in microbes and in stars,
say,
These are my people,
Russian and Ukrainian, Cossack and Tartar, my brothers—
even Ishmael and Esau;
know myself a stitch, a nail, a word
printed in its place, a bulb screwed in its socket,
alight by the same current as the others
in the letters of this sign—*Russia.*
Or better still,
there is no Russia;
there are no peoples, only man!

Stay or go;
be still the shining piston
moving heavy wheels;
the propeller
before whom ocean and the heavens divide:
the steamer seen from the land
moves slowly
but leaves a tide
that washes shore and banks;

the airplane from the ground—
an insect crawling
but filling all the heavens with its drone;
a small cloud
raining its sound
from the wide sky.

SEPARATE WAY

1

HEART AND CLOCK

I

Now the sky begins to turn upon its hub—
the sun; each leaf revolves upon its stem;

now the plague of watches and of clocks nicks away
the day—
ten thousand thousand steps
tread upon the dawn;
ten thousand wheels
cross and criss-cross the day
and leave their ruts across its brightness;

the clocks
drip
in every room—
our lives are leaking from the places,
and the day's brightness dwindles into stars.

II

If my days were like the ants,
I might carry away this mountain;
therefore, you must be precious to me,
seconds;
let them step and stamp upon you as they can,
I shall escape with a few grains.

III
Evening

The dark green leaves
of grass, bushes, and trees—
the jays are hushed,
I see no squirrel scamper;
but the street lamps along the winding path
burn brightly—
the work of man is not yet over.

IV

How pleasant
the silence of a holiday
to those who listen
to the long dialogue of heart and clock.

2

Malicious women greet you saying, So this is Marie!
She was such a beautiful girl, my dears!
And afterwards you study your glass for wrinkles and hair graying,
as if the face of a Greek goddess were less beautiful
because its paint has been washed away a thousand years;
your beauty is like that of a tree whose beauty outlasts the flowers,
like that of a light constantly
losing its rays through the hours
and seasons, and still aglow
through twilight and darkness, through moths and snow.

3

I

I will write songs against you,
enemies of my people; I will pelt you
with the winged seeds of the dandelion;
I will marshal against you
the fireflies of the dusk.

II

I eat and am happy;
I am hungry—and sad;
that so little means so much
means that among the little
I am such.

4
Epitaphs

I

Drowning
I felt for a moment reaching towards me
finger tips against mine.

II

You mice,
that ate the crumbs of my freedom,
lo!

III

The clock strikes:
these are the steps of our departure.

IV

A brown oak leaf
scraping the sidewalk
frightened me.

V

Proserpine
swallowed only six seeds
of the pomegranate
and had to stay six months among the dead—
I was a glutton.

5
Walking and Watching

I
Summer Evening

The black sloop at anchor
has a light in the rigging;

the waters of the river
twinkle;
the stars spring up
on the smooth twilight;
row after row,
the street lamps burst into light.

II

The branches,
sloping towards each other,
sway in the wind;
the leaves quiver
in the rain;
flashing when the lightning flashes,
drops of rain
become falling sparks.

III
Desert

The swift river, foaming into waves,
waves bursting into foam,
mile after mile,
under a windless and unclouded sky;
not a beast or bird,
neither tree nor bush, no weed or grass:
a plain of white sand
on which are scattered
black stones and boulders,
or ledge on ledge
rising in barren cliffs.

IV

The water is freezing in straight lines across the ripples;
the ice is so thin the brown leaves
are seen moving along underneath;
the wheels of the automobiles hiss
on the wet pavement;
the bridge has become only a few lines in pencil
on the grey sky—
even lines made by rule and compass.

The street curves in and out, up and down
in great waves of asphalt;
at night the granite tomb is noisy with starlings
like the creaking of many axles;
only the tired walker knows how much there is to climb,
how the sidewalk curves into the cold wind.

6

MILLINERY DISTRICT

The clouds, piled in rows like merchandise,
become dark; lights are lit in the lofts;
the milliners, tacking bright flowers on straw shapes,
say, glancing out of the windows,
It is going to snow;
and soon they hear the snow scratching the panes. By night
it is high on the sills.
The snow fills up the footprints
in the streets, the ruts of wagons and of motor trucks.
Except for the whir of the car
brushing the tracks clear of snow,
the streets are hushed.
At closing time, the girls breathe deeply
the clean air of the streets
sweet after the smell of merchandise.

7

SEPARATE WAY

Take no stock in the friendly words of friends,
for in such kindness all their kindness ends;
we go our separate ways to death.

The love of father or of mother knows
the fear of sickness, the need of food and clothes,
but otherwise—we go our separate ways to death.

Kiss after kiss of the head beside you on the cushion,
but faithful only in its fashion—
we go our separate ways to death.

If you would see the phoenix burn
and in the traffic hunt a unicorn,
well, ride the subway till your death
and hold your job till you are out of breath.
We heard your jokes, your stories, and your songs,
know of your rights and all your wrongs,
but we are busy with our own affairs.
Sorry? O yes! But after all who cares?
You think that you have something still to say?
Perhaps. But you are growing old, are growing grey.
And we are too.
We'll spare another friendly word for you;
and go our separate ways to death.

8

DEPRESSION

So proudly she came into the subway car
all who were not reading their newspapers saw
the head high and the slow tread—
coat wrinkled and her belongings in a paper bag,
face unwashed and the grey hair uncombed;

simple soul, who so early in the morning when only the poorest go
        to work,
stood up in the subway and outshouting the noise:
"Excuse me, ladies and gentlemen, I have a baby at home who is sick,
    and I have no money, no job"; who did not have box or cap to
        take coins—
only his hands,
and, seeing only faces turned away,
did not even go down the aisle as beggars do;

the fire had burnt through the floor:
machines and merchandise had fallen into
the great hole, this zero that had sucked away so many years
and now, seen at last, the shop itself;
the ceiling sloped until it almost touched the floor—a strange curve
in the lines and oblongs of his life;
drops were falling
from the naked beams of the floor above,
from the soaked plaster, still the ceiling;
drops of dirty water were falling

on his clothes and hat and on his hands;
the thoughts of business
gathered in his bosom like black water
in footsteps through a swamp;

waiting for a job, she studied the dusty table at which she sat
and the floor which had been badly swept—
the office-boy had left the corners dirty;
a mouse ran in and out under the radiator
and she drew her feet away
and her skirt about her legs, but the mouse went in and out
about its business; and she sat waiting for a job
in an unfriendly world of men and mice;

walking along the drive by twos and threes,
talking about jobs,
jobs they might get and jobs they had had,
never turning to look at the trees or the river
glistening in the sunlight or the automobiles
that went swiftly past them—
in twos and threes talking about jobs;

in the drizzle
four in a row
close to the curb
that passers-by might pass,
the squads stand
waiting for soup,
a slice of bread
and shelter—
grimy clothes
their uniform;
on a stoop
stiffly across the steps
a man
who has fainted;
each in that battalion
eyes him,
but does not move from his place,
well drilled in want.

9
MESSIANIC

The night is warm,
the river is brimming over
with the light
of street lights and electric signs;
the wires of a star
shine in the mist;
the fine spring rain will fall
smelling of earth,
the sunshine
brighten the streets;
the sparrows will wheel about the shining twigs—
a sparrow flying into a budding tree
curves about a twig to alight on another.

How far and wide
about the upper and the lower bay,
along the rivers and beside the sea,
how close and evenly
the street lamps shine:
you shall know the forests of your fathers
among these posts,
and you their deserts
upon these miles of pavement
whose mica
glistens in the sunlight and the lamplight,
in the heat of summer or the frost of winter,
wet with rain or white with snow.
Though your tribe is the smallest and you are the least,
you shall speak, you shall drill, you shall war;
and, dying,
wheeled away so swiftly
you see the sun
no larger than the evening star,
their boots shall carry your blood—
its corpuscles
seeds
that will grow in the sandy lots,
between the cobblestones of alleys and on the pavement of avenues.

10

The Socialists of Vienna*

The rain is falling
steadily. Two by two,
a column of policemen marches
in the twilight. (Revolution!
Against our boots
strike,
flickering tongues!)
A company of soldiers
with machine-guns,
squad by squad, turns within a square
and marches down a street. (Revolution!
We are the greyhounds—
unleash us!—
to hunt these rabbits
out of the fields. *Listen to me,*
my two wives,
I have killed a man!)
Workingmen troop down the stairs
and out into the rain;
hurrah!
Revolution! (The gentleness of the deer
will never persuade the tiger from his leap.
Strong as a million hands,
what Bastille or Kremlin withstands us
as we march, as we march?)
Who minds the rain now?
How bright the air is;
how warm to be alive!
No children
in the hallways;
the stores closed,
not a motor car;
except for the rain,
how quiet.
Revolution!
Hurry to the power-house;
let the water out of the

---

* I am indebted to Ilya Ehrenbourg's *Civil War in Austria* (*New Masses*, July 3, 1934) for
information.   —C. R.

boilers! The wires of the lamps burn dimly,
the lights in the houses
are out. Tie the red flag to the chimney,
but do not go through the streets,
where the steel-helmets have woven nets
of barbed wire;
bring guns and machine-guns
through the sewer
to each beleaguered house;
and send couriers throughout the land.
Arise, arise, you workers!
Revolution!

Put on your helmets;
troopers, tighten the straps
under your chins;
strap on revolvers;
tighten your belts,
and mount your horses; mount!
Send bullets flying through the panes of glass—
windows, mirrors, pictures;
forward, trot!
I am Fey,
I am Prince Starhemberg;
behind me is The Empire—
the princes of Austria
and the captains of Germany,
armored tanks and armored aeroplanes,
fortresses and battleships;
before us only workingmen
unused to arms and glory!

The bones in his neck part as they hang him,
and the neck is elongated;
here is a new animal
for the zoo in which are
mermaid, centaur, sphinx, and Assyrian cherub—
the face human, like their faces,
but sorrowing for a multitude,
hands and feet dangling
out of sleeves and trousers become too short,
and the neck a giraffe's—

as the neck of one who looks away from the patch of grass at his feet
and feeds among clouds should be.

Tell of it you who sit in the little cafés,
drinking coffee and eating whipped cream
among the firecrackers of witticisms;
tell of it you who are free to gallop about on horseback
or to ride in automobiles, or walk in gardens,
who say, Do not speak of despondency—
or any ugliness;
"Wie herrlich leuchtet
Mir die Natur!
Wie glaenzt die Sonne,
Wie lacht die Flur!"*

Karl Marx Hof, Engels Hof,
Liebknecht Hof, Matteotti Hof—
names cut in stone to ornament a house
as much as carving of leaves or fruit,
as any bust of saint and hero;
names pealing out a holiday among the ticking of clocks!—
speak your winged words, cannon;
shell with lies, radios,
the pleasant homes—
the houses built about courtyards
in which were
the noise of trees and of fountains,
the silence of statues and of flowers;
cry out, you fascists,
Athens must perish!
Long live Sparta!

---

* How splendidly Nature is alight before me! How the sun is shining, how the meadows
laugh! —Goethe.

11

New Nation*

I

Land of Refuge

A mountain of white ice
standing still
in the water
here forty fathoms deep
and flowing swiftly
from the north;
grampuses and whales
going by in companies,
spouting up water in streams
(these wonders of the Lord, I, Francis Higginson,
saw on the way to Salem);
a fair morning,
and still many leagues from land,
but the air warm and spiced—
yellow flowers on the sea,
sometimes singly,
sometimes in sheets;
high trees on every hill and in every dale,
on every island,
and even on the stony cliffs;
banks of earth
on which are groves of trees,
and no undergrowth of bush or brambles;
the sandy shore overrun with vines
of melons and of grapes
which the beat and surging of the sea
overflows
(this I, Arthur Barlowe, saw);
trees of sweet-smelling wood
with rind and leaves sweet-smelling
as the bark of cinnamon and leaves of bay;
soil dark and soft,
strawberries everywhere,
hickory nuts and sassafras;
here are grapes white and red,

---

* Based on Albert Bushnell Hart's *American History Told by Contemporaries.* —C. R.

very sweet and strong,
and plums, black and red,
and single roses, white and red and damask;
we have eaten venison with the Indians,
and drunk water with spice in it—
Indian corn, even the coarsest,
makes as pleasant a meat as rice.
(Without any show of anger
the Iroquois crunched our fingers in their mouths,
and with their teeth tore off the nails;
then hacked our fingers off, joint by joint,
with stone hatchets, or with a shell too dull
to cut the sinews;
and in the stumps of our thumbs drove up spikes
until the elbow;
but so great the help of Jesus,
with this maimed hand I, Isaac Jogues,
Jesuit and priest,
baptised an Indian among the captives,
using the raindrops on a long leaf of corn.)

Let others cry, "New lands!
where Indians shall bring
kernels of gold, wagons full of gold;
whatever spills upon the way
we shall tread carelessly,
for we shall have so much of gold—
so many pearls to sew upon our clothes;
away,
unthrifty gentlemen,
to the forests of Virginia!
There are lands
to feed all the poor of England,
trees
to build each a home;
give us but axes, shovels, and ploughshares,
and away then to America,
all you poor!"
In England a watch is set about us
and we are clapt in jails,
and Holland is a dear place,
for there they live by trading—
but we are a plain country people

whose trade is husbandry,
and we would worship God as simply as the shepherds
and Galilean fishermen,
live as plainly;
away,
dissenters,
to New England!
A great wind is blowing,
heavy rain—
thick darkness;
the sailors running here and there,
shouting at one another
to pull at this and at that rope,
and the waves pouring over the ship;
landing in the rain—
the cold rain
falling steadily;
the ground wet,
all the leaves dripping,
and the rocks running with water;
the sky is cloud on cloud
in which the brief sun barely shines,
the ground snow on snow,
the cold air
wind and blast;
we have followed our God
into this wilderness
of trees heavy with snow,
rocks seamed with ice,
that in the freezing blasts
the remnant of this remnant
kindle so bright, so lasting a fire
on this continent,
prisoners of ice and darkness everywhere
will turn and come to it
to warm their hands and hearts.

        II
        Brief History

Glaciers pushing so far and surely
thaw and withdraw;
even the deep,

while the explosion of its waves
dynamites the cliffs,
leaves new lands,
new groves and habitations
beside the glittering currents flowing quickly
into the silver waters of the sun.

Here are men who find
a comfortable bed
among the rocks,
who wrap themselves
in their coats
to sleep upon the ground
while their horse feeds in the grass beside the lake;
who catch trout in the brook
and roast them on the ashes;
eat the flesh
of bear for meat, the white meat of turkeys
for their bread, and whose salt is brought
in an iron pot across the mountains;
who live
where two hundred acres may be had
for a calf and a wool hat;
or walk where there is no road
nor any man, except the savage.

All the bells of Boston
are tolling
a solemn peal;
the market men will take no more paper money—
hard money only;
soldiers with bare feet showing through their shoes
in the snow, the smoke of the camp-fires blowing into their eyes;
for food a bowl of beef soup full of burnt leaves;
no house or hut, and even the sick in tents.
The rays of your light,
like the sun's, Republic of France,
shone first in the west; the eater shall give meat,
and out of the strong sweetness—
out of the bones of the French monarchy
the honey of freedom;
the bells of Philadelphia are ringing
as if for a fire,

and the crowds,
shouting and hallooing,
fill the streets;
ring, bells, throughout the night,
let no one sleep;
ring, clash, and peal
until the log cabins and cottages of cedar shingles,
the houses of grey stone or of brick,
tremble,
and the listeners
feel in their flesh
the vibrations of your metal voices
ringing,
Proclaim liberty,
proclaim liberty throughout the land!

Wrongs,
like molecules of gas that seep into a house,
explode
in particles of fire!
A captain gallops down the street,
wheels,
and the hoof of his horse
sends the pie plates shining in the sun;
his horse stops
at what is
flowing from the battlefield,
sniffs at it, and will not cross:
this is not water—
it is blood
in a thick and ropy stream.
(The dying Negress says,
I cannot eat dry hominy:
I lived in *Massa's* house,
and used to have white bread and coffee;
and I want something sweet in my mouth.)
On the lawn the Negroes dance
and clap their hands,
So glad! so glad!
Bless the Lord for freedom!
So glad! so glad!

Do not mourn the dandelions—
that their golden heads become grey
in no time at all
and are blown about in the wind;
each season shall bring them again to the lawns;
but how long the seeds of justice
stay underground,
how much blood and ashes of precious things
to manure so rare and brief a growth.

Currents of waste
wind
along the river
between the factories—
the colonnades
and sacred groves
of chimneys;
where once the road
in ruts and ridges—lines of rails
hold to a gleaming purpose,
come wind, come rain, come winter or the night;
build storey on storey out of glass;
light electric lights,
row after row, whose shining wires
will not flicker in the wind;
let the streets sound
with the horns and hosannahs of motor cars!
Man, you need no longer
drudge at plow or oar, no longer trudge;
proclaim this liberty to all!
If bread may be as plentiful,
shall we not share it
as we share water?

12

PALESTINE UNDER THE ROMANS*

The east is alight as far as Hebron.
In the room of hewn stone, the vaulted room,
the priests would hear the noise of the opening of the great gate of
     the Temple;
and the goats on the mountain would sneeze
at the smell of the incense.
Colonnades, a forum, and a basilica,
the camping-grounds of the legions; the tents or the Arabs;
an olive tree beside the winepress or the gap in the wall,
and paths that lead towards cisterns, pits, caverns, and winepresses:
hilly or rocky country,
and a place over which the sea rolls during a storm.

Israel is like a bird
that a creeping weasel has wounded in the head
or a man knocked against a wall—
the cattle have trampled it but still it flutters;

if there is bone enough to make the tooth of a key,
and ink enough to write two letters of the alphabet—
the house is sold and the door but not the key;
the ship is sold, the mast, the sail, the anchor, and all the means
     for steering,
but not the packing-bags or lading.
The cord that holds the balances of dealers in fine purple
and a harlot's shift that is made like network;
the hooks of porters or a weaver's pin
and the point of the sun-dial;
oil dripping into the trough from between the pressing-stone and
     the boards of the olive-press
and lamps in synagogues, in houses of study, in dark alleys.

Put out the lamp for fear of gentiles,
for fear of thieves or of an evil spirit;
when will heart and mouth agree?
Make ready all that is needful for the dead,
and anoint it, and wash it,
bind up the chin, and hire a wailing woman
and two to play dirges on the flute.

---

* Based on the *Mishnah* as translated by Herbert Danby.

Go with a staff and a bag and a scroll of the law,
and fear not the rush of tramping shoes, at the sound of the shouting!
Cut it with sickles, uproot it with spades;
if it grows into the blade, it must be hoed up;
if into the ear, it must be broken off;
if into the full corn, it must be burnt.
In the evening, until midnight, until dawn,
as soon as we can tell between blue and green,
between blue and white,
when we lie down and when we stand up,
each in his own way
(though we stop to return a greeting or greet a man
out of respect, out of fear),
bringing grapes in baskets to the winepress or figs in baskets to
        the drying-place,
trampling the grain and binding it into sheaves,
or the women spinning their yarn by moonlight,
a workingman on the top of a tree or a course of stones,
or a bridgroom on the first night,
or he whose dead lies unburied before him,
and they that bear the bier and they that relieve them—
if our faces cannot, our hearts
turn towards Jerusalem
and you, the God of our fathers,
of Abraham, Isaac, and Jacob.

13

KADDISH

"Upon Israel and upon the Rabbis, and upon their disciples and upon all
the disciples of their disciples, and upon all who engage in the study of
the Torah in this place and in every place, unto them and unto you be
abundant peace, grace, lovingkindness, mercy, long life, ample sustenance
and salvation, from their Father who is in Heaven. And say ye Amen."
—*Kaddish de Rabbanan*, translated by R. Travers Herford

Upon Israel and upon the rabbis
and upon the disciples and upon all the disciples of their disciples
and upon all who study the Torah in this place and in every place,
to them and to you
peace;

upon Israel and upon all who meet with unfriendly glances, sticks and
        stones and names—

on posters, in newspapers, or in books to last,
chalked on asphalt or in acid on glass,
shouted from a thousand thousand windows by radio;
who are pushed out or class-rooms and rushing trains,
whom the hundred hands of a mob strike,
and whom jailers strike with bunches of keys, with revolver butts;
to them and to you
in this place and in every place
safety;

upon Israel and upon all who live
as the sparrows of the streets
under the cornices of the houses of others,
and as rabbits
in the fields of strangers
on the grace of the seasons
and what the gleaners leave in the corners;
you children of the wind—
birds
that feed on the tree of knowledge
in this place and in every place
to them and to you
a living;

upon Israel
and upon their children and upon all the children of their children
in this place and in every place,
to them and to you
life.

Going To and Fro and Walking Up and Down

A Short History of Israel; Notes and Glosses

I

The prince who once left an ancient city
for the sands in which were only snakes and lizards,
the vulture and the owl—wilderness that led to wilderness—
has become this stranger,
whose pillow is a stone,
who leads a flock from well to well
no faster than the lambs can walk,
afraid
of those whose water and whose land it is;

the servant who once served a master well—
Potiphar and Pharaoh—has become a tribesman with matted hair,
this slave, the son of a slave;
a desert fox
become a faithless dog, fawning
upon the sleek Egyptian for a fish,
afraid,
and snarling at the whip
that lifts him from his sleep.

The water is bitter—you must learn to drink it;
the food you gather will not last—
wormy by morning;
you must gather it again.

Your enemies have forbidden you this peace—
this place;
you will find another—
a land of milk and honey,
of springs and fruit trees.

The timid folk that once ran before the horses of their masters
into the wilderness
to cry out at last for bread and remember with longing
the fish and cool melons of Egypt and find nothing
except pools of bitter water to drink—
serpents underfoot and swords in the hands of enemies,
until the weak and meek, the kind and gentle, died,

have become these savages
from the rocks

who troop down howling
to take no man alive
either to draw water or gather twigs,
to whom the women and their children are as baleful,
who burn pots and jugs,
clothing and ornaments,
in the fire
that leaves a heap of blackened stones
where once a quiet people lived;

those wanderers who, fainting in the
heat of day and freezing by night,
still led a few sheep and goats
from wilderness to wilderness, picking their food
from the bushes and scrabbling in the sand for roots,
are now these churls,
become fat
in fenced cities and walled towns—
in ivory houses,

among olive trees and fig trees, vineyards
and fields of barley and wheat,
with cattle feeding beside streams and fattening in stalls,
with men servants and maid servants,
jugs of oil and jars of wine, jewels of silver and jewels of gold;
for whom the Tyrians
bring embroidered shirts and swords with jewelled hilts
and slaves with sticks
to run before the chariot shouting, "Kneel, kneel!"

This meat is forbidden—you must not eat it;
lusts of the belly and the loins!
Your neighbor's house, your neighbor's cattle,
your neighbor's wife, and the stranger's god—
all are forbidden!

Be just
to each other, to your servant, to the needy and stranger;
for you were needy in the wilderness
and servants and strangers in Egypt.

Those who were farmers and herdsmen
in the villages of Judah,
owners of vineyards and olive-yards in the hills—
far from great rivers and cities,
walking slowly as their cattle,
and for whom time was measured slowly
by the seasons,
now live from day to day among the weeds
where the streets end

and the sewers of Babylon empty
into the river,
hurry along,
searching the gutter and rubbish heaps
or selling salt
in the bustle of Rome—
are now carried by the waves and winds
to the uttermost islands and lands,
exiles and captives;

those who left their land
for all the neighboring countries—
standing in the
puddles of the galleys
or following
the chariots, chained together,
to be howled at in towns
and stared at
by the shepherds—

are these Jews
in the cities of Persia and Spain,
in Egypt and England,
who have houses of stone and green fields,
chests heavy with coins and books,
who ride out gingerly on mules and horses
to sell damask and furs and spice,
lend money to the lords,
and become uneasy physicians and counsellors of kings.

Among men who gorge and swill
and sleep in their vomit,
be temperate and clean;

among men who lust and whore
be true; among men in armor
be men of peace; among men in robes who fast and scourge themselves and
      go about
in hair shirts, preaching love and hell fire,
be men of sense; among men who torture
be Jews.

Those who lived in villages and alleys,
in huts and cellars,
selling a calf shrewdly
and buying a sack of wheat cheap
to sell cupfuls
for a copper—
who were pillaged and murdered
in the cities of Germany,
in Spain and Russia,

from York to Ispahan—
their sons
stand up to plead—
in every language—
for the poor
and wronged,
teach by formula and picture,
speech and music—
heal and save!

You who envied Edom
and were afraid of
Egypt, whose soldiers were like the sands for number,
like the stars,
Judah was buried in Jerusalem
to flourish;
burnt—
to step out of the sea
among the breaking waves.

    II

Despite this and despite this,
despite this and despite this, too;
for we are a stubborn people.

The bulls of Assyria gored and trampled us
and the jackals and hawks of Egypt tore us to bits
and the eagles of Rome feasted upon us,
and yet despite that and despite that—
why not, Israel,
despite this and despite this, too?

III
After Reading Translations of Ancient
Texts on Stone and Clay

The Pharaoh of the Exodus is eight feet tall;
of black granite; a god and a sun.
You must have seemed very small, Moses,
standing before him pleading for Israel;
hide, Jacob,
between two rocks in the water, bow down
among the bushes of the desert!

All is well with Assyria; all is well with the temples;
all is well with every fortress of the King!
Let the magicians recite the litanies beside the river,
and send the King his amulet, "To-rest-in-the-wilderness-and-sleep-
        again-in-the-palace";
lead out the white horse in trappings of silver;
muster the bowmen with waterskins and baskets;
set the tents of Israel on fire, set his cities on fire!

The colored tiles fall from the walls,
weeds lift the flags of marble;
the tame lions pace the corridors,
and the spearmen with frizzled beards
lean on their spears in the palace.

IV

Wouldn't they have been surprised, Saint Louis and his knights,
still bleeding from the scimitars,
if, crowding forward to greet the Queen of Heaven,
she were to turn from them and say, pointing to a wretched Jew,
"The bravest of you all is he,
who alone,
hedged in by monks and knights, by staves and swords,

in answer to your question
still denied me!"

V
Glosses

Moses, who left a cool palace and pleasant walks
in a garden beside the Nile
to become a shepherd in a desert,
thought it, no doubt, a small matter
that his people leave their drudgery,
the commands of princes and blows of the masters,
for the wilderness—
just to be free.

As I sit in the street-car and hear the chatter about me,
I do not envy Solomon
who understood the language of birds as well.
What do the birds talk about?
The weather, I suppose.
O yes, they brought Solomon news
of what was said about him
so that it became a proverb not to speak of the king,
even in one's bedroom, lest a bird tell it.

Loquacious Gauls and Greeks,
will you not learn from Caesar
to be brief;
and you, zealous Jews,
still compassionate,
will you not learn
merely to understand
like Caesar?

Scorn
shall be your meat
instead of praise;
you shall eat and eat of it
all your days,
and grow strong on it
and live long on it, Jew.
You will not find it poison
as the Gentiles do.

VI
The Letter

I have heard of this destruction—
it is in our books.
I have read of these rains and floods,
but now I have only to go to the window
and see it.

I was always with Noah and the animals,
warm and comfortable in the ark,
and now—
is it possible?—
am I to drown
in the cold flood
with the wicked,
among the animals that have crawled upon the rocks and hills
in vain?

I walk slowly in the sunshine watching
the trees and flowers,
smelling a pungent weed, noting a bird's
two notes.

VII

On a seat in the subway, staring out of the window at
the noisy darkness, why are you sad?
You are not a Hebrew:
you would have no trouble getting a job
(even a Hebrew would be glad to hire you)
with your blond hair, blue eyes,
straight nose and square chin.
Why, you might be a Viking just jumped from his ship
without helmet or shield, or even a shirt,
and a long sword in his hand;
yet, neither very poor nor drunk,
why are you unhappy, Aryan?

VIII

A dead gull in the road,
the body flattened

and the wings spread—
but not to fly out of the dust
over the waves;
and a robin dead beside a hedge,
the little claws drawn up
against the dusty bundle:
has there been a purge of Jews
among the birds?

IX

I will go into the ghetto: the sunlight
for only an hour or two at noon
on the pavement here is enough for me;
the smell of the fields in this street
for only a day or two in spring
is enough for me.
This peace is enough for me;
let the heathen rage.

They will take away
our cakes and delicacies,
the cheerful greetings, the hours of pleasant speech, the smiles,
and give us back
the sight of our eyes and our silent thoughts;
they will take away our groans and sighs
and give us—
merely breath.
Breathe deeply:
how good and sweet the air is.

X

To wake at midnight,
to wake at dawn,
to say, This is too sweet for me
because of you . . .
If I fast
because of you who are hungry,
if I am silent
because of you who dare not speak . . .

I stutter. How shall I speak to Pharaoh?
I was a dresser of sycamore trees;

how shall I speak to the king and his priest?
I am the least of my house
and my house the least in Israel;
am I also among the prophets?

XI

A hundred generations, yes, a hundred and twenty-five,
had the strength each day
not to eat this and that (unclean!)
not to say this and that,
not to do this and that (unjust!),
and with all this and all that
to go about
as men and Jews
among their enemies
(these are the Pharisees you mocked at, Jesus).
Whatever my grandfathers did or said
for all of their brief lives
still was theirs,
as all of its drops at a moment make the fountain
and all of its leaves a palm.
Each word they spoke and every thought
was heard, each step and every gesture seen,
by God;
their past was still the present and the present
a dread future's.
But I am private as an animal.

I have eaten whatever I liked,
I have slept as long as I wished,
I have left the highway like a dog
to run into every alley;
now I must learn to fast and to watch.
I shall walk better in these heavy boots
than barefoot.
I will fast for you, Judah,
and be silent for you
and wake in the night because of you;
I will speak for you
in psalms,
and feast because of you
on unleavened bread and herbs.

AUTOBIOGRAPHY: NEW YORK

I

It is not to be bought for a penny
in the candy store, nor picked
from the bushes in the park. It may be found, perhaps,
in the ashes on the distant lots,
among the rusting cans and Jimpson weeds.
If you wish to eat fish freely,
cucumbers and melons,
you should have stayed in Egypt.

II

I am alone—
and glad to be alone;
I do not like people who walk about
so late; who walk slowly after midnight
through the leaves fallen on the sidewalks.
I do not like
my own face
in the little mirrors of the slot-machines
before the closed stores.

III

Walking along the highway,
I smell the yellow flowers of a shrub,
watch the starlings on a lawn, perhaps—
but why are all these
speeding away in automobiles,
where are they off to
in such a hurry?
They must be going to hear wise men
and to look at beautiful women,
and I am just a fool
to be loitering here alone.

IV

I like the sound of the street—
but I, apart and alone,

beside an open window
and behind a closed door.

V

Winter is here indeed; the leaves have long been swept
from the winding walks; trees and ground are brown—
all is in order.
Only the lamps now flourish in the park.
We walk about and talk;
but the troubles of the unsuccessful middle-aged
are so uninteresting!

VI

Now it is cold: where the snow was melting
the walk crackles with black ice beneath my careful steps;
and the snow is old and pitted,
here grey with ashes and there yellow with sand.
The walks lie in the cold shadow
of houses;
pigeons and sparrows are in a hollow
for cold, out of the wind; but here,
where the sunshine pours through a narrow street
upon a little tree, black and naked of every leaf,
the sparrows are in the sun, thick upon the twigs.
Those who in their lives braved the anger of their fellows,
bronze statues now,
with outstretched arm or sword
brave only the weather.

I find myself talking aloud
as I walk;
that is bad.
Only Don Juan would believe
I am in conversation with the
snow-covered statues;
only St. Francis
that I am talking to the sparrows
in the naked bushes,
to the pigeons
in the snow.

VII

The ropes in the wind
slapping the flag-pole
(the flag has been hauled down);
behind the bare tree-tops
the lights of an aeroplane
moving away slowly.

A star or two shining
between factory chimneys;
the street dark and still
because the street-lamp has been broken
and it is cold and late.

VIII

Bright upon the table
for your birthday,
the burning candles will dissolve
in rays
and lumps of wax.
Unlike a skull,
they say politely,
This is you!

IX

I am afraid
because of the foolishness
I have spoken.
I must diet
on silence;
strengthen myself
with quiet.

Where is the wisdom
with which I may be medicined?
I will walk by myself
and cure myself
in the sunshine and the wind.

X

I do not believe that David killed Goliath.
It must have been—
you will find the name in the list of David's captains.
But, whoever it was, he was no fool
when he took off the helmet
and put down the sword and the spear and the shield
and said, The weapons you have given me are good,
but they are not mine:
I will fight in my own way
with a couple of pebbles and a sling.

XI

"Shall I go there?" "As you like—
it will not matter; you are not at all important."
The words stuck to me
like burrs. The path was hidden
under the fallen leaves; and here and there
the stream was choked. Where it forced a way
the ripples flashed a second.
She spoke unkindly but it was the truth:
I shared the sunshine like a leaf, a ripple;

thinking of this, sunned myself
and, for the moment, was content.

XII

There is nobody in the street
of those who crowded about David
to watch me
as I dance before the Lord:
alone in my unimportance
to do as I like.

XIII

Your angry words—each false name
sinks into me, and is added to the heap
beneath. I am still the same:
they are no part of me, which I keep;
but the way I go, and over which I flow.

XIV
The Bridge

In a cloud bones of steel.

XV
God and Messenger

This pavement barren
as the mountain
on which God spoke to Moses—
suddenly in the street
shining against my legs
the bumper of a motor car.

XVI

A beggar stretches out his hand
to touch a fur collar, and strokes it unseen,
stealing its warmth for his finger tips.

XVII

The elevator man, working long hours
for little—whose work is dull and trivial—
must also greet each passenger
pleasantly:
to be so heroic
he wears a uniform.

XVIII

This subway station
with its electric lights, pillars of steel, arches of cement, and trains—
quite an improvement on the caves of the cave-men;
but, look! on this wall
a primitive drawing.

XIX
Subway

People moving, people standing still, crowds
and more crowds; a thousand and ten thousand iron girders

as pillars;
escape!
But how,
shut up in the moving train?
And upstairs, in the street,
the sun is shining as it shines in June.

XX
Poet with Whiskey Bottle and Sailor

There is anguish there, certainly,
and a commotion
in the next room;
shouts of
words and phrases that do not make sentences
and sentences that do not make sense.
I open the door:
ah, the hallway is crowded—
descendants of the three wise men,
now male and female,
come again to worship in a stable.

XXI

The white cat on the lawn,
lying in the sun against the hedge,
lovely to look at—
but this stout gentleman,
who needs a shave badly,
leaning in an arbor hung with purple grapes,
purple grapes all about him,
is unpleasant.
Am I becoming misanthropic?
An atheist?
Why, this might be the god Bacchus!

XXII

The bearded rag-picker
seated among heaps of rags in a basement
sings:
It was born that way;
that is the way it was born—

the way it came out of some body
to stink:
nothing will change it—
neither pity nor kindness.
A paralytic,
hands trembling like water,
listens.

Behind her
the sparrows cluster upon one tree
and leave the others barren;
and the town clock,
that stern accountant,
tells us it is six,
and would persuade us that the night is spent.

XXIII
Cooper Union Library

Men and women with open books before them—
and never turn a page: come
merely for warmth
not light.

XXIV

A row of tenements, windows boarded up;
an empty factory, windows broken;
a hillside of dead leaves, dead weeds,
old newspapers and rusted cans.
Now come a group
in old clothes and broken shoes
who say politely,
The way, sir? If you don't mind
tell us
the way, please.

XXV

The young fellow walks about
with nothing to do: he has lost his job.
"If I ever get another, I'll be hard!
You've got to be hard

to get on. I'll be hard, all right,"
he says bitterly. Takes out his cigarettes.
Only four or five left.
Looks at me out of the corner of his eye—
a stranger he has just met; hesitates;
and offers me a cigarette.

XXVI

I am always surprised to meet, after ten or twenty years,
those who were poor and silly
still poor and silly, of course, but alive—
in spite of wars and plagues and panics,
alive and well.
Is it possible
there is a Father in Heaven,
after all?

XXVII

On a Sunday, when the place was closed,
I saw a plump mouse among the cakes in the window:
dear ladies,
who crowd this expensive tea-room,
you must not think that you alone are blessed of God.

XXVIII

A fine fellow, trotting easily without a sound
down the macadam road between the woods,
you heard me,
turned your pointed head,
and we took a long look at each other,
fox and man;
then, without any hurry, you went into the ferns,
and left the road to the automobiles and me—
to the heels and wheels of the citizens.

XXIX

The sun sinks
through the grey heavens—
no brighter than the moon;

from the tower
in single notes
the winter music of the bells.

A stooping Negress walking slowly
through the slowly falling snow.

XXX

In your warm room,
do not judge by that line of clothes
behind the wall of the warehouse—
in the sunshine;
on other roofs
other lines of clothes
turn and twist;
yes, a cold wind is blowing.
The pigeons will not rise
from their roof;
fly to the coop, find the door closed,
and huddle on top,
facing east, away from the wind.

XXXI

The sky is cloudy
but the clouds—
as the long day ends—
are pearl and rose;
spring has come
to the streets,
spring has come to the sky.

Sit still
beside the open window
and let the wind
the gentle wind,
blow in your face;

sit still
and fold your hands—
empty your heart of thoughts,
your mind of dreams.

XXXII
Dawn in the Park

The leaves are solid
in the gloom;
the ledges of rock
in this new world are
unsubstantial.
The sole inhabitants, it seems,
are birds—

until these two,
his arm about her waist.

XXXIII

Stream that a month ago
flowed between banks of snow
and whose grey ripples showed
a sky as grey—
now the stream is seen
clear and as green
as are the willows on its banks,
for it is May:
this stream was turbid, grey,
that now is clear and green—
for it is May!

Your hair be dyed and curled the more,
your dress be gayer than before—
your beauty had its praise,
your anxious eyes now ask it;
but your face will soon be crumpled
like a ball of paper tossed
in the trash-basket,
in the trash-basket.

XXXIV

Holding the stem of the
beauty she had
as if it were still
a rose.

XXXV
Going West

The train leaves New York—leaves the tunnel: yesterday's snow
in the corners of roofs, in the furrows of ploughed fields,
under the shelter of the naked trees,
on one side of roads and one bank of streams—
wherever the morning sun did not reach it;
turbulent streams running in twenty parallel currents;
slopes showing on top a dark band of naked woods.
Bits of coal rain on the roof of the car,
smoke from the engine is blown in front of the window,
and on the flat land beside the rails
the snow is blown about.

Next morning, across the lots, blocks of brand-new houses;
old wooden houses with back porches facing the tracks;
the railway yard widens and the ground is evenly lined with rails,
and we are in Chicago.
The flat fields on either side covered with dried corn-stalks,
broken a little above the ground and flat on the black earth;
ice in the hollows; shaggy horses
trot away from the train; a colt with lifted hoof
looks at us; towers of steel girders, in an endless row,
carry wires on three pairs of arms across the fields. A beam to
        guide planes
flashing in the night.

At last only the morning star is shining;
the plain is covered with sparse yellow grass;
a great herd of cattle—red cattle with white faces and legs—grazing.
Hills with flat tops; snow in the hollows on the steep sides;
a cement bridge with a bright new railing;
reddish ground; above a ridge of hills
black mountains, sheets of snow on their sides, black mountains veined
        with snow.
Low rolling hills covered with sage; neither house nor cattle. By nightfall
        it is snowing.

The dark ground is flat to the river—bright with dawn;
beyond rise the mountains blue and purple;
the blue of the sky becomes purple, in which a star is shining.
The desert is white with snow, the sage heaped with it;

the mountains to the north are white. The train turns
south. We are among rocks:
grey rock and red rock; yellow rock and red rock;
cliffs bare of any growth; walls of red rock crumbling;
a mountain covered with boulders, rocks, and stones;
and not a living thing
except a large bird
slowly flying.

The ground beside the roadbed is green with bright grass;
the trees along the muddy river are bright with buds;
trees in the hollow have budded and are green with leaves.
Palms in the streets of a town.
Purple and white flowers on the desert.
White sand in smooth waves.
A gravel plain like rippling water.
Single lights; many lights; lights along highways, lights along streets,
and along the streets of Los Angeles.

3

AUTOBIOGRAPHY: HOLLYWOOD

I

A street of strange trees
thick with small leaves; a grove of dark pines
with heavy branches thick with needles;
a sparrow that flutters to the sunny ground
unlike the brisk birds that I know.

I like the streets of New York City, where I was born,
better than these streets of palms.
No doubt, my father liked his village in Ukrainia
better than the streets of New York City;
and my grandfather the city and its synagogue,
where he once read aloud the holy books,
better than the village
in which he dickered in the market-place.

I do not know this fog,
this sun, this soil, this desert;
but the starling that at home
skips about the lawns
how jauntily it rides a palm leaf here!

II

I wish that they were with me here
to walk under the palms
and feel the silken air—
my wife, three thousand miles away, my mother,
farther yet, being dead.

You write that you work and are tired.
I know—and remember your dream:
I was looking at the stars and saying
they were like this and like that,
and you, my wife, beside me,
making similes better than mine—
when an animal ran out of the bushes
to bite your foot and gnaw it; you screamed and I,
horrified and compassionate,
stood bravely watching.

III

I like this secret walking
in the fog;
unseen, unheard,
among the bushes
thick with drops;
the solid path invisible
a rod away—
and only the narrow present is alive.

IV

I like this walk in the morning
among flowers and trees.
Only the birds are noisy.
But if they talk to me,
no matter how witty or wrong,
I do not have to answer;
and if they order me about,
I do not have to obey.

V

Shining on grass and flowers,
this is too wet for dew—
it is last night's rain;
yes, the bottom leaves of the bushes beside the walk
are still pasted to the asphalt.
The birds that merely cheeped at dawn
are whistling, chirping and twittering,
wherever I turn. Why then do I look askance
at this man
plodding along talking to himself?

VI

These plants
which once halted the traveller
with thick thorny leaves
and clusters of spines
have become ornaments
to guard beds of flowers.

VII

In the picture,
a turbaned man and a woman are seated in a garden
in which—this very tree
with large white blossoms like tulips.
It is a long way from Persia to the Pacific,
and a long time from the Middle Ages;
yet both picture and blossoming tree
have lived through time and tide.

VIII

A clear morning
and another—yet another;
a meadow bright with dew;
blue hills
rising from a lake of mist;
single flowers
bright against a white-washed wall
and scattered
in the grass;
flowers in broad beds
beside the narrow walk;
look, soldiers of Ulysses,
your spears
have begun to flower, too!

IX

The grass is high beside the asphalt
and yellow poppies and small blue flowers are growing
where the rains have washed earth upon it from the bank.
I see only the old prints of a dog.
A bird runs before me,
stops and runs again
with a querulous cry:
I suppose it would be no use telling it
this is a sidewalk
made by a man for men.

X

I look at the opaque red of the passion-flower coldly
and at these bright odorless flowers
that grow so closely. The poppies are still most beautiful
(that grew in the fields before any gardener)
through whose yellow translucent petals
the sun shines
as they stand straight on the slender stems,
native to the soil and sun—
a bright democracy, a company yet each alone.

XI

The bush beneath my window has grown
until now a twig
is reaching over the sill
as if to show
its cluster of delicate leaves.
You are beautiful, leaves, and silent:
you ask nothing—
neither food nor a fee
nor even that I look at you.

XII
Rainy Season

It has been raining for three days.
The faces of the giants
on the bill-boards
still smile,
but the gilt has been washed from the sky:
we see the iron world.

XIII

The cold wind and black fog and the noise of the sea.

XIV

An actress
powdered yellow for the camera—
daughter of the Greek princess buried in Mycenæ

with a gold mask on her face. The hush
when into the restaurant crowded with faces
a star comes:
the painted lips are silent, the painted eyes turn.
The Mexican has finished playing;
he lifts his guitar and kisses it.

XV

The paths are deserted as always;
below, lights of houses and motor cars
and the broad wash of foam;
here, under the stars, beds of flowers, gloom of thick hedges,
and the orderly clusters of palm leaves.
If this were in Italy, you say,
the walks would be crowded,
and here would be rows of tables—
a band would be playing.
Is silence too strong for you?
Must it be diluted
with alcohol, conversation, and music?

XVI

The Greeks would have made a myth about you, my fine girl,
and said a god, because of this indifference,
because you walk away quickly, turning
your beautiful head with its sleek black hair away,
changed you into the starling that flies with angry cries
from branch to branch
after the indifferent passer-by.

XVII

These gentlemen are great; they are paid
a dollar a minute. They will not answer
if you say, Good morning;
will neither smile nor nod—
if you are paid only a dollar or two
an hour. (Study
when to be silent, when to smile.)
The director who greets my employer loudly
and smiles broadly, reaching for his hand and back,
scowls and glares at my greeting. Now I understand

why he managed to give me only his fingers
when we were introduced. Why do you go to such trouble
to teach me that you are great?
I never doubted it until now.

XVIII

The flies are
flying about
and about
the middle of the room—
jerkily
in geometrical figures:
what are they trying to prove—
my guardian angels?

I have said good morning to the man at the door,
good morning to the man polishing the stairs.
Seated in my arm-chair,
on a cushion,
I, the shepherd, stare at my flock—
ten flies.
I came penniless
and found only a few,
never bothered my head about them,
did not pay them,
neither gave them to eat or to drink
nor even spoke to them,
and, look!
I shall cross the Jordan with at least twelve flies,
maybe, twelve times twelve:
how unworthy am I
of all this generosity!

I have become poor, it seems:
my flies are gone—except one
flying jerkily
about the room.
You do not buzz, my fly:
deep in thought, no doubt.
That is well.
I, too, am learning how to be silent,
and have learnt long ago how to be alone.

XIX
Automobiles in a Fog

In the thick fog
under trees thick with leaves
all you clever people are going about
on wheels
with private lights
to your business and pleasures:

your headlights pour their light
before your wheels
for you alone;
no, these are not street-lamps
to light the way for me.

XX

At twilight, twenty years or so ago,
two or three mice would come into the room,
in and out
under the radiator beside the desk;
now
two or three sparrows stop at the window
to chirp a while—pleasanter company.
Surely, I am not unblessed of God.

XXI

I never thought that I should knock
into a post, reel and feel that I was falling
under the broad wheel that came steadily
along the sunny pavement:
my time-table did not call for any stops.

But the world that slides so smoothly
will suddenly, as it has, fly all to pieces
for us—just us.

XXII

I will not question the sunshine
that shines so pleasantly

on my face. I know the answer:
it will not last—for me.

Tomorrow it will rain, we say, and tomorrow is as clear as yesterday;
the mountains are green and yellow—clear of mist;
and the sea, free of fog, is bluer than ever.
But we do not believe this sunshine;
it will not last, we say darkly:
an earthquake will tumble a wall upon our heads
or a thorn scratch a finger and we shall die.

XXIII

The cloudy afternoon is as pleasant
as silence. Who would think
one would ever have enough of sunshine?
A good epitaph, I suppose, would be
He liked the sunshine;
better still, *He liked to walk.*
And yet the dead, if it could speak, might say,
I had grown tired of walking,
yes, even of the sunshine.

XXIV

I will take off my coat and tie; unbutton
my collar; sit in a soft chair;
cross my legs and close my eyes;
open them only
to see the bush in front of the window
stir in the wind.
The bush in front of the window is crowded
with bunches of red flowers among the narrow leaves:
flowers and leaves
have the same colorless shadow.

The single fly that went jerkily about is
resting somewhere;
outside a bird is chirping slowly
a single note.
The room is growing dark,
but the brass knob of the closed door shines—
ready for use.

XXV

I would be the rock
about which the water is
flowing; and I would be the water flowing
about the rock.
And am both and neither—
being flesh.

XXVI
Heroics

In the discipline I set myself
a spoonful of porridge is a breach;
how much more a careless word.
I charge you, Captain Abstinence, put down the rebels;
and you, Captain Diligence, see to the borders—
where are the laurels
to hide my grey hair?

To march, to hurry, yes, to hide day after day,
month after month, eating, so they say, bread green with mould
and drinking water green with scum
to live, crowded in camps or in ditches or alone in a pit,
but glad to be alive, losing day after day,
year after year, perhaps life itself,
at the beck of others;
yet you boggle
at a little hunger, a little thirst.
The forty winks you oversleep, the blade of grass you overeat—
this is the straw that will break your back at last.
If you were walking along a highway,
a step to the right or left
would not matter at all;
but, if you climb the rocks of the wild goats,
watch yourself.

I never tasted food that was better
than the bread and apples I used to buy
for a dime; nor anything to drink
better than water from the faucet
after a long walk.
Here, beggar, three pennies—

your fare to serenity:
abstinence, reticence, diligence—
hunger, silence, and sweat.

XXVII

Strangers would say
these flowers have no fragrance,
but we who loiter
smell them.
You sun yourself.
Very well.
You begin to look at trees and flowers
like a connoisseur of painting. Very well.
I have read of travellers
who fell asleep
to die,
but that was in the winter and in snow;
is it possible
this can happen
in a land of sunshine—
among flowers?

4

TESTIMONY*

I

The company had advertised for men to unload a steamer across
      the river. It was six o'clock in the morning, snowing, and
      still dark.
There was a crowd looking for work on the dock;
and all the while men hurried to the dock.
The man at the wheel
kept the bow of the launch
against the dock—
the engine running slowly;
and the men kept jumping
from dock to deck,
jostling each other,
and crowding into the cabin.

Eighty or ninety men were in the cabin as the launch pulled away.
There were no lights in the cabin, and no room to turn—whoever was
      sitting down could not get up, and whoever had his hand up
      could not get it down,
as the launch ran in the darkness
through the ice,
ice cracking
against the launch,
bumping and scraping
against the launch,
banging up against it,
until it struck
a solid cake of ice,
rolled to one side, and slowly
came back to an even keel.

The men began to feel water running against their feet as if from a hose.
      "Cap," shouted one, "the boat is taking water! Put your rubbers
      on, boys!"
The man at the wheel turned.
"Shut up!" he said.
The men began to shout,

---

* Based on cases in the law reports.

ankle-deep in water.
The man at the wheel turned
with his flashlight:
everybody was turning and pushing against each other;
those near the windows
were trying to break them,
in spite of the wire mesh
in the glass; those who had been near the door
were now in the river,
reaching for the cakes of ice,
their hands slipping off and
reaching for the cakes of ice.

II

Amelia was just fourteen and out of the orphan asylum; at her first job—
  in the bindery, and yes sir, yes ma'am, oh, so anxious to please.
She stood at the table, her blonde hair hanging about her shoulders,
  "knocking up" for Mary and Sadie, the stitchers
("knocking up" is counting books and stacking them in piles to be
  taken away).
There were twenty wire-stitching machines on the floor, worked by a
  shaft that ran under the table;
as each stitcher put her work through the machine,
she threw it on the table. The books were piling up fast
and some slid to the floor
(the forelady had said, Keep the work off the floor!);
and Amelia stooped to pick up the books—
three or four had fallen under the table
between the boards nailed against the legs.
She felt her hair caught gently;
put her hand up and felt the shaft going round and round
and her hair caught on it, wound and winding around it,
until the scalp was jerked from her head,
and the blood was coming down all over her face and waist.

III

They had been married in Italy in May.
Her husband had been in America before,
but she had never been in this country;
neither had her husband's cousin.
The three of them had landed in New York City

that morning, and had taken a train north.
As they left the station, she carried a bundle, her husband a little trunk,
　　　and his cousin a satchel.
It was almost midnight and freezing cold.
Her husband had a paper on which an address was written.
He asked a man near the station the way,
but the man shook his head and walked on.

The saloon was still open, and her husband went inside.
The saloon-keeper knew the man they were looking for,
but he had moved.
Three men were sitting at a table, playing cards and drinking beer:
one was very short, the other dark
with curly hair and a cap on his head,
and the third was tall. That was Long John.

The saloon-keeper's wife poured her a little glass of anisette,
and the saloon-keeper put up two glasses of beer
for her husband and his cousin; and they warmed themselves at
　　　the stove.
The saloon-keeper said to the dark fellow with curly hair,
"Take them to my brother's—maybe he knows where the man lives."
　　　When they were gone,
Long John stood up and said,
"I think I'll get myself a little fresh air," and finished his beer.
Long John and the little fellow followed the others, overtook them,
and went along. Long John rang the door-bell, knocked and kicked at
　　　the door
until the saloon-keeper's brother—in his underwear—
opened the door, and all went in together.
The saloon-keeper's brother said to Madelina, "If you and your husband
　　　and the cousin
want to stay here tonight—
for going where the man you are looking for lives will take a little time—
you can stay in my place tonight. It's so late!
I'll put a mattress for the three of you in the kitchen."
Long John answered, "They will get there quickly—
we will go with them!" And the six went out,
Madelina, her husband and his cousin, Long John and the dark fellow
　　　with curly hair and the silent little fellow.

They had left the streets of the city
and were on the railroad tracks.
Long John went on ahead and the other two

who had been sitting with him in the saloon,
walked behind. Madelina carried the bundle, her husband the little
        trunk, and his cousin the satchel.
She said at last, "When will we get there?"
Long John answered, "In four or five minutes.
You have walked so far, can't you walk a little longer?"
At last he stopped. "This is the place," he said.
Madelina looked about and saw only the railroad tracks
and the ground covered with snow.
"Is this the place? But I don't see any houses."
"They are only three or four steps further on."
Madelina turned to her husband. "Give them some money—
they have earned it." "No," said Long John,
"we don't want any money." And all at once
he had a pistol in his hand and was shooting.
Her husband started to run,
crying out, and holding his hands to the wound in his belly.
Madelina ran after him,
until Long John caught her by the neck
and held her. Then the little fellow came up
and they took her back to where her husband's cousin was lying on
        the ground
dead, beside the satchel, the bundle, and the little trunk.

Long John said, "Don't cry! You've got to be my wife.
Don't think of your husband any more.
You should be glad to be my wife."
"Yes," said Madelina, "yes, yes."
He took the wedding ring from her finger,
but the rings on her other hand would not come off;
and they walked on in silence.
Long John told the other two to go ahead;
turning to Madelina,
he pushed her down on the snow.

Afterwards, they began to walk again,
and came up to the others;
and all walked on until dawn.
In the morning, Long John saw the necklace.
"Give me your gold," he said. She took the necklace off and gave it to him.
They came, at last, to a car on a siding
in which was a store for the workers on the railroad,
and went up the little ladder.

The storekeeper knew Long John. He brought soap and water,
and Long John made Madelina wash her hands
and slipped the rings off.
The storekeeper called Long John aside and asked who she was.
"A whore," said Long John.
"You must go away," the storekeeper answered.
"If a foreman should come around, he'd kick if he saw you.
Warm yourselves a while—I'll make some coffee;
but then you must go away."
They were all silent until the coffee was ready.
Long John and his companions drank it,
but Madelina did not want any. She sat weeping.
Long John brought her a cup of coffee.
"Drink it," he said. "Never mind, never mind!"

IV

Outside the night was cold, the snow was deep
on sill and sidewalk; but in our kitchen
it was bright and warm.
I smelt the damp clean clothes
as my mother lifted them from the basket,
the pungent smell of melting wax
as she rubbed it on the iron,
and the good lasting smell of meat and potatoes
in the black pot that simmered on the stove.
The stove was so hot it was turning red.
My mother lifted the lid of the pot
to stir the roast with a long wooden spoon:
Father would not be home for another hour.
I tugged at her skirts. Tell me a story!

Once upon a time (the best beginning!)
there was a rich woman, a baroness, and a poor woman, a beggar.
The poor woman came every day to beg and every day
the rich woman gave her a loaf of bread
until the rich woman was tired of it.
I will put poison in the next loaf, she thought,
to be rid of her.
The beggar woman thanked the baroness for that loaf
and went to her hut,
but, as she was going through the fields,
she met the rich woman's son coming out of the forest.

"Hello, hello, beggar woman!" said the young baron,
"I have been away for three days hunting
  and am very hungry.
 I know you are coming from my mother's
  and that she has given you a loaf of bread;
  let me have it—she will give you another."

"Gladly, gladly," said the beggar woman,
  and, without knowing it was poisoned, gave him the loaf.
 But, as he went on, he thought, I am nearly home—
 I will wait.
 You may be sure that his mother was glad to see him,
  and she told the maids to bring a cup of wine
  and make his supper—quickly, quickly!
"I met the beggar woman," he said,
"and was so hungry I asked for the loaf you give her."
"Did you eat it, my son?" the baroness whispered.
"No, I knew you had something better for me
  than this dry bread."
 She threw it right into the fire,
  and every day, after that, gave the beggar woman a loaf
  and never again tried to poison her.
 So, my son, if you try to harm others,
  you may only harm yourself.

And, Mother, if you are a beggar, sooner or later,
  there is poison in your bread.

5

KADDISH*

I

In her last sickness, my mother took my hand in hers
tightly: for the first time I knew
how calloused a hand it was, and how soft was mine.

II

Day after day you vomit the green sap of your life
and, wiping your lips with a paper napkin,
smile at me; and I smile back.
But, sometimes, as I talk calmly to others
I find that I have sighed—irrelevantly.

III

I pay my visit and, when the little we have to say is said,
go about my business and pleasures;
but you are lying these many weeks abed.
The sun comes out; the clouds are gone; the sky is blue;
the stars arise; the moon shines; and the sun shines anew
for me; but you are dying,
wiping the tears from your eyes—
secretly that I may go about my business and pleasures
while the sun shines and the stars rise.

IV

The wind that had been blowing yesterday has fallen;
now it is cold. The sun is shining behind the grove of trees
bare of every leaf (the trees no longer brown
as in autumn, but grayish—dead wood until the spring);
and in the withered grass the brown oak leaves are lying,
gray with frost.
"I was so sick but now—I think—am better."
Your voice, strangely deep, trembles;
your skin is ashen—
you seem a mother of us both, long dead.

---

* A portion of the ritual of the synagogue recited by mourners.

V

The wind is crowding the waves down the river
to add their silver to the shimmering west.
The great work you did seems trifling now,
but you are tired. It is pleasant to close your eyes.
What is a street-light doing
so far from any street? That was the sun,
and now there is only darkness.

VI

Head sunken, eyes closed,
face pallid,
the bruised lips parted;
breathing heavily,
as if you had been climbing flights of stairs,
another flight of stairs—
and the heavy breathing
stopped.
The nurse came into the room silently
at the silence,
and felt your pulse,
and put your hand
beneath the covers,
and drew the covers to your chin,
and put a screen about your bed.
That was all:
you were dead.

VII

Her heavy braids, the long hair of which she had been proud,
cut off, the undertaker's rouge
on her cheeks and lips,
and her cheerful greeting
silenced.

VIII

My mother leaned above me
as when I was a child.
What had she come to tell me

from the grave?
Helpless,
I looked at her anguish;
lifted my hand
to stroke her cheek,
touched it and woke.

IX
Stele

Not, as you were lying, a basin beside your head
into which you kept vomiting; nor, as that afternoon,
when you followed the doctor slowly with hardly the strength to stand,
small and shrunken in your black coat;
but, as you half turned to me, before you went through the
      swinging door,
and lifted your hand, your face solemn and calm.

X

We looked at the light burning slowly before your picture
and looked away;
we thought of you as we talked but could not bring ourselves to speak—
to strangers who do not care, yes,
but not among ourselves.

XI

I know you do not mind
(if you mind at all)
that I do not pray for you
or burn a light
on the day of your death:
we do not need these trifles
between us—
prayers and words and lights.

INSCRIPTIONS: 1944–1956

Where is that mountain of which we read in the Bible—
Sinai—on which the Torah was given to Israel?
Perhaps it is in Egypt
where the wild Israelites left the little idols
of the sons of Jacob, the little idols
which stood in the corners of the tents
and rode with the rider
under the saddle-cloth; perhaps it is in Egypt—
a land of such affliction
three thousand years or so afterwards
we speak of it to this day.
Blessed are You, Lord, God of the Universe,
Who has kept us alive.

Where is that mountain of which we read in the Bible—
Sinai—on which the Torah was given to Israel?
Perhaps it is in Palestine;
for Sinai was built out of the skeletons
of much suffering,
in which the lives of the Israelites
were like the sands—
that become in the centuries rock, ledges of rock,
a mountain, and at last
the Law,
cut into tables of stone.
Blessed are You, God, King of the Universe,
Who has kept Israel alive.

Where was the Bible written?
Some of it in Babylon
where the Jews wept when they remembered Zion;
exiles among the hosts of Persia,
to be given away by a nod of a drunken king
to a Haman for slaughter,
or, in another whim of the king,
to be saved by an Esther and a Mordecai.
Yes, they sang the songs of Zion
in a strange land,
even in the land of their captivity.
Blessed are You, Lord, God of the Universe,
Who has kept Israel alive.

Where was the Mishnah written?
In Palestine
where bands of Jews had fought against the legions
until Jewish slaves were so many
a Jewish slave was not worth as much as a horse
and no Jew might enter the city
where Jerusalem had been
except by stealth to weep there
on the day of its fall;
and the Torah might not be taught,
and the houses of study were darkened,
and the scholars and their disciples
were hunted down and crucified
or flayed alive
or wrapped in a scroll of the Torah and burned to death.
But still the Jews at dawn
before binding the grain into sheaves,
before the women turned to their spinning,
or the dealers set out the wares in the market place,
and the porters lifted their burdens,
turned towards the hills of Jerusalem and the God of their fathers.
Blessed are You, God of the Universe,
Who has kept Israel alive.

As when a great tree, bright with blossoms and heavy with fruit,
is cut down and its seeds are carried far
by the winds of the sky and the waves of the streams and seas,
and it grows again on distant slopes and shores
in many places at once,
still blossoming and bearing fruit a hundred and a thousandfold,
so, at the destruction of the Temple
and the murder of its priests, ten thousand synagogues
took root and flourished
in Palestine and in Babylonia and along the Mediterranean;
so the tides carried from Spain and Portugal
a Spinoza to Holland
and a Disraeli to England.
God, delighting in life,
You have remembered us for life.

One man
escapes from the ghetto of Warsaw
where thousands have been killed

or led away in tens of thousands, hundreds of thousands,
to die in concentration camps,
to be put to death in trucks, in railway cars, in gullies of the woods,
in gas chambers,
and yet he who escapes—
of all that multitude—
in his heart the word *Jew* burning
as it burned once in Jeremiah
when he saw the remnant of Judah
led captive to Babylon
or fugitives in Egypt,
from that man
shall spring again a people
as the sands of the sea for number,
as the stars of the sky.
Blessed are You, God of the Universe,
delighting in life.

Out of the strong, sweetness;
and out of the dead body of the lion of Judah,
the prophecies and the psalms;
out of the slaves in Egypt,
out of the wandering tribesmen of the deserts
and the peasants of Palestine,
out of the slaves of Babylon and Rome,
out of the ghettos of Spain and Portugal, Germany and Poland,
the Torah and the prophecies,
the Talmud and the sacred studies, the hymns and songs of the Jews;
and out of the Jewish dead
of Belgium and Holland, of Rumania, Hungary, and Bulgaria,
of France and Italy and Yugoslavia,
of Lithuania and Latvia, White Russia and Ukrainia,
of Czechoslovakia and Austria,
Poland and Germany,
out of the greatly wronged
a people teaching and doing justice;
out of the plundered
a generous people;
out of the wounded a people of physicians;
and out of those who met only with hate,
a people of love, a compassionate people.

The Indian of Peru, I think,
chewing
the leaf of a shrub
could run all day.
I, too,
with a few lines of verse, only two or three,
may be able
to see the day through.

One of my sentinels, a tree,
sent spinning after me
this brief
secret on a leaf:
the summer is over—
forever.

This is the old familiar twilight:
the river flowing blue and rose;
the hero's tomb we used to visit—
and now each to his own tomb goes.

Some have reached their goal already,
become well off, well known—and died;
and some—grey-haired or bald—planning still and hoping,
walk in the twilight beside the rosy tide.

You are young and contemptuous.
If you were the sentry,
you would not fall asleep—
of course.
Wounded
you would not weep.

It was raining and the street
empty. I passed an old woman selling newspapers.
As I bought one
I glanced at her feet.
"So big
in these rubbers.
But it's better than to get them wet," she added,
dubious, "and be sick.
A man lent them. They are rubbers for a man, not me,
and I have to tie them on with a string.
But how big my feet look!" I looked at her again:
only this was left—vanity.

7

Two girls of twelve or so at a table
in the Automat, smiling at each other
and the world; eating sedately.
And a tramp, wearing two or three tattered coats,
dark with dirt, mumbling, sat down beside them—
Miss Muffit's spider.
But, unlike her, they were not frightened away,
and did not shudder as they might if older and look askance.
They did steal a glance
at their dark companion and were slightly amused:
in their shining innocence seeing
in him only another human being.

8

He had with him a bag, a heavy bag,
big and crammed to the mouth with useless slag
of her scolding, fleer and flout,
and as he walked he flung the words about
among the rushes
of the river and under the bushes
on the ground,
until of all her scolding he had not left a sound,
not a sound.

But walking back lightly he saw where there had sprung
from all that he had flung
weeds—and wives with bright knives
digging them up
to have a fresh salad on which husbands sup.

9

The two have told each other all that they have brooded
upon, and now each has concluded
the other is a fool. *The flowers of the earth are withered away;*
the time of the singing of birds is gone. The sky is grey.
In its shadow
are street and meadow;
the park
and all its paths are dark.

10

The golden sun hangs in the shining mist
and lights a noisy world—
not mine.
I will be Adam in his paradise this hour
and never think of ploughing.

11

Put it down in your ledger
among the profits of this day:
the dark uncertain path of the wind
on the bright water;
snow on the yellow branches of the sycamore.

12

Hardly a breath of wind
starts the leaves falling:
the little purposes are lost
in the great designs.

Fortunate man,
where the fugitives
are only birds and leaves.

13

MEDITATIONS ON THE FALL AND WINTER HOLIDAYS

I
New Year's

The solid houses in the mist
are thin as tissue paper;
the water laps slowly at the rocks;
and the ducks from the north are here
at rest on the grey ripples.

The company in which we went
so free of care, so carelessly,
has scattered. Good-bye,
to you who lie behind in graves,
to you who galloped proudly off!
Pockets and heart are empty.

This is the autumn and our harvest—
such as it is, such as it is—
the beginnings of the end, bare trees and barren ground;
but for us only the beginning:
let the wild goat's horn
and the silver trumpet sound!

Reason upon reason
to be thankful:
for the fruit of the earth,
for the fruit of the tree,
for the light of the fire,
and to have come to this season.

The work of our hearts is dust
to be blown about in the winds
by the God of our dead in the dust
but our Lord delighting in life
(let the wild goat's horn
and the silver trumpet sound!)—
our God Who imprisons in coffin and grave
and unbinds the bound.
You have loved us greatly and given us
Your laws
for an inheritance,

Your sabbaths, holidays, and seasons of gladness,
distinguishing Israel
from other nations—
distinguishing us
above the shoals of men.
And yet why should we be remembered—
if at all—only for peace, if grief
is also for all? Our hopes,
if they blossom, if they blossom at all, the petals
and fruit fall.

You have given us the strength
to serve You,
but we may serve or not
as we please;
not for peace nor for prosperity,
not even for length of life, have we merited
remembrance; remember us
as the servants
You have inherited.

II

Day of Atonement

The great Giver has ended His disposing;
the long day
is over and the gates are closing.
How badly all that has been read
was read by us,
how poorly all that should be said.

All wickedness shall go in smoke.
It must, it must!
The just shall see and be glad.
The sentence is sweet and sustaining;
for we, I suppose, are the just;
and we, the remaining.
If only I could write with four pens between five fingers
and with each pen a different sentence at the same time—
but the rabbis say it is a lost art, a lost art.
I well believe it. And at that of the first twenty sins that we confess,
five are by speech alone;
little wonder that I must ask the Lord to bless
the words of my mouth and the meditations of my heart.

Now, as from the dead, I revisit the earth and delight
in the sky, and hear again
the noise of the city and see
earth's marvelous creatures—men.
Out of nothing I became a being,
and from a being I shall be
nothing—but until then
I rejoice, a mote in Your world,
a spark in Your seeing.

III
Feast of Booths

This was a season of our fathers' joy:
not only when they gathered grapes and the fruit of trees
in Israel, but when, locked in the dark and stony streets,
they held—symbols of a life from which they were banished
but to which they would surely return—
the branches of palm trees and of willows, the twigs of the myrtle,
and the bright odorous citrons.

This was the grove of palms with its deep well
in the stony ghetto in the blaze of noon;
this the living stream lined with willows;
and this the thick-leaved myrtles and trees heavy with fruit
in the barren ghetto—a garden
where the unjustly hated were justly safe at last.

In booths this week of holiday
as those who gathered grapes in Israel lived
and also to remember we were cared for
in the wilderness—
I remember how frail my present dwelling is
even if of stones and steel.

I know this is the season of our joy:
we have completed the readings of the Law
and we begin again;
but I remember how slowly I have learnt, how little,
how fast the year went by, the years—how few.

IV
Hanukkah

The swollen dead fish float on the water;
the dead birds lie in the dust trampled to feathers;
the lights have been out a long time and the quick gentle hands that
       lit them—
rosy in the yellow tapers' glow—
have long ago become merely nails and little bones,
and of the mouths that said the blessing and the minds that thought it
only teeth are left and skulls, shards of skulls.
By all means, then, let us have psalms
and days of dedication anew to the old causes.

Penniless, penniless, I have come with less and still less
to this place of my need and the lack of this hour.
That was a comforting word the prophet spoke:
Not by might nor by power but by My spirit, said the Lord;
comforting, indeed, for those who have neither might nor power—
for a blade of grass, for a reed.

The miracle, of course, was not that the oil for the sacred light—
in a little cruse—lasted as long as they say;
but that the courage of the Maccabees lasted to this day:
let that nourish my flickering spirit.

Go swiftly in your chariot, my fellow Jew,
you who are blessed with horses;
and I will follow as best I can afoot,
bringing with me perhaps a word or two.
Speak your learned and witty discourses
and I will utter my word or two—
not by might nor by power
but by Your spirit, Lord.

14

FROM JEHUDA HALEVI'S SONGS TO ZION*

My heart in the East
and I at the farthest West:
how can I taste what I eat or find it sweet
while Zion
is in the cords of Edom and I
bound by the Arab?
Beside the dust of Zion
all the good of Spain is light;
and a light thing to leave it.

And if it is now only a land of howling beasts and owls
was it not so
when given to our fathers—
all of it only a heritage of thorns and thistles?
But they walked in it—
His name in their hearts, sustenance!—
as in a park among flowers.

In the midst of the sea
when the hills of it slide and sink
and the wind
lifts the water like sheaves—
now a heap of sheaves and then a floor for the threshing—
and sail and planks shake
and the hands of the sailors are rags,
and no place for flight but the sea,
and the ship is hidden in waves
like a theft in the thief's hand,
suddenly the sea is smooth
and the stars shine on the water.

---

* There was some question in my mind if I should try to use rhyme as Jehuda Halevi did
or at least follow his rhythms. Franz Rosenzweig, translating him into German, said it was
sheer laziness not to do both. Perhaps. But the reproduction of a meter in another language
does not necessarily have the effect it had in the original: rhyme and rhythm stirring in the
Hebrew may be cloying and merely tiresome in English; it may be light instead of grave
and so clever as to be nothing else. And it is of interest to note that Jehuda Halevi himself
said (Jewish Publication Society's edition, p. xxii): "It is but proper that mere beauty of
sound should yield to lucidity of speech."
—C. R.

Wisdom and knowledge—except to swim—
have neither fame nor favor here;
a prisoner of hope, he gave his spirit to the winds,
and is owned by the sea;
between him and death—a board.

Zion, do you ask if the captives are at peace—
the few that are left?
I cry out like the jackals when I think of their grief;
but, dreaming of the end of their captivity,
I am like a harp for your songs.

15

FROM THE APOCALYPTIC EZRA*

Because I saw the desolation of Zion,
and the wealth of the buildings of Babylon,
I said to myself:
Have the inhabitants of Babylon behaved so well?

And the angel, Uriel, came to say:
"Is your heart troubled
because of this world, Ezra,
and would you understand the Most High?
Then weigh for me the weight of fire,
measure the blast of the wind,
or call back a day that is past."
And I answered: "My lord, what man can do these things?"

---

* This is a rearrangement and versification of parts of the Fourth Book of Ezra (so desig-
nated in the appendix to the Vulgate) or 2 Esdras of the Protestant Apocrypha. I based this
rearrangement and versification upon a translation of the apocalyptic Ezra from the Syri-
ac by Joshua Bloch for his edition of Ezra, in the series of Jewish Apocrypha sponsored by
The Dropsie College for Hebrew and Cognate Learning; and I did so with Dr. Bloch's
kind permission and that of the sponsors.

The apocalyptic Ezra, to be distinguished from the Ezra of the Old Testament,
was written by several persons during the miseries and persecutions of the struggle against
Rome in the first century of the Christian era. It is G. H. Box's opinion that the book as
we have it—without the Christian additions—was edited and first published about 120 C.E.
(see R. H. Charles's edition of the Apocrypha and Pseudepigrapha). At one time, some
scholars believed that the original was in Greek. Dr. Box argues that it was in Hebrew. Dr.
Bloch, however, did not believe that there ever was a Greek or Hebrew original or version,
but only an Aramaic original.   —C. R.

And the angel said: "If I asked you how many springs in the sea?
what are the paths of Heaven? or the gates of Hell?
you would say, I have never gone down into the depths of the sea
or to the gates of Hell,
nor have I ever climbed up into the sky.
But I asked you about fire and wind and the day—
which you know well—
and yet you could not answer;
how then are you to understand the way of the Most High?"

And I answered: "It would have been better for me
not to have been born
than to live and suffer without knowing why;
else, why have I been given a mind?
Why has Israel been abandoned to the heathen,
and the people God loved to godless tribes?
If the world was designed
for the righteous,
why do they not have it,
and are ruled by a people that are like spittle?
Why?"

The angel, his face as bright as lightning, cried:
"Do you think that you love Israel more than his Maker does?
The days come when the evil men do
will be greater than whatever you see
and whatever you heard as of long ago;
and those of one city will ask in the neighboring cities:
Has any good man passed through?
and in the neighboring cities they will answer: No.
Chasms will open in many places
and out of them fire will not cease to blaze;
and even the birds will leave the land.
The sweet waters will turn salt,
and friend suddenly turn upon friend;
women will be in labor and unable to give birth.
Just as a farmer sows many seeds and plants much
but the seeds do not all take root nor do all the plants sprout;
so of those who have come upon the earth:
out of a cluster a grape will be saved,
and out of a great forest a fern.
Mourn not for the multitudes that perish;
for they are like a breath and like smoke and like a flame that burns
        until it goes out."

And I, Ezra, prayed:
"God at Whose word
the hosts of Heaven change into winds and fire—
and it was so when all was dark and silent
before the sun and moon were shining
and the voice of man was heard—
what is man that You are angry at him?
Give us
the flowering of a new heart and the fruit of it—
light a candle of understanding
in our hearts, Lord—
that everyone who is corruptible and whoever is made in the image
       of man
may live."

16

"The lamps are burning in the synagogue,
in the houses of study, in dark alleys . . ."
This should be the place.
This is the way
the guide-book describes it. Excuse me, sir,
can you tell me
where Eli lives, Eli the *katzev*—
slaughterer of cattle and poultry?
One of my ancestors.
Reb Haskel? Reb Shimin? My grandfathers.

This is the discipline that withstood the siege
of every Jew;
these are the prayer-shawls that have proved
stronger than armor.

Let us begin then humbly. Not by asking:
Who is This you pray to? Name Him;
define Him. For the answer is:
we do not name Him.
Once out of a savage fear, perhaps;
now out of knowledge—of our ignorance.

Begin then humbly. Not by asking:
shall I live forever?
Hear again the dear dead greeting me gladly
as they used to
when we were all among the living?
For the answer is:
if you think we differ from all His other creatures,
say only if you like with the Pharisees, our teachers,
those who do not believe in an eternal life
will not have it.

In the morning I arise and match again
my plans against my cash.
I wonder now if the long morning-prayers
were an utter waste of an hour
weighing, as they do, hopes and anguish,
and sending the believer out into the street
with the sweet taste of the prayers on his lips.

How good to stop
and look out upon eternity a while;
and daily
in the morning, afternoon, and evening
be at ease in Zion.

17

IN MEMORIAM: S. R.

This I light for you
will last longer, perhaps,
than if it were on a wick
in a glassful of wax,
than if it were shining wires
and safe in a glass bulb
from any gust of wind.

And you are still here
shining like a star that has
crumbled out of heaven.

18

In Memoriam: L. R. W.

A shadow on the bright sidewalk:
death was beside us
showing his pistol.
No!

So skillful have the undertakers become
that when they buried you
they led us straight away from the grave
and did not let us see how deep the coffin lies.
To the savage, perhaps, each bird has a message;
I know that they shriek only to themselves.
The stars in their courses did not fight for us.

19

I died last week, last year.
I know these streets so well, these skies,
yet look about me with a stranger's eyes.

I bring a message from the wind and worms,
from darkness, dust, and stones;
I wear a shroud beneath this suit
but talk of trifles or am mute.

Many, many that I meet
greet me politely and I greet them, too;
but, once behind,
out of sight, out of mind.

I have no word of blame, no stick or stone,
because I died. The fault, the weakness,
was mine, of course. Mine alone.

20

As I was wandering with my unhappy thoughts,
I looked and saw
that I had come into a sunny place
familiar and yet strange.

"Where am I?" I asked a stranger. "Paradise."
"Can this be Paradise?" I asked surprised,
  for there were motor-cars and factories.
"It is," he answered. "This is the sun that shone on Adam once;
  the very wind that blew upon him, too."

21

I have neither the time nor the weaving skill, perhaps,
for the intricate medallions the Persians know;
my rugs are the barbaric fire-worshipper's:
how blue the waters flow,
how red the fiery sun,
how brilliant a green the grass is,
how blinding white the snow.

22

Te Deum

Not because of victories
I sing,
having none,
but for the common sunshine,
the breeze,
the largess of the spring.

Not for victory
but for the day's work done
as well as I was able;
not for a seat upon the dais
but at the common table.

23

> Thou shalt eat bread with salt and
> thou shalt drink water by measure,
> and on the ground shalt thou sleep
> and thou shalt live a life of trouble . . .
> *Mishnah, Aboth* 6: 4

Salmon and red wine
and a cake fat with raisins and nuts:
no diet for a writer of verse

who must learn to fast
and drink water by measure.

Those of us without house and ground
who leave tomorrow
must keep our baggage light:
a psalm, perhaps a dialogue—
brief as Lamech's song in *Genesis*,
even Job among his friends—
but no more.

Like a tree in December
after the winds have stripped it
leaving only trunk and limbs
to ride and outlast
the winter's blast.

24

Scrap of paper
blown about the street,
you would like to be cherished, I suppose,
like a bank-note.

25

A well-phrased eulogy, a low-pitched dirge,
faces politely sad
before the expensive, well-polished coffin;

a thick green cloth about the deep grave
to keep loose earth
from the sod:
a funeral
punctual, well-mannered, neat.

I see that from the rude young man you were
you have gone far.

26

EPISODE IN ICELAND

I know you did not approve of the struggle at all—
sure that I could not possibly win—
and thought that I should go from the homestead meekly
into exile;
but I have this against you, my dear,
that when, as in the saga, an arrow cut the string of my bow
and the foe were closing in
and I turned and asked you to cut off your long hair,
your beautiful hair
that reached to your waist when you combed it,
to make another string for my bow,
you would not.

I did not die as the hero of the saga did.
Now stay if you like
but, if you want to, go.

27

Again cool windy days,
grey skies and sidewalks black with rain;
again the solitary walks,
and a quiet room in which to sit and work
and see mankind—
only through a windowpane.

28

It had been snowing at night
and the snow could still be seen
on the roofs, parapets, and water-tanks.
Slowly the sky grew brighter,
the room lighter;
morning came—almost at noon.

29

Now on our way through the park one meets
birds not unlike the sparrows of our streets

but smaller and colored a softer grey—
without the sparrow's brownish hue
and with a tinge of green, a hint of white:
a soothsayer might read a message in their flight
and I can spell a good omen, too.

30

Here where the bushes are beginning to bud
in the bright sun of March,
a man comes walking stiffly all in black:
grim, grey beard, toes out.

Is this a granite angel that has climbed down from a church?
Michael, perhaps, without his sword?
No, no, my friend, it is only Adam,
too old to plough and Cain and Abel dead.

31

This added kindness:
as when, revisiting a grove
for the symmetry of trunk and twigs,
we find the trees in flower.

32

SAINT AND BIRD

After the rain that fell all of last night
the wet street is almost as blue as the sky;
a shining black bird in the grass,
head cocked—
a crafty eye upon me as I pass.

I mistrust the shrewd archaic smile
of your saint
in spite of the big book in the crook of his arm
and two fingers raised in blessing.

33

The park is green and quiet
except for a bush
with as many white flowers as leaves
and the gardener—crooked leg, malicious eye—
tearing at the weeds.

Beneath the trees
strut robber knights
in black speckled armor:
I know them,
although they look like starlings.

34

Blue flowers in the hot sun
and the brown birds flying
through the cool tunnels
between the bushes and the ground.

I listen to the chatter of my fellows—
alien as a bird:
who cares, who cares?

I see their smiles
but am the silent dog that hurries on,
nose to the ground,
busy about his own affairs.

35

Another generation of leaves is lying
on the pavements;
each had a name, I suppose,
known to itself and its neighbors
in every gust of wind.

Now the wind
taking, taking . . .

36

Silent and sullen, in a bitter debate with the dead—
their sentences still touching his heart like icicles—
stiffly as if he had spent the night
on a park bench;
summer long gone and his shoes—to be worn in summer—
no longer white;

laces not even tied
and the tin tips dragging along the ground
with the thin persistent sound
of an insect's song
as if—in the machine of which they are a part—
something has gone wrong.

37

The nail is lost. Perhaps the shoe;
horse and rider, kingdom, too.

38

The dogs that walk with me are Now and Here
and a third dog I do not trust at all,
for he would lead me far into the past
and there I'd lose myself: his name is If.

39

My parents were of a great company
that went together, hand in hand;
but I must make my way alone
over waves and barren land.

My grandfathers were living streams
in the channel of a broad river;
but I am a stream that must find its way
among blocking rock
and through sands and sand.

40

Because, the first-born, I was not redeemed,
I belong to my Lord, not to myself or you:
by my name, in English, I am of His house,
one of the carles—a Charles, a churl;
and by my name in Hebrew which is Ezekiel
(whom God strengthened)
my strength, such as it is, is His.

41

Of course, we must die.
How else will the world be rid of
the old telephone numbers
we cannot forget?

The numbers
it would be foolish—
utterly useless—
to call.

42

I remember very well when I asked you—
as if you were a friend—whether or not
I should go somewhere or other,
you answered: "It does not matter:
you are not at all important."

That was true. But I wonder
whom you thought important.
He who has been in his grave
these ten years or more?
He is not important now.
Or he who is wearing out a path
in the carpet of his room
as he paces it
like a shabby coyote in a cage,
an old man hopelessly mad?

Yourself, no doubt:
looking like one
who has been a great beauty.

These days when I dare not spend freely
and the friends I meet are uneasy
that I might ask for a loan, I dreamt of you:
my friend at school.
I was going to ask you a question
and afraid you might find it foolish
(you were somewhat older and sensible).
The faces about you were shadowed
but yours was smiling, fresh and pink.
And I must be in my dotage
for I find myself weeping that you are dead—
who have been dead for a long time.

44
SIGHTSEEING TOUR: NEW YORK

I

The sky is a peculiar blue
with small clouds,
numerous and white: not the luminous blue
seen in paintings but a cheap opaque blue,
once painted in the vestibules of tenements
with the same small clouds;
yet here it is—
real sky, real clouds.

A young woman dressed in white
is seated on a bench in the park,
eating an apple
and reading a magazine: the apple is a summer pippin,
green outside;
but the inside is brown and decayed,
and she eats it with small, dainty bites.

II

The barber shop has curtains
but it must have been a long time since they were washed
for they are a dark grey
and falling apart;

the window itself is dirty
and whatever signs it has are grey with dust.
The barber stands in the doorway
wearing a coat of uncertain white
over dirty trousers—
and he needs a shave badly.
The shop is called in bold letters
"Sanitary Barber Shop,"
and there are those, I suppose, who believe it.

45

Fraser, I think, tells of a Roman
who loved a tree in his garden so much
he would kiss and embrace it.

This is going pretty far
even for a lover of nature
and I do not think it would be allowed
in Central Park.

46
NOTES ON THE SPRING HOLIDAYS

I
Purim

The Jewess, Hadassah, takes the name of the moon-goddess, Esther;
her kinsman, Mordecai, whatever his Hebrew name,
has the name of the Babylonian god.
If you have intelligence and beauty, Esther,
"tell no one of your people or your kindred,"
and you will live in the king's palace and be a queen.

"We are sold, I and my people, to be destroyed, to be slain, and
            to perish!"
The hands, heavy with rings, are Esther's
but the voice is the voice of Hadassah.

II
Passover

"Begin with the disgrace and end with the glory," the rabbis say.
The disgrace was not in being a slave—that may happen to anyone—
but to remain such.
What was the glory?
To choose the Lord:
that is, the bread of affliction and freedom.

III
Hanukkah

In a world where each man must be of use
and each thing useful, the rebellious Jews
light not one light but eight—
not to see by but to look at.

47

"O Lord, be with us!"
At my pious ejaculation
all the pigeons flew away
in terror.
Truly, our God is not like Aphrodite
"with her doves about her"
but the God of battles.

48

Blurred sight and trembling fingers—
these alone are not the ills of age:
the gluttony for *mine*
that still would feed
the failing *me*, the dying *I*.

49

How grey you are! No, white!
I see the body has struck its colors
and flies the white flag.

Your friends are growing old
and even the dog, after a block or two,
scratches her master's coat
to show she is tired.

50

FABLE

It is very pleasant to walk in the woods
singing together and telling joke for joke,
but sooner or later you will find yourself alone
and a bear's cold muzzle nudging you.

Then do not tell your friend that he was false
just because he ran away—as you might, too—
and you are a fool to look for anything else
than song for song and joke for joke.

51

PUERTO RICANS IN NEW YORK

I

She enters the bus demurely
with the delicate dark face
the Spaniards first saw
on an island in the Caribbean
and he follows—
a tall gentle lad.
He smiles pleasantly, shyly,
at her now and then,
but she does not look at him,
looking away demurely.

She holds a small package in her hand—
perhaps a nightgown—
and he a larger package:
a brand-new windowshade.

II

A young man, wearing a loose jacket of light brown with a yellow muffler
     tied loosely about his throat,
is singing loudly to himself
a Spanish song.

"In my country," he says in English, "sing all the time:
money, sing;
no money, sing."
Then he adds *staccato* as beginners in a language do:
"Doughnut, five cents.
Four cents—no doughnut!
Coffee, five cents.
Four cents—no coffee!
Restaurant.
Come in, please!"
And he bows deeply.
"No money!"
And he draws back, hands lifted,
the indignation of owner and waiter on his face.

"Girl."
He takes off the hat he does not have
and looks earnestly into the eyes of a girl that isn't there;
then smiles and looks aside coyly.
"No money!"
And he turns away in disgust.
"Ah, tragic, tragic, tragic!"

52
NIGHT-PIECE

I saw within the shadows of the yard the shed
and saw the snow upon its roof—
an oblong glowing in the moonlit night.

I could not rest or close my eyes,
although I knew that I must rise
early next morning and begin my work again,
and begin my work again.

That day was lost—that month as well;
and year and year for all that I can tell.

53
EXODUS

We who had known the desert's grit and granite,
saw the river, the wide and brimming river,
watering the fields of wheat and barley,
of cucumbers and onions, and bringing fish for food.
Come, he had said, I am no Egyptian—
who fears and hates the tribesmen of the desert—
I am your brother, Joseph.
Come and bring your herds and flocks;
here is land, ample land, for grazing;
here is plenty; come and prosper.

We who had known the desert's angry god,
saw the well-ordered life of Egypt,
its fields and ancient cities;
shelter from the heat by day, the wind at night;
saw the ancient river, wide and brimming—
all of Egypt's plenty;
and, turning to each other who had famished in the desert,
languished in the desert,
said: let us stay in Egypt;
here the gods are many—kind and wise.

But there came a Pharaoh who knew not Joseph
and set us building treasuries and cities,
set us making brick for him and building cities:
we who had been masters of our days and daylight,
free to wander, free to stay.
King and servants, priests and laymen;
soldiers, overseers, and slaves:
this was Egypt's peace and order,
and in this order we were slaves:
Israel like a bird that a creeping weasel has wounded in the head
or a man knocked against a wall;
the cattle have trampled it—but still it flutters.

But there came a shepherd from the desert,
speaking in the ancient tongue
all but our eldest had forgotten;
and we saw an old man-withered hands and haunches;
and he said to us, stuttering as he spoke:

I bring a message from the God of your fathers
and, in place of these burdens,
I bring you—the yoke of His law.
How pleasant it is, distinguished from the beasts,
to feed upon His law,
tasting in each syllable
the radiance of our Lord!
If there is bone enough to make the tooth of a key
and ink enough to write two letters of the alphabet—
then fear not the rush of tramping shoes nor the sound of the shouting
and hurry out of this land!*

---

* The three lines at the very end of the third stanza and those at the end of the last stanza
(lines 13–15) are from the *Mishnah* (Hullin 3:3 and other places, Danby's translation).
—C. R.

By the Well of Living and Seeing

By the Well of Living and Seeing

> "And Isaac came from the way of the
> well Lahai-roi . . ."
>
> *Genesis* 24: 62

|

I

My grandfather, dead long before I was born,
died among strangers; and all the verse he wrote
was lost—
except for what
still speaks through me
as mine.

2

My grandmother in her old age
sold barley and groats at a stall
in the market place. She did not measure her cereal
more carefully
than I must minutes.

3

Whenever my sister used to practice
a certain piece on the piano
and came to a certain part—
not particularly good she thought—
a bird would fly to the windowsill
and sing along for a few notes.

The bird must have heard
what the player,
and perhaps the composer himself,
did not hear; and I am reminded of a Hindu saying:
a work of art has many faces.

4

The windows opened on blank walls,
the work was under lamps all day,
summer and winter, spring and fall;
on every desk a bulb was shining.

One morning, I sat down at home
to read or write and for a moment thought:
how wonderful the light!
It lit up table, room, and street,
the neighboring houses and the sky;
how clear each object in the room,
how clear the sight of room and street;
how even, mild, and wonderful the light—
just sunlight.

5

The birds sing
in the spring woods:
here now, here now,
here, here, here!

Spring has come again
and with it the robins:
the bird takes a few brisk steps,
stops
and lifts its head—
a wasted motion!

You will never find a worm
by looking up, my bird;
I see that nature, too,
can use an efficiency engineer.

6

Please do not underestimate the starling:
it hasn't the beautiful feathers of the jay;
and its song,
to say the most for it,
is nothing to speak of.

But it has been doing pretty well
in numbers
and has taken over some of the handsomest houses of the city
to roost on.

7

The blue jay is beautiful
as it flies from branch to branch—
but its cries!

8

The pigeon saunters along the path—
towards me.
Will it turn aside?
Of course.
Not only Athena's owl
knows the history of man.

9

The cat behind the windowpane
stares
at the pigeons walking about on the lawn.
Dreams, idle dreams.

10
Neighbors

The horse that draws a cab through the park
now digs his mouth into the pail
in front of him
and is as annoyed at the pigeons
pecking away at the oats he scatters
as they are at his active hoof.

11

You must not suppose
that all who live on Fifth Avenue
are happy: I have heard the gulls screaming
from the reservoir in Central Park.

12

The dying gull
alone on a rock,
wings spread and unable to fly,
lifting its head—
now and then—
with a sharp cry.

13
Death of an Insect

The sparrow with its beak taps the beetle
and it begins to buzz loudly
as if the bird has set off an alarm-clock.

The beetle flies into the air
in a series of clumsy gyrations
and the sparrow follows it gracefully.

14

Horsefly,
on the window of the automobile agency:
you're out of business now.

15

Ah, the drill
breaking open the pavement
again—
and yet again.
This is the nightingale
that sings in our streets.

16

A grove of small trees, branches thick with berries,
and within it, the constant twitter of birds.
The trees of the park this cold windy day
for want of leaves
are hung with paper—strips of dirty paper.

17

Too early in the morning
for many to be in the park
but a couple ahead of me
every now and then
stop to kiss and embrace:
a tall heavy-set man,
still wearing his dark winter overcoat,
and the slighter figure in slacks.

They hold their arms about each other
and no sooner do they stop kissing
than they fall to kissing again,
as if they could never have enough.
Nothing, indeed, seems more suitable
this beautiful morning—
the first warm day of spring.

As I pass them,
the figure in slacks turns and smiles—
a fixed smile
not unlike that of an archaic Apollo—
the grey eyes shining and glazed—
not a girl at all
but a young man
badly in need of a shave.

18

At the zoo, the camel and zebra are quarreling:
trying to bite each other
through the bars between them.
Of course, they come from different continents.

19

The flowers of the garland at the base of the statue
are withered:
time has written its epilogue
to the inscription.

20

The face of the old woman
sitting alone on a park bench
is suddenly flushed
and she begins to curse and scream.
I can understand the horns of the automobiles
screaming at each other
as they stream out of the park
into the crowded street;
but, sitting alone on a park bench,
at whom is she screaming?

21

The beggar who has been sitting and sleeping
on the same bench in the park
day after day,
surrounded by paper bags stuffed with her belongings,
has now become a donor:
feeding with crumbs the pigeons and sparrows
in a broad circle about her.

22

This Puerto Rican—just an ordinary laborer—
how he goes to his work in the park
jauntily
swinging his rake
like a cane!

23

The park is growing dark and quiet
and lights are beginning to shine among the trees;
here and there, near a light
leaves and lawn are green again.

24
Autumn

The plebian leaves of the trees
are all over the wet sidewalk;

but what are you doing here,
rose petals?

25
Heat Wave: Third Day

In the blaze of sunshine,
an old man comes slowly down the empty street
pushing the heavy cart
in which he gathers
corrugated paper and iron scrap.

A young Negro is bending over a pressing-machine
in the tailorshop on the corner,
the white steam rising into his face.

26

The autumn rains have begun
but are over for the moment;
leaves float
on the pools of water on the pavement.
The lonely walker hears
only the swift motor-cars.

27

A row of brownstone buildings—
houses of the well-to-do
years ago—
in a quiet neighborhood.
Now empty:
windows with Venetian blinds
at crazy angles;
window after window broken,
showing teeth of glass
at the passers-by.

Suddenly a door opens
and an angry old man
is sweeping a cloud of dust
along the dim hallway
upon us.

Excuse me, sir,
are you Father Time?

    28
    Millinery District

Many fair hours have been buried here
to spring up again as flowers—
on hats.

    29

The first ten stories are used as offices for business
and the hotel itself is above them;
in its lobby a narrow trunk of steel
with a few slender metal twigs,
swaying slightly in the breeze of an electric fan;
and only a single leaf—
of metal too.
But what tree could be more fitting
in a hotel lobby
ten stories above the ground?

    30

In the subway car all are reading intently
their newspapers;
students of current events, no doubt.
War in Viet Nam, crisis in the Middle East, clashes between the
        Russians and the Chinese.
But when the train reaches the station at the race-track,
young and old rush out;
they have been merely students of the racing-charts, it seems.

But not all:
one man remains seated,
pencil in hand,
deep in thought—
doing a cross-word puzzle.

31
Graffito

Do not underestimate the value of an education;
how else could one scribble
this on a wall?

32

The princess
on the way to the guillotine
saw a stain on her gown
and was annoyed.

33
La Belle Dame Sans Merci

White, bloodless face, red eyes
and tight bitter mouth.

34
In Memoriam: Peter Freuchen

In the lobby of one of the best hotels
men and women seated or walking about;
outside, the winter night has fallen
but the lobby is warm
and we cannot see the snow falling
nor hear the wind.

Out of the darkness comes a tall man,
bearded—
the long square beard of an Assyrian cherub
guarding the king's palace—
but wearing the blue pea-jacket of a sailor
and the cap of a sea-captain.

He has only one leg and a wooden peg for the other.
As he walks about the lobby
all the others,
stiff in their expensive clothing
and massaged faces radiant,
look like dolls
and he the only living creature.

35

The rabbi would read off the names of the congregation he used to head
and as he read aloud each name would add: "Dead!"
A note of satisfaction in his voice
that he was still alive—
feeble in body and feebler still in mind.

36

The invitation read: not to mourn
but to rejoice in a good life.
The widower, his false teeth showing in a wide smile,
entered
and, turning from side to side,
greeted us.
He began by reading a long essay on his dead wife.
And as he read, we heard those who were washing dishes in the rear of
        the hotel's restaurant
joking and laughing about some matter of their own.
At the end, we were asked to stand
while the widower recited the ancient prayer of mourning—
used at first at all religious gatherings of Jews only to glorify God—
and yet, even as he read,
he began to cry.

37

In my dream,
long dead, he stood in front of me
before an open door;
head high and confident,
looking as he used to
when about to leave on a business trip.
And, indeed, he had his hat and coat on
and held a valise.
At the moment I was as fond of him
as I used to be when a boy;
and I called out, "Uncle, uncle!"
But he paid no heed to me
and was going away.

Through the open door I could look into other rooms
with open doors
that led into other rooms—
all with open doors.

38
Hail and Farewell

Waiting to cross the avenue,
I saw a man who had been in school with me:
we had been friendly
and now knew each other at once.
"Hot, isn't it," I said,
as if we had met only yesterday. "It hit ninety-five."
"O no," he answered. "I'm not ninety-five yet!"
Then he smiled a little sadly and said,
"You know I'm so tired
I thought for a moment you were talking about my age."

We walked on together and he asked me what I was doing.
But, of course, he did not care.
Then, politely, I asked him about himself
and he, too, answered briefly.
At the stairs down to the subway station he said,
"I know I ought to be ashamed of myself
but I have forgotten your name."
"Don't be ashamed," I answered,
"I've forgotten yours, too."
With that we both smiled wryly,
gave our names and parted.

39
Lesson in Homer

A god could have brought the body of Hector back,
just as Phoebus kept it from decay,
but Priam had to get it himself;
so Pallas could have killed Hector easily,
but Achilles had to do it.
She would hand him his spear when he missed
but he had to throw it again.

40

The victorious Greeks before Troy, according to Homer,
spoke "winged words" and Achilles
was "swift of foot."
Why then should we in New York
reproach ourselves
about our hurry?

41

When the prophet of the Greeks, Kalchas,
was called upon by Achilles
to account for the plague—
killing the Greeks faster than the Trojans did—
he first asked the great captain
to protect him, so Homer tells us,
before blaming King Agamemnon.
Now would the Hebrew prophets, Nathan, Amos, or Jeremiah,
        for example,
trusting in the Lord,
have hesitated
and looked to a mere mortal for protection?

Of course, the man of God who came out of Judah
to denounce King Jereboam of Israel
was killed on his way back from Beth-El.
Is it possible that he was killed by a captain of the king?

42
Lesson of Job

To see a god plain
was to die at once;
even the girls Zeus loved
could see him only
as a bird, a beast, or a shower of gold.
And Moses,
to whom God Himself spoke,
could catch no more than a glimpse of Him
as He turned away.

43

Three clouds—
steps
leading into the blue sky:
is this part of the ladder
Jacob saw
when he slept in the wilderness?
But, unless my eyesight is failing,
there are no angels, ascending and descending,
upon it now.

44

Fireworks against the evening sky
are pretty and even dramatic:
but I prefer the crescent moon and evening star.

45
Similes

Indifferent as a statue
to the slogan
scribbled on its pedestal.

The way an express train
snubs the passengers at a local station.

Like a notebook forgotten on a seat in the bus,
full of names, addresses and telephone numbers:
important, no doubt, to the owner—
but of no interest whatever
to anyone else.

Words like drops of water on a stove—
a hiss and gone.

46

You understand the myths of the Aztecs
and read with sympathy
the legends of the Christian saints
and say proudly:

though you were born a Jew
there is nothing Jewish about you.
But the ancient Greeks would still have thought you a barbarian
and even the Christian saints might not have liked you;
and the Nazis
would have pried from your witty mouth
your golden teeth.

47

Malicious but polite,
she said the usual things against the Jews;
and you, the Jew,
went her one better, of course.
This is the smooth cloth
that polishes
the facets of my Jewishness.

48

You would crack my bones
and with your supple tongue
picking out every drop of marrow
lift your bloody mouth at last and say:
Ah, these little animals:
what a waste of my time!

49

The man who planned the bridge
had his foot crushed between the piling and the dock
by a ferryboat.
That was useless, ferryboat!
He died
but the ferryboats, too, are gone.

50
The Old Man

The fish has too many bones
and the watermelon too many seeds.

51
Epitaph

Not the five feet of water to your chin
but the inch above the tip of your nose.

52

Give me the strength
to dance before Your ark
as King David did.

53
Epilogue

Blessed
in the light of the sun and at the sight of the world
daily,
and in all the delights of the senses and the mind;
in my eyesight blurred as it is
and my knowledge slight though it is
and my life brief though it was.

I

Leaving the beach on a Sunday in a streetcar
a family of three—mother, son and daughter:
the mother, well on in the thirties, blond hair, worried face;
the son, twelve years of age or so, seated opposite,
and the daughter, about eight or nine, beside her.
The boy was blond, too; a good-looking little fellow
with dreamy eyes. The little girl was quite plain;
mouth pulled down at the corners,
sharp angry eyes behind eyeglasses.

No sooner were they seated than the boy, speaking gently, said,
"Today was one of the most wonderful days I ever had."
The girl said shrilly, "I wish we could live in one of those houses"—
looking at the bungalows along the shore—
"then we could go to the beach every day."
The mother did not answer either.
The beach they were coming from was crowded with poor people;
and the family was dressed cheaply but was neat and spotless,
even after the day's outing.
I wondered idly where the father was: at work? dead? divorced?

After a while the mother said, weighing her words,
"You know Mister . . ."
I did not hear the name: it was spoken so softly.
She was talking to the boy.
"He goes fishing every Wednesday.
I think I can get him to take you along."
The boy did not answer for a minute or two
and then said, in his gentle voice,
"I should like it very much."
"Can I go too?" asked the little girl shrilly,
but no one answered her.

Mother and son had eyes only for each other.
She took out her handkerchief and wiped his face.
He complained of something in his eye—
certainly not enough to make him blink—
and she raised the upper lid
and lowered the lower lid to look for it.

The little girl stood up to look out of the window
and the boy said to his mother, "She stepped on my toes
and did not even say, Excuse me, please."
The mother turned to the little girl and said sharply,
"Why didn't you say, Excuse me?
You should have said, Excuse me, brother."
The little girl said nothing,
face turned toward the window,
the corners of her mouth far down and her eyes,
bright and dry, looking sharply through her glasses.

2

The fat Italian restaurant-keeper and his wife with big breasts
were standing at the bar
quarreling. Finally she said coldly
but not loud enough to be heard throughout the restaurant:
"Not before people! No hollering before people!"
He recognized the force of the rule and walked away,
lighted a cigarette and glared at the customers,
but could not contain himself and returned to the bar,
said something or other in a loud, angry voice
and picking up a glass
brought it down with a bang
on the bar. He concluded sarcastically
before walking away again:
"All right, boss! All right, *madame!*"
His wife was silent
and the Irish barkeeper, who had been looking straight ahead,
his wrinkled face pink and malicious,
lowered his head to hide a smile.

3

Would I write a letter for him?
Rather homely, no longer young.
His speech had an accent
but I could not place it
and supposed he had come to this country
as a young man
and gone right to work.
"Certainly."

"I have paper and an envelope—

two if you spoil one."
He smiled, took note paper and an envelope out of his pocket,
and we went to one of the desks in the post-office.
I picked up a pen.
The letter was to go to a girl named Sadie,
somewhere in a small town
in Connecticut or Pennsylvania.
I wrote the full name and address on the envelope
as he watched me.
"Now, what shall I write?"

"Dear Sadie," he began, "I love you.
  Got that?" "Yes. Next."
"I love you."
"You said that. What next?"
"I love you. Write it again."
"All right. Next?"
"I love you."
  I looked at him. "Have you nothing else to say?"
"Yes."
  He thought a while and said:
"I love you very much. Got it?"
"Yes."
"Now write—." I was tempted to say,
  I love you,
  but I didn't want to make fun of him.
"Write: Please excuse me, Sadie."

"You see," he said, turning to me,
"she went out with another man
  and I call her, 'Bitch! Whore!'
Now she do not want to see me.
Write: Please excuse me, Sadie. I love you."

I thought of a plain bird with only two or three notes
piping away on a tree in winter.

              4

The cook in a little Italian restaurant
came grimly out of the kitchen;
"I am chef," he was saying loudly and bitterly to the pretty waitress,
"not dishwasher!
'No dishes!' I say when they hire me."

The waitress, it seemed, knew no Italian
and the cook had to complain in English.
"I was here till three o'clock in the morning," he went on,
"three o'clock las' night and back here nine this morning,
and when I go out for a little while before noon—
a little fresh air—
they tell me to eat while I am out:
I am the chef and mus' eat outside!"

"Why don't you tell it to the bosses?" said the waitress cheerfully.
"Why tell me? Before them you keep still;
  when they are out, you talk loud."
"I will tell them, too," said the cook, knitting his brows.
"I am a chef—a good chef.
A good chef is hard to find."
"There are plenty of chefs walking around
  looking for a job," said the waitress unimpressed,
  as unconsoling as if she were married to him.
The cook, however, was not unimpressed by what she had said.
"You must be good to a chef," he muttered after a while,
"or he can do plenty!
A couple of steaks in the garbage can!"

He opened the ice-box and took out a salad
and seated himself at a table;
a man of fifty with mustachios and a ruddy face—
because of much wine or long hours before the fire.
After he had refreshed himself somewhat
by a couple of mouthfuls,
he began to complain again of his long hours.
But this time the waitress said sharply:
"It is your own fault!
You are taking away another man's job.
You are doing the work of two.
There are plenty of people out of work.
Why do you do two men's work?"
The cook stabbed away at the salad with his fork,
unhappy and angry.
"You don't say anything to the bosses.
You are afraid!
You talk to me but when they are here—
you are quiet."

5

The experienced waitress was impatient:
she turned to look for the spoons that were kept on a shelf under
    the counter:
"Where are the spoons?"
"I have been trying to get spoons all morning,"
  the other girl began in a Southern accent;
"every time the bus boy comes here, I ask for spoons—."
"I didn't ask for conversation," said the first girl curtly.

The second girl was having trouble filling her orders.
She had brought the man who had ordered an omelette
a fried butterfish and, when he had refused it,
returned with the same fish again after a while.
She realized her mistake
when she saw the look on his face
and brought his omelette.
"I know you didn't want any potatoes," she said brightly;
the cook had put rice instead of potatoes beside the omelette.
But the customer did want potatoes
and did not want rice at all—
it must have been another customer who had told her that—
but he was not going to wait any longer and took the omelette.
When she gave him his check
she had made it out for the butterfish
and corrected it testily
when he told her about it, pleasantly enough.

Now it was the customer's turn to lose his patience
and he said angrily, "Why get sore about it?"
"Oh," she said, "I am not sore. I am just tired, dreadfully tired,"
and she looked at the long row of customers at the counter,
waiting impatiently to be served.
The other waitress and the bus boy were making fun of her.
"Honey chile," they were saying and grinning to each other.
"Honey chile!"

6

The beggar was making his rounds:
a sturdy fellow in his thirties;
blond hair carefully combed,

blue eyes in a square German or Slav face;
but the sooty look of people who cannot wash regularly.
I never gave him anything
and always looked at him coldly,
and pretty soon he stopped asking me.

One afternoon crossing a driveway
leading into the park—the green light with me—
an automobile shot out of the traffic
past my face.
I looked after it startled and angry—
and kept on walking.
Suddenly I heard a voice, just behind me, saying sharply,
"Stop!"

I stood stock-still
and another car whizzed past:
I might have been killed
if I had not stopped.
I turned to see who had spoken
out of a common humanity:
it was the beggar,
and he walked on before I could even thank him.

7

The highway I was walking on
went through a marsh. There were no houses:
nothing but the marsh.
No one else was walking on the highway
in the blazing sun.

I saw the dog a hundred feet away—
a burly fellow, half chow, I thought,
half German shepherd,
shaggy hair plastered with mud.
The dog saw me, too, and came running towards me.
I walked on, afraid the dog would bite.

I could hear the nails of his paws
clicking on the pavement.
But he passed me—never looked at me—
and ran along as I walked;

ten or twenty feet ahead,
ten or twenty feet behind.
I did not like his looks at all,
the heavy brow, the square jaws—
a shaggy dirty fellow.
The road was as lonely as ever:
marsh under the blazing sky
and the motorcars speeding past.

I could see the pavement of a street on the other side
and the bright blue sea. It would be cooler there,
and I might be rid of the dog.
The dog looked up, after a while,
saw me on the other side,
and came towards me, straight through the traffic.
I stood stock-still,
waiting for the dog to be hit.
Sure enough, the second or third car struck him
and sent him sprawling on his back, squealing.
The brakes of the car screeched;
the dog leaped to his feet,
and was knocked down again,
and then came running towards me.

"You dope!" I said.
But I was touched at his devotion.
Now we went on side by side:
the dog close to me and I no longer afraid.
Now and then we came to a stairway
leading to the beach. Below, other dogs were running about on the sand
and the dog was eager to go down. But he stopped,
waiting for me at the head of each stairway,
and as I went on followed.
The street turned at last and we were back on the highway.

Now I was afraid to cross for fear the dog would be hit.
He stood beside me, looking up at me,
watching my hands and feet,
ready to spring forward.
At last there was a break in the traffic—
only two cars coming. I could cross easily:
go part of the way, let the cars pass, and then cross over.
But I was afraid the dog would rush on

and be hit. "No," I said to him,
"no!"
And we walked along the edge of the highway without crossing.

As the dog ran on beside me, sturdy and true,
I thought of his lifted face,
the deep brown eyes watching mine;
yes, I should like to keep him.
Walking so together, we came to some houses.
These were at the sea—
cottages, refreshment stands, even a small merry-go-round.
I stopped at a stand.

"What should I get my dog to eat?" I asked the pleasant girl
behind the counter. She smiled at me,
and leaned over the counter to smile at the dog
as he stood beside me, wagging his tail.
"Hamburger," she said. "Dogs love it."
"All right."
"One or two?"
"Two."

She took the fresh cakes out of the icebox
and put them on a square of wax paper.
I walked to the corner of the stand. The dog followed
and I put the meat down.
The dog looked at it;
his tail drooped, his eyes were glazed with fear,
and he was off
as fast as he could go
bolting over the sand hills.

8

When I came for my laundry, I found a shirt missing.
The laundryman—a Jew—considered the situation:
"There are four ways of losing a shirt," he said thoughtfully;
"in the first place, it may never have been delivered by the steam laundry;
in the second place, it may be lying around here, unpacked;
in the third place, it may have been delivered and packed in someone
        else's bundle;
and in the fourth place it may be really lost.
Come in again at the end of the week and I'll know what has happened."

And his wife, recognizing a fellow Jew,
smiled and spoke up in Yiddish,
"We won't have to go to the rabbi about it, will we?"

9

In my neighborhood there is a small congregation of Puerto Ricans.
They meet in a room on the street level
to pray, sing hymns, and listen to a sermon.
The room has a window facing the street and an upper pane of the glass
    is cracked:
the cracks run like crooked rays
from a small hole in the glass—
it might be the image of a star.

There is a cheap colored print in the window—
the picture of a path going up a hill
and many people on it.
The framed print is below the cracked pane
at an angle:
leaning backward from the window
and hanging from a cord fastened to a nail in the sash.
If you look at the print,
the people are really going up the path
and above it, in the pane above, is the star
with the cracks in the glass for rays.

10

The new janitor is a Puerto Rican;
still a young man and he has four small children.
He has been hired because he is cheap—
not because he is the handy man
a good janitor is supposed to be.
I doubt if he ever saw any plumbing
before he came to this country,
to say nothing of a boiler and radiators.
Anyway, he was soon overwhelmed by requests from the tenants
to do this and fix that.
He does his best and spends hours at simple jobs,
and seldom does them well—or can do them at all.
He was in my flat once
to do something or other and, when he was through,

asked me if he might sit down.
"Of course," I said and offered him a drink,
 but he would not take it.
"It is so quiet here," he explained.
 And then he began to talk about a man who lived in the house
        and taught Spanish.
"He talks to me in Spanish," the janitor said,
"but I do not understand.
 You see, I am not an educated man."
His eye caught the print of a water-color by Winslow Homer
which I have hanging: a palm tree in the Bahamas.
"That is my country," he said,
 and kept looking at the print
 as one might look at a photograph of one's mother
 long dead.

        11

The Chinese girl in the waiting-room of the busy railway station
writing on a pad
in columns
as if she were adding figures
instead of words—
words in blue ink
that look like small flowers
stylized into squares:
she is planting a small private garden.

        12

Four sailors on the bus, dressed in blue denim shirts,
ill-fitting jackets,
shoddy trousers that do not match the jackets:
one a Negro, another has some Negro blood,
the other two white—Spanish or Portuguese.
The mulatto or octaroon is the eldest—
a handsome fellow in the thirties.
The others chatter away, laugh and talk,
but he says little
although they keep looking at him to say something.
He speaks once, briefly, dryly—
and the three burst out laughing with delight.

One of the white men gives him a packet of photographs
to look at—snapshots;
and the other white man reaches for it.
The mulatto stops him with a gesture.
You would think the mulatto would slap his hand
or push him away
but he merely lifts his own hands
and keeps them lifted for a moment—
a moment in a dance.
Then when he has glanced through the pictures,
instead of giving them back or to his companion
who has snatched at them,
he offers them to a young woman seated nearby.

She is a stranger but her eyes
caught by the flicker of the photographs—
as anybody's would—
had strayed to them. And this time his gesture
has the grace of a man plucking a spray of flowers
from a bush he is passing
and giving them to the girl beside him.

13

Most of the stock in the hardware store
is the odds and ends of auctions.
An old Negro is looking at a cup in his hand
and turning to me says gently:
"Do you see this picture?"
The cup has a picture on it
which is not too clear—
a Watteau group in the silks, ribbons, and wigs of the French court;
and the rest of the cup is covered by a coarse web of gilt.
"If you look at the other pieces of the set,
you will see that the pictures tell a story—
a wooing, a wedding, and the birth of a child."
The cups and saucers—thick with dust—
are in a basket marked ten cents each.
I watch him picking up one
and then another
and studying them as if they were rarities.

He holds the sugar-bowl of the set in his hands
and is saying to the young man taking the cash:

"How much is the sugar-bowl, did you say?"
"Thirty-nine cents."
"As much as that? Are you sure?"
"Sure.
The sugar-bowl is always the dearest."
"I can't take it now,
  but will you keep it for me until tomorrow?"
"If you give me a deposit."
"I can't.
But keep it for me, won't you, until tomorrow?
I am buying these now,"
and he lifts two cups from the counter.
"I have bought here before. You know me."
"Sure I know you," says the young man, taking the cash for the cups,
and adds by way of a joke:
"And I am sick and tired of seeing you.
But I will keep it for you until tomorrow."
"Be careful not to break it," the Negro says in the same gentle voice.

Straw by precious straw,
he is building himself a home.

14

The dark subway-station was almost empty at a little after ten
that summer morning. The man who sold tokens for the turnstiles
was going back to his booth with a broad smile on his face.
I supposed he had been engaged in an amusing conversation
with the Negro alone on the platform.
The black man's face was wrinkled. As he stood there,
stooped over a stick, he kept on talking:
"I cuss my mother in her grave," he was saying in a loud angry voice,
"because she borned me!"
What a line for a "Mammy" song, I thought.
By this time there were two or three other passengers on the platform
and we stood at a distance from the Negro and watched him,
though we pretended not to. He turned to us and said,
"I wonder how it feels to be white."

Just then the train came in and we went inside
hoping that the Negro with his disturbance
would not enter the brightly-lit car.

15

Two men were seated near me in a bus:
well-dressed, well-fed; in the forties;
obviously respected members of their community;
talking together calmly,
the way men of good breeding and education talk,
and the speech may have been Greek or Italian.
I could not hear enough of it to decide.
Suddenly a woman seated directly behind them
began in a loud voice:
"Why don't you talk American?
You live here, don't you?
You make your living here!
Talk American!"

One of the men turned to glance at her
and then the two went on talking in Greek or Italian,
calmly, quietly
although every now and then the woman cried out,
"Talk American, why don't you?"

If these men were Jews, I thought,
how uneasy they would have become,
and their faces would show it.
One of them might even say to the woman—
if he knew enough English—
"This is a free country, isn't it?"
And there would be a noisy argument.
Or they might become silent.
The two men, however, continued to talk
as they had been doing
and neither turned to glance at the woman
or show by gesture or grimace
that they heard her.
Finally, she jumped up and sat down beside me.
"What do you think of these men?" she asked.
"Why don't they talk American?
They live here, don't they?
They make their money here!"

"You must not be so impatient," I said.
"English is not an easy language to learn.
Besides, if they don't learn it, their children will:

we have good schools, you know."
She looked at me suspiciously
and, when the bus stopped, hurried off—
fleeing our contamination.
One of the men then turned to me and said quietly
in the best of American with not a trace of a foreign accent:
"She's a little cracked, isn't she?"

16

A husky red-faced young fellow
pushed his way through the crowded subway train
selling Father Coughlin's "Social Justice,"
and a man with a thin face, reading a thick book, leaned forward
to shout, "You dirty Fascist! Coughlin is a Fascist!"
The young fellow turned to shout back,
"Prove it! Prove it!"
but did not wait. However, the young fellow had a defender.
At first, I took him for a Jew
because of his long nose and eyeglasses.
Leaning forward from his seat, he said:
"This is a free country!
He can sell what he likes!
Try and stop him!"
Now I could see that his hair was dark blond
and his profile not at all Jewish.

The two passengers began to shout at each other.
Others joined in. A girl stopped to yell something
just before she left at a station.
It was hard to make out above the roar of the train—
if anyone wanted to—what they were saying.
Three of the passengers, well-dressed women in a group,
were much amused at this sudden storm;
but other passengers—among those who were silent—
became grim and sad,
particularly the Jews.

17

It was a pleasant restaurant
with an open fireplace and a crackling fire—
not for use but ornament—
and good-looking colored girls to bring the food.

At a table a handsome old man
with a ruddy face and white hair,
speaking to his companions in a gentle voice
about the Jewish refugees then coming to this country
from Nazi Germany,
expostulated in his well-bred way
that any were allowed to come in at all;
his face never losing its smile
at the folly of the politicians.

Innocent people—men, women, and children—
ordered from their beds in the dead of night
and carted through side streets not to disturb the Aryan citizens,
and then standing with their bundles in railroad yards
waiting for the freight trains to take them—
where?
We who lived through those years finally knew.
And these people with calm intelligent faces
in snug restaurants and rooms
talking against them in the best of tempers
with smiling faces and cheerful well-bred voices.

    18

I saw him walking along slowly at night
holding a tray of candy and chewing-gum:
a Jewish boy of fifteen or sixteen
with large black eyes and a gentle face.
He sidled into a saloon
and must have been ordered away
because he came out promptly
through the swinging doors.

I wondered what he was doing
far from a Jewish neighborhood.
(I knew the side streets
and the roughs standing about on the corners and stoops.)
What a prize this shambling boy with his tray!
I stepped up to warn him
against leaving the brightly-lit avenue.
He listened, eyed me steadily, and walked on calmly.
I looked at him in astonishment
and thought: has nothing frightened you?

Neither the capture of Jerusalem by the Babylonians, by the Romans,
    by the Crusaders?
No pogrom in Russia;
no Nazi death-camp in Germany?
How can you still go about so calmly?

19

We have a print of Marc Chagall's picture of a green-faced Jew:
like a corpse, a doctor visiting us once said.
But the green-faced Jew is smoking peacefully,
holding tightly in his opened hand between thumb and forefinger
a cigarette stub or bit of a cigar—
to smoke the very last of it—
and looking at you calmly.
An open book, brown with age, such as my grandfather used to read,
is in front of him,
and behind him a silken hanging over the scrolls of the Torah.
The hanging is green, too;
embroidered on it, the shield of David
and a single word in Hebrew, "hai,"
meaning "life."
When we moved, the moving-men dropped the picture
and the glass that protected the print cracked;
the crack ran over the word "hai"
but the cracked glass held in the frame.

20

I was wearing a belt buckle
with the initial of my family name on it
in a cheap design. A friend noticed it
and I said apologetically:
"This was my father's. He had no taste."
"Perhaps," my friend answered gently,
"he wore it because it was a gift."

21

I sat at home writing, using up my savings,
impatient at any interruption.
I could hear our neighbors in the next flat:
a young couple with a baby; the husband, I gathered from their talk,

drove a truck for a living.
Radios were becoming common
and his wife played hers all day—
so it seemed to me—
and the ragtime she liked disturbed me no end.

One night I heard them quarreling:
she was speaking in a tearful voice
and he in a strange thick voice.
(I had never seen them
although they lived next door,
but I judged from her thin, girlish voice
that she was still very young
and his voice was that of a young man
barely out of his teens.)
"You are drunk," she was saying
and I could hear her sobbing.
"Can I help it?" he answered.
"He's my boss. I have to drink when he asks me to,
don't I? Can't you understand?
It's our bread!"

Next morning I did not hear the radio,
nor was it turned on that day
or the next. I would stop my work now and then
and listen for it.
When I did hear the radio again with its cheap music,
it no longer bothered me at all.

22

Hillel said: "trust not in thyself until
the day of thy death . . ." *Aboth*: 2,5

I finally found a berth with a firm publishing law books:
the work was superficial for the most part
and dull; poorly paid
and it deserved no more.
However, it offered me a living.
In the long panic that began in 1929,
just as in a storm a captain may jettison the cargo
without blame
to save ship and crew,

in that panic many a firm began to jettison the crew
to save the ship; and the firm I was working for
closed the department I was in.
To be sure, it was not the only firm publishing law books
but the others were as badly off.

I had played with the thought of doing something pleasanter
for a living, if not more profitable;
and now I tried this and that:
answered advertisements without pride—
or reply;
and finally, as the saying goes in Yiddish,
ran about like a poisoned mouse.
In no time, it seemed to me,
I had used up my savings.
I would soon be out in the street!
Just as I had seen, when a boy,
the furniture of a family on the sidewalk
in the rain
with a white saucer on the table
to catch pennies from the passers-by.
I had made the acquaintance of an accountant who had clients
in various kinds of business, and I asked him
if he could get me a job. He looked at me closely
as if he had never seen me before,
scrutinizing me as a possible employee.
"Do you understand Yiddish?" he said slowly.
I nodded.
"One of my clients is in the textile business.
His customers are mainly from Mexico
and other Latin American countries;
they can't speak English but they speak Yiddish,
and he must have someone in the office
who will understand them.
He himself is away most of the time
buying goods or out with customers.
He can't pay much.
He has a young fellow working with him now
but my client is dissatisfied.
However, he can't remain without someone in the office
even for a day.
Now, don't say you are interested unless you really are!"
"Of course, I am," I said.

"He can't pay more than twenty dollars a week.
But you will have the place to yourself
most of the time: to read or do whatever you like."
I wondered how I could make twenty dollars a week do;
but it would be better than nothing
and give me a chance to catch my breath.
"If he hires you, he will have to give the young fellow notice,"
the accountant went on;
"my client is not a man to send anybody away without notice,
especially in times like these.
Well, I'll talk to him about you. But, before I do,
are you sure you are interested?"
"Certainly!"

"I know," he said, scrutinizing me again,
"that you are a man of your word."
With that we shook hands, I thanked him warmly and we parted.
Sure enough, he called me up in a few days
and arranged that I meet the dealer in textiles.
I knew the neighborhood where the man had his place of business:
my father worked there when he first came to this country,
and I did not feel particularly happy
to be back at my age where my father began.

The man's place of business was in a loft building—
probably one of the first of that height in the city.
No doubt, my father had seen the building daily
and admired it. It was nine stories high,
a narrow building on a corner,
with windows on all sides.
There was no entrance to speak of:
I walked through an old wooden doorway
and was right at the elevator;
a winding iron stairs with narrow steps
went up around the elevator shaft;
and the elevator-operator, a stocky man of forty,
summoned from the basement by my ring,
gave me an unpleasant glance, and we shot upward.
The elevator was of the oldest type,
run by a cable which the operator pulled;
a battered wire net around the platform
kept passengers and freight from falling off;
and I could see the shaft sliding

swiftly past.
The elevator stopped at the sixth floor.
The operator slammed the folding wicket shut
to let me out,
and I stepped into the hall:
a large window facing me,
the sill only a foot or so from the floor
and the window wide open
because the day was warm.
A step or two
and I would be out of the window!
I looked back at the elevator operator
hoping that the man would stay
to give me the support of his companionship—
such as it was. But he saw no reason for waiting
and, as if he read my fear,
grinned and shot away.

I almost ran to the door of the textile-dealer,
opened it quickly—thank God it opened!—
and entered a large loft.
The heavy wooden cases that textiles come in
were lined up along the length of it,
and here the large windows were also wide open.
The accountant and his client were seated at a desk
talking quietly to each other.
The accountant stood up at once when he saw me
and motioned to me to come towards him;
and when we were out of earshot of a young fellow doing something
        or other
in a corner of the loft,
the accountant spoke, low and gravely
as if this were a matter between representatives of nations, no less.
"It is important that the young fellow over there
does not suspect
that my client is thinking of discharging him.
I explained to you that my client must have someone here
all the time—
someone he can trust."
"I understand," I said.

"Wait here!"
The accountant's voice had become crisp and military.

The man at the desk arose: a pleasant-looking man,
well-fed and looking well-to-do,
with a ruddy face and a pleasant smile;
and when he spoke
I found the voice pleasant and cheerful.
He brought over two chairs, motioned me to a seat,
and sat down facing me.
However, the young fellow suspected that something was up,
and took occasion to pass near us once or twice
trying to catch something of our conversation,
and threw at me, now and then, a sharp nervous glance.
His face was thin and sallow, eyes large and dark:
such a face as I had seen in the art museum
painted on a coffin from Hellenist Alexandria.
"It is surprising how little young men know these days,"
the textile-dealer began. "Why, he can't even type!
You type, I suppose?"
"O yes," I said. "But only two fingers."
"Good enough. Part of the work here is to make out bills of lading.
And, when a case of goods comes, you'll have to bring it upstairs."
I knew how heavy cases of textiles were
and thought of myself with hook and hand-truck bringing up a case;
the elevator-man, I could see, would be of little help unless tipped—
out of my own money, I supposed.
The dealer must have seen the doubt on my face but misread it for pride.
"Why," he said, "I do it myself when I am here."
At that it occurred to me that if I were the only employee—
as I would be—
I would have to sweep the loft and open and close the windows;
and the thought of going near them, particularly if I were alone,
made me sick at heart.
I turned away and looked at the cases blankly.

The dealer followed my gaze
and said smiling, again misreading my troubled face:
"Yes, they're empty. I have them to fill up the place."
I smiled too. "Of course," I said.
"I was told that you speak Yiddish:
that is important."
I answered in Yiddish to show that I knew it:
"My Yiddish is not as good as that of a man born on the other side;
but I understand it
and have always been able to make myself understood."

"It is good enough," said the dealer.
"Well, then, there is nothing more to say.
  You know the salary. The hours are the usual hours—
  nine to six. Sometimes you may have to stay a little later;
  but then we are closed on all the Jewish holidays.
  You can come to work a week from Monday.
  I want to give the young fellow at least a week's notice.
  He is very poor. Very poor," he said again slowly,
  thinking about it and sad.
"And he must support his old parents, too.
  I must give him a chance to find another job.
  All right," he concluded briskly,
"you will be here?" He looked at me with a smile.
"All right," I answered cheerfully
  as if I were really pleased, and we shook hands.
  The accountant, making entries in the dealer's books,
  had also been watching
  and was now beside me. "Thank you," I said,
  and we, too, shook hands.
  But all I could think of just then
  was about the open window in the hall.

  If there was terror in my face,
  the others could not see it
  as I closed the door gently behind me
  thinking that I could open it again at once,
  although I knew it would be silly
  to return without an excuse.
  My heart beating loudly,
  I thought of running down the stairs
  without waiting for the elevator;
  but I would have to be as careful as a cat
  on the narrow winding steps,
  and the elevator-man would certainly see me
  and wonder what the devil I was up to.
  I forced myself to ring the elevator-bell
  and stood as far away as I could from the window,
  feeling quite faint.
  The elevator came quickly enough,
  and the operator looked at me quizzically and amused.
  Afterwards, when I thought about what had happened,
  I said to myself: how idiotic!
  I don't want to jump out of any window.

Besides, the sixth floor is not very high.
And I made up my mind to go that very evening
and see from the street
just how high the sixth floor in that building was.

I did go and saw that the sixth floor was really high.
As I walked home slowly,
I found myself counting the floors of each building that I passed:
to my surprise there was a great variation—
the sixth floor of some buildings might be as high as the ninth in others
or as low as the fourth.
I had never noticed this.
But really, as I told myself, what difference did it make?
To jump from the fourth floor would probably be just as fatal
and a good deal more painful.
Nor had I ever noticed before in the newspapers
so many items about people jumping from a roof or window.
I read each carefully;
and I kept going over and over in my mind what the work would call for:
first, the swift ride upward as if into the sky itself
as it shone through the windows in the hallway
into the open cage of the elevator;
the stop at the sixth floor before the wide-open window;
the door where I might very well have to wait
until my employer arrived to unlock it—
before I could escape into the loft—
and it would never do to arrive after my employer.
The loft itself with its rows of windows which I—who else?—
would have to open
and near which I would have to be alone most of the day.
Of course, after a while—a few months or just a few days—
I would become used to the open windows
and might never give them another thought.
But until then?
Just a step and I would be plunging to my death.
It was inevitable, too, that I should think,
in simple self-defense,
of not showing up at all. In spite of the hardship to my employer
who had been pleasant enough; in spite of the harm
in the employer's esteem to the accountant;
in spite, too, of the hardship and unnecessary harm to the young man
who had lost a job he needed badly—
because of me. I tried to console myself

by thinking that the young man would be discharged
sooner or later, anyway.
I remembered, too, a story I had read—
from some "midrash" or other—
that Job was given the choice of escaping his future sufferings
by being poor but preferred his wealth
because it was difficult for a poor man to remain righteous.
However, I knew well enough that poverty was no excuse
for a self-respecting man. What tormented me most
was simply that I would not keep my word,
and whenever I thought of that I drew my hand back
as if from the hands I had shaken by way of pledge.

The day before I was to go to work
I could think of nothing else
but the open window in the hall.
The night before I did not sleep a wink.
I hoped it would turn unseasonably cold
so that at least the window in the hall might be closed;
but it dawned warmer than ever.
I left my bed, since I was not sleeping anyway,
shaved and bathed slowly, putting off the moment
when I would have to leave for work. I left the house at last
and went quickly—
in the opposite direction.

I stopped at a telegraph-office
and sent the man who had hired me a telegram
saying that I was sick and could not come:
a childish lie,
although I tried to persuade myself there was some truth in it.

23

When I was beginning to go to school,
I found out that the owner of a candy-store nearby
was a friend of my parents—at least an acquaintance.
One evening, my father took me along to visit the man
and he gave me candy and spoke kindly to me
and after that I thought of him as a friend.
After a while, we moved from that neighborhood—
or perhaps he did—
but now and then my parents spoke of him

and always with respect.
Twenty or so years afterwards, I met his daughter
and she told me that her father was stopping with her briefly
on his way to some Home for the Aged
a thousand miles away
where, she assured me, it was very pleasant
and he would be well taken care of,
for now he was feeble and had lost all his money;
and, of course, neither his son nor daughter could take care of
      him properly.

I said that I should like to visit him before he left,
for I still thought of him in the way I did when I was a child;
she gave me the telephone number
and I called up.
I told him whose son I was and to my surprise he answered gruffly,
"Well, what is it?"
I went on to say I remembered him from the days when he had
      a candy-store.
He cut me short and said sharply, "What do you want?"
I brought the conversation—if one may call it that—lamely to a close
and hung up
and thought him unreasonably rude.

Years afterwards, when I, too, had spent what money I had
and was at my wits' end as to what to do next,
I was told that I had answered the telephone brusquely—
to the indignation of the person who had called—
and then I remembered the old man and understood:
he just did not feel like meeting anyone
or even talking.

    24

Every now and then I buy a German newspaper
for the pleasure I still have in the language:
it is really the speech of soldiers
or rather of sergeants—
a good mouthful of consonants, accented and crisp;
the English of Hengist and Horsa.

I like the advertisements in a newspaper;
for this is a glimpse at how people live

and earn their living.
This time—in a German newspaper published in this country—
I read under Female Help Wanted:
"Here is the position you are looking for!
Good pay, beautiful little apartment, one child,
very little housework, simple cooking:
a good home for a lucky person!"
"A lucky person!"
What American would try to assure any servant
she was "lucky" to be that,
no matter what the pay and how easy the job!

25

I was walking along Forty-Second Street as night was falling.
On the other side of the street was Bryant Park.
Walking behind me were two men
and I could hear some of their conversation:
"What you must do," one of them was saying to his companion,
"is to decide on what you want to do
and then stick to it. Stick to it!
And you are sure to succeed finally."

I turned to look at the speaker giving such good advice
and was not surprised to see that he was old.
But his companion
to whom the advice was given so earnestly,
was just as old;
and just then the great clock on top of a building across the park
began to shine.

26

The nurse who had been working all night
entered the bus. White shoes and white silk stockings;
her body willowy and her hands big and strong;
still a pretty woman
with her bright blond hair carefully combed.
It is after six this May morning
and the sunlight, shining on the automobiles along the curb
and the chromium decorating the store-windows,
shines on her face.

But there are lines on her throat and the forehead is lined;
she closes her eyes for weariness now and then
and her strong hands are folded quietly in her lap.
When she leaves the bus her shoulders are stooped:
no longer the proud carriage of head and body
with which she entered the bus—and life.

27

A sign on a store window: no fancy name—just "Mrs. Smith's Cafeteria";
come in, if you like.
The street was dingy, the houses small and shabby,
but it was not a side street,
not a quiet street, by any means.
Streetcars and buses, motorcars and motor trucks,
ran along it all day long
until late at night, and it was lined with stores.
The stores were small, the merchandise cheap;
clearly a street where poor people walked and shopped.

The window was clean; in the window, a canary bird in a bright
        gilt cage—
nothing else.
Two or three men were eating at the small tables
and two or three waiting at the counter;
behind it an old woman—
she must surely have been seventy—
hair white as the chinaware,
small and hunchbacked with age,
and alone.
Serving everybody and everything—
the meat or fish, the vegetables,
white bread or corn bread, the salad, dessert and coffee or milk;
and she took the money, too,
brought a glass of water to the table when the customer was seated,
and carried off the dirty dishes.

The food was plain and cheap.
She filled each order quickly
before a customer changed his mind—if he was that sort;
nothing dropped from her fork or spoon
as she lifted it to the plate;
the water did not slop over as she put the glass on the table;

there was no fumbling. She kept them waiting, of course,
as she briskly served each customer in turn,
but she made no apology, wasted no words.
What do you wish, young man? Young woman?—
they were all young as they stood before her—
choose and pay,
then eat and dawdle as much as you like;
but I have no time to dilly-dally;
I am old and alone.

28

During the Second World War, I was going home one night
along a street I seldom used. All the stores were closed
except one—a small fruit store.
An old Italian was inside to wait on customers.
As I was paying him I saw that he was sad.
"You are sad," I said. "What is troubling you?"
"Yes," he said, "I am sad." Then he added
in the same monotone, not looking at me:
"My son left for the front today and I'll never see him again."
"Don't say that!" I said. "Of course, you will!"
"No," he answered. "I'll never see him again."

Afterwards, when the war was over,
I found myself once more in that street
and again it was late at night, dark and lonely;
and again I saw the old man alone in the store.
I bought some apples and looked closely at him:
his thin wrinkled face was grim
but not particularly sad. "How about your son?" I said.
"Did he come back from the war?" "Yes," he answered.
"He was not wounded?" "No. He is all right."
"That's fine," I said. "Fine!"
He took the bag of apples from my hands and groping inside
took out one that had begun to rot
and put in a good one instead.
"He came back at Christmas," he added.
"How wonderful! That was wonderful!"
"Yes," he said gently, "it was wonderful."
He took the bag of apples from my hands again
and took out one of the smaller apples and put in a large one.

29

In the street, nine stories below, the horn of an automobile out of order
began sounding its loudest
steadily—without having to stop for breath.
We tried to keep on talking
in spite of that unceasing scream;
raised our voices somewhat, no longer calm and serene.
Our civilization was somewhat out of order, it seemed.

But, just as we began to knit our brows,
tighten our jaws, twist our lips,
the noise stopped;
and we dipped our heads,
like ducks on a stream, into the cool silence,
and talked again quietly, smiling at each other.

30

When I reached the park, the fog
had become so thick
I could not see the houses on either side.
I had met no one
from the time I left the streets.

I could see only a few feet into the fog:
the cinder path beneath me,
the fence of heavy wire,
the grey stones below that lined the reservoir.
Suddenly a siren began to sound
and grew loud and shrill as it came closer,
but I could not tell whether it was a police car
or an ambulance;
now it was on this side,
now on that,
louder and louder in the fog—
and just as suddenly as it had sounded
it was silent.

Then a little bell began to ring,
quite closely.
I imagined it was in a police-box.
It rang persistently for a while

and then it, too, was silent.
I walked on, hearing no one and meeting no one,
tense as a wild animal in a cage.

31

A cold wind was blowing down the street in gusts;
the streetlamps were merely threads and points of light.
In the morning my mind had been like a spool of cotton;
now all the thread had been stitched away at my job
and only the wooden spool was left.

The straight street really went up and down in waves
and only the tired walker knew
how often it rose into the teeth of the wind.

32

The hillside facing the river was much used by the citizens last night
and now, in the morning, newspapers and empty beer cans are
        scattered about.
A grey bird, piping on a twig,
interrupts my melancholy calculations.
Next to the path are some bushes growing wild;
among them a tall weed with small blue flowers.
I stop to admire them
and a bright yellow insect
has come fluttering out of the sunshine
to admire them, too.

33

It was after midnight before I got into bed
and then I found that I could not sleep
and kept thinking about the vexations of the day.
It seemed to me an excellent idea
to get up and take a long walk through the quiet streets
but I was too tired to leave my bed:
even dressing again seemed too much.
As I kept turning my head restlessly
I caught sight of the garage in the yard:
the roof covered with a smooth level of snow.
From where I lay I could not see the moon

nor the yard itself
but the garage roof was shining like a quadrangle of light
against the darkness:
a quadrangle of light
against the darkness.
Looking at it I forgot myself
and fell into a deep and untroubled sleep.

EARLY HISTORY OF A WRITER

I

My mother and I were going to the park
and as soon as I smelled the earth I could no longer walk sedately
but ran away—as fast as I could—
upon the forbidden grass;
up, up
a steep slope
until I had to stop for breath.

I turned to look proudly down at my mother
far below.
The tall policeman, who stood in the middle of the drive
among the horses and carriages
and who, it seemed to me, had never as much as glanced at us,
was walking slowly towards my mother
scolding her.
She called me back sharply
and I came down from the heights
to walk meekly beside her
along the asphalt path;
guilty and ashamed,
unworthy to be trusted among the splendors of the park.

2

When a child of four or five,
I would sit beside the rubber plant at night
if unable to sleep;
the stiff starched curtain pushed aside.
The lights were out in the stores
and the street, in spite of the arc-lamps,
dark and still.
After a while the trolley wire would begin to hum and sing
in the darkness
until the trolley itself rushed past,
ablaze with light.
Content
at the periphery of such wonder
I would lean back in the chair
to wait patiently for the next car.

3

The game was to walk—run if you dared—
along the curb
and never step off upon the sidewalk or into the gutter;
if you did, you went to the back—
last in line.
I was last but did not mind;
I could step as I liked
and, if without any honor,
I was also without the weight of it.
The leader turned the corner into a side street
where I had never been;
"I am going around the block!" he shouted boldly.
"Around the block, around the block!"
shouted the other boys and girls gaily
and followed.
Hesitant, I followed too.

In the side street, the autumn afternoon had grown dark and cold.
The roots of the great trees that stood along the sidewalk
had lifted the flags of the pavement in places;
and, unlike the bright avenue where we lived,
the gutter was heaped with leaves:
a dark and awesome street.
Silent,
we ran along the curb,
eager to be back before the familiar doors.

4

On Election Night,
there was a great bonfire in the street;
luckily just in front of our windows.
The fleeting lines of the flames were dimly outlined
on the walls and ceiling of the parlor;
what a glare in the room,
although we lived on the third floor!
Boys, and even men, were bringing whatever they could lay hands upon—
barrels and boxes—
to throw upon the fire.
They have broken into the grocer's cellar!
What cheers for the boys dragging a sofa from a storage bin!

The fire sank under its wealth—
it is going out!—
but then leaped higher than ever.
In the morning,
there was a great hole burnt in the asphalt,
in which were scattered hundreds of blackened nails of all kinds—
blunted and good only to kick at.

   5

We had just moved again
and I went into the street
to see what the new neighborhood was like:
it was noisier and more crowded
than any we had ever lived in.
There were pushcarts along the curbs
and the elevated railway was only half a block away.

I walked on to look about me,
unafraid, a big boy now
as my parents had so often told me.
But, as I turned a corner,
I saw a bigger boy swinging a ball of newspaper by a string.
The boy saw me, too, and gleefully ran towards me,
striking me with the hard dirty ball.
I tried to run past him to get home
but could not: the ball struck my face and head
until I turned and ran.
I found myself at last in a street
where the sidewalk was broad and crowded—
here I was hidden in the moving crowd:
the boy with the swinging ball
would never find me.
But how should I ever get out of this crowd
which, time and again,
almost knocked me down?

   6
   Carl

Next to the house in which we now lived was a stable;
from this, my mother complained, came the roaches, mice and spiders
that plagued her. But the landlord's little son, Carl,

assured me it was the stable that made the house healthful,
and for proof pointed out how strong the men were
who worked about horses. I did not mind the smell of the stable,
even in August, and liked to hear the horses stamping on the
  wooden floors
and the sound of their hoofs, at evening,
on the long incline that led from the street right to the stalls.

Carl was older than I but not so much older
that he would not talk to me, at times, even as to a familiar:
summer evenings we would sit on the bottom step of the stoop,
still warm with the sun, and, while our parents sat above us,
he would tell me what he had just read or heard.
Instead of playing in the street or park Saturday afternoon,
we often went together to the museum of art
and wandered dutifully through the galleries,
glancing about idly and rather bored.
But our mothers thought well of us, and we thought well of ourselves,
for going. The way back from the museum,
beside the stone wall of the park, was long,
when I was seven and even when I was nine;
and I was always glad to see the lake near 110th Street
and know that I was only half a mile from home.

(One cold Sunday morning, I heard my father telling my mother
how he and the head cutter in the shop where both worked,
coming home from a Turkish bath,
had stopped to slide on the ice of the lake like boys.
Whenever I passed the lake afterwards,
I thought of my father, the foreman, and the head cutter
sliding on the ice together in the dawn.)

I belonged to the neighboring branch of the public library
and was diligent in bringing books home and taking them back
but read little—
perhaps a page or two before I lost interest.
Carl was the reader:
on the walk to the park with our mothers,
he would carry his book along
and remain seated among the women and the baby-carriages,
biting his nails over the page,
while I, merely a savage, ran up and down the asphalt walks
with other boys. (The grass, of course, was forbidden.)

Once, about to take a walk, I stopped for Carl
but he was too busy to talk to me, let alone walk,
for he was writing a story
under the admiring eyes of his mother and grandmother.
I looked outside at the sunny street regretfully
and waited for him:
his mother let me stay a while when I promised to be silent.
He must have been all of ten years old at the time, perhaps eleven.
He sat in the middle of the parlor, where he used to practice on
        the violin,
writing away at a little table that had been cleared for him of its
        knicknacks,
and had almost filled a blank book when I came.
Soon he was asking his proud mother for a penny
with which to buy another blank book
and raced downstairs to get it without even turning to greet me.

Like the little Teutonized Jew that Carl was—
his parents had been born in Germany—
when we walked together, he would not let me take my cap off;
nor could we ever walk along indolently leaning on each other's
        shoulders;
and we had to finish our bread and butter, every bit,
for if we threw any away,
we should surely, some day, want it.
As we walked, Carl kept stopping to rub his shoes on his stockings;
that his stockings became shiny with blacking did not matter, it seemed.
He was, to tell the truth, not very friendly:
made fun of me and ordered me about;
but I was eager for his companionship
and took his gibes and commands meekly
as from a superior person—
which, indeed, he was.

Perhaps to a German Jew I was ill-mannered—
like all Russians.
Certainly, our mothers did not discipline us alike.
Carl's mother would lock him in a dark closet—
for even he was naughty at times—
and when my mother thought that too harsh,
Carl's mother answered:
"It is good for him! It breaks his spirit!"
My mother, in her uninstructed way, would sooner break my arm.

Though she threatened me when I misbehaved:
for example, when I lost my temper
and thrust my head forward to shout,
she would say calmly
I might end by becoming always as stooped as I was at the moment;
but the punishment was not one she would inflict
but that I was inflicting on myself.

I saw less of Carl as we grew older
and our parents moved from Harlem.
I heard, now and then, of honors he had won at school.
Once, when I was twelve or so and Carl fourteen or fifteen,
I visited him at his new home.
He went to the ice-box to help himself to some strawberries
and I saw a great bowl heaped with all it could hold.
I had heard that his father had come into money
and, though the new home was full of shiny new furniture—
they had not moved next to a stable for all its healthfulness—
it was not until I saw that great dish of berries
that I knew it was true:
they had indeed come into money.
Carl offered me some strawberries but did it hesitantly,
and I took none. When his parents were poor,
really poor for all that his grandmother owned the house
and his father was called the landlord,
they used to offer a sandwich of sausage—
or whatever else there was for supper—
so heartily and cheerfully
I never waited a moment before taking it.

Years afterwards,
when Carl had a good job and was smoking cigars,
I met him at a dinner that our fathers' lodge was giving
and tried to get him to go to the museum with me
as we did when we were children.
He said—somewhat unwillingly—he would
but when we met to go excused himself,
for he had, so he said, something important to do.

A year or so later, when I was nineteen,
I read a long humorous poem by Carl
that took all of a column in a much respected newspaper.
I read the poem carefully, twice,
and found it good.

So Carl is somebody, I thought;
no wonder he did not want to spend a Saturday afternoon with me.
And that very summer, perhaps that month,
I was reading a newspaper one hot night;
as I read on, turning the unimportant inner pages,
too lazy to go out on the porch or up to bed,
I saw at the bottom of a column,
just before a joke that was used for filler,
an item of three lines or so:
a young man had been drowned the day before at one of the beaches—
Carl.
Yes, that humor, learning and discipline
were quenched in a casual wave.

7

I had been given a box of water colors—
not only delightful to look at
but with wonderful names—
for, as children commonly do, I liked to draw and paint.
My parents found this to their liking, too.
I would sit at the dining-room table,
upon which the tablecloth had been rolled back
that I might not smear it, working away,
head to one side and the tip of my tongue between teeth and lips,
snug as a kitten near the stove.

A friend of my parents, skilled in these matters—
at least in their eyes—
had taken lessons in drawing at a settlement-house
on the East Side. He brought me there, the first time.
A small charge, just a few pennies,
and I was equipped with a board, paper pleasantly white and thick,
and a stick of charcoal—
which I found confoundedly brittle.
I was set to drawing from plaster casts of fruit and flowers:
easy enough compared to the heads and torsos
older boys and girls were at. When, doubtful of my work,
I showed it to the instructor,
the young man would smile and say nothing
but would spray it as freely as he did other drawings
with whatever it was that kept the charcoal from rubbing off.
I took this for approval, after a fashion.

On the way home with my charcoaling,
I would stop at my father's store.
Here I found, to my surprise, that I was a person of consequence
to a pale little girl who lived in the house.
It was an old tenement that did not even have a stoop;
the hallway had a foul smell
and was dark—
a single gas-jet flaring near the stairs.
The little girl's father had a pushcart—
he sold bananas for a living—
and she was shyly polite to the son of a man who owned a store.
The two of us would stand in the doorway of the house
and speak of my wonderful life uptown
with two parks—Central Park and Mount Morris Park—in which to play.
Her frank, yet timid, admiration
was very pleasant
to one who had known only the indifference of girls,
and even their impertinence,
and the rude fellowship of boys.

8

My father's parents were a strange pair:
my grandmother tall, even for a man,
and she walked, when more than seventy,
straight and stiff like a grenadier;
a good-looking woman with strong regular features
and bright blue eyes.
My grandfather was no taller than five feet—
if that much:
in the Ukrainian village where he had lived most of his life,
his fellow Jews—who used to make fun of each other—
would call him, because of his size, "Simon the Flea."
He was timid, too, when I knew him,
and would walk along a street with a glance, now and then,
behind him,
as if he were waiting for a stone to come flying at his head.
No doubt many had.

When my grandfather was a boy,
perhaps no more than six or seven,
his father had jumped into the water of the neighboring river—
swollen with melting ice and snow in the spring,

it had overflowed its banks and was sweeping away the stalls of the
    market place—
to save an old woman from drowning.
He took sick with pneumonia because of this
and died.
His son, now that he was an orphan,
never had enough to eat
or a decent place where to sleep,
and did well enough to grow up at all.
But in the synagogue the orphan found himself
at ease in Zion,
and, in the teaching of the rabbis,
became more than the equal of many a man.

Men spoke well of him;
and my grandmother's father, somewhat of a scholar himself,
thought he could find no better husband
for his tall pretty daughter, now all of fifteen.
Since she had no say in the matter,
married she was
to this little timid lad,
so unlike the strapping peasants
and even the Jews of her village.

My grandfather had a great deal of trouble earning a living
at first,
but in time God blessed him,
as He had blessed Abraham, Isaac, and Jacob.
Although never the butcher himself,
he bought cattle and sold beef,
and became the richest, as he was the most learned, Jew of his village.
However, his wife's temper and tongue
became proverbial.
My mother used to explain this
by saying that her mother-in-law had little love for learning;
but my grandmother knew how to read and write better than most
    women of her kind
and, when she was old and had a little time for herself at last,
she found pleasure in reading.

When my grandfather was about fifty, he fell sick,
and my grandparents thought it best to go to America
where my father and their other children were.

My father went to the pier to bring his parents to our home
and could hardly recognize his father—
the face was swollen
and the man could hardly move his hands and feet.
I had been watching from the window
and my brother and I ran downstairs
to meet them. My father turned to my grandfather
and said: "These are my sons."
My grandfather looked at us with his bleary eyes,
whose rims were red,
and turning to my father murmured in Hebrew
what the patriarch Jacob had said to his son Joseph:
"I did not think to see your face
and God has shown me your sons also,"
and, putting his swollen hands slowly on my head,
began to bless me. Even as he did so,
my grandmother who was standing beside him
poked him in the ribs and said sharply in Yiddish:
"Well?"
My grandfather hurriedly brought the blessing to a close.
Shoving his fist into his pocket he took out a gold coin
and put it in the hand I had stretched out to greet him.
"No, no," I said
and would have given the coin back,
for I had been brought up to think it disgraceful
to take money from my elders: the purpose of the instruction
was that I should not ask for pennies,
as ill-bred children did; in good Talmudical style
the prohibition was wider than the evil.
But this time my father smiled and said:
"Keep it—to remember your grandfather by."
As they went into the house,
I stopped to glance at the coin
and saw the monstrous eagle of czarist Russia,
with two open beaks,
from which my father and mother and so many others had fled.

9

The bright boys of the East Side,
of whose competition my father had warned me,
were not in great number
in any class I was in.
Many Jewish boys were in my school, of course;

for the most part, they were duller
than those I had known in Harlem.
Perhaps the poverty of their parents had humbled them early.
Some, instead of believing in the Jewish maxim
that learning was the best merchandise,
were only waiting until they were fourteen
and old enough to get "working papers"
and begin looking for a job.

There were a few German boys, too;
quiet, sturdy fellows
who in those days troubled no one;
the poorest remnant
of many who had been in the neighborhood.
They lived in the oldest and worst houses of the block:
houses of three or four storeys built right up to the sidewalk
without stoops or even yards—
for in back of each house was another just like it.
Each house had a low wooden doorway—
without a door—
as simple as the entrance to a room.
These were the flats of poor people, indeed,
and there was no pretense to be otherwise
in a stoop with stone steps and iron and brass railing,
a doorway of stone and a tiled vestibule.
Several of our teachers were Irish,
children of earlier immigrants,
bright men and women with a sparkle in their blue eyes
and quick smiles,
who taught well and, except for one or two, worked hard.

But graduation itself was not the promised triumph—
at least for me,
except that I was not quite twelve
and two years younger than most in my class.
I was neither first nor second, neither valedictorian nor salutatorian—
had neither imposing title.
Indeed, I felt discredited
because I was fourth or sixth in an examination for a gold medal,
which some unkindly soul had offered to make us all,
except the winner, unhappy.
I was, in fact, pretty bad in arithmetic—
my father's subject:
he was so good at it he liked to do all sorts of problems in his head

for fun
and was surprised and somewhat disgusted
to find that his son was bad at arithmetic
and, of course, disliked it.

At the class meeting, before graduation,
the question that agitated the pupils
was whether they were each to buy a class-pin for seventy-five cents
or one for twice as much.
One of the teachers was petty enough to think
that the cheaper pin would do.
But most of the children scorned it,
for it was only silver instead of gold,
and they called it "tin."
When the teacher urged that some of the boys—the class had only boys—
could not buy the more expensive kind,
I and others grandly offered to "chip in"
and let any such have, if need be,
a pin, ice cream, class picture and all—
free.
We thought ourselves generous,
although it was our parents' money, of course,
which we offered. The end of all the talk
was that it was decided for the pupils by this teacher
that those boys who had to have—
for surely no one wished to—
cheaper pins, might;
but, at that,
some could get no money at all from parents
who had none to spare.
I noticed the face of one such boy,
who stood a little beyond the crowd
at the jubilant class party
and, to the surprise of those boys who thought that he should be happy
to have his ice cream free,
ate it sadly and in silence.
As for my gold pin, I wore it proudly that summer
but was quickly ashamed of it,
for it marked me as a beginner in high school.
I left it about in drawers
until I lost it
and only found it again, after many years,
among my mother's treasures.

10

My grandmother could not get along
with any maid hired to help her.
At night, when my parents came from work,
they heard little but her complaints;
and my mother had to clean and dust until late
to keep our rooms somewhat in order.
Once my grandmother said to her:
"You don't have to go to work to help my son—
and never had to.
But you worked with needle and sewing-machine when you were a girl
and you want to work in a shop instead of doing your own housework,
although you are married:
the dog that ran after the wagon runs after the sleigh."

I remembered very well my father's stories
of how quick my grandmother had been to hit him—
when a boy—
with the rolling-pin. But my grandmother never touched me,
never told me to do this or that
or forbade me anything;
her rolling-pin was now busy,
as God intended it to be,
making cookies—
plain, hard cakes with a little sugar sprinkled on top
or speckled with poppy seed,
good with tea or milk or to nibble at any time.

My grandfather hardly ever left the house.
When we lived on the East Side,
my parents on Fourth Street and my grandparents on Tenth, near
        the East River,
my grandfather would sometimes come to see us.
I went back with him one cold night.
Our way led through a little park. The trees were bare
and the benches, crowded when it was warm,
had nobody sitting on them—nobody at all.
Two strapping Germans—or were they Russians?—
were larking with a girl
in the middle of the wide asphalt path.
They saw my grandfather—
a little sick Jew with a short greyish brown beard

ruffled by the cold wind.
He knew that their merry glances
boded him no good, and hurried ahead of me
to get past them. Hands deep in his coat pockets,
head drawn into his coat, the narrow shoulders hunched,
he seemed to be even smaller than he was.
The two young fellows kept slipping out of each other's grasp
until one of them
managed to push the other into my grandfather.
The girl stopped laughing for a moment to say, "Oh!,"
and even stretched out her hand,
but her reproach was only half in earnest and too late:
my grandfather had been sent rolling on the pavement
until the iron railing along the path stopped him.
I helped him to his feet,
and then ran to catch his hat which had gone farther still
and was being blown away.
When I came back with it,
my grandfather was leaning against the railing,
holding the icy iron bar in his bare hands.
The men, having had their fun with him,
were not even looking that way,
and were larking again with the girl.
I asked my grandfather if he was hurt
and wanted to brush his coat with my palms,
for it was dirty;
but my grandfather would not stop,
and did not say a word
to those who had hurt him or to me.

Now that we had moved to Brooklyn,
my grandfather sat in a sunny corner
beside the window facing the yard three storeys below,
and read the Bible and the commentaries printed in the margin
or a book of the Talmud. To show that he was pleased,
as when my father brought him a package of shredded tobacco
and a little machine for making his own cigarettes,
he would merely say "Ah!" and nod his head
or, if displeased, as when my grandmother was scolding,
he would say "Ah!" again sharply.
He rarely spoke,
except to pray or read a sacred book aloud to himself—
as if words were too precious
for lesser thoughts.

The Brooklyn street was sunny
and the air fresh after the East Side.
But my parents had moved far from their shop
that their children might be happy and healthy
into a most unhappy neighborhood—for me.
It was a mile from Brownsville,
the ghetto where I was born twelve years before.
The neighborhood was chiefly laborers and clerks
who lived in small houses or flats like that of my parents,
without steam-heat or hot water
except when the kitchen stove would heat the boiler next to it.
Among their children, if not among themselves,
the hatred for Israel smoldered,
sending out a tongue of flame now and then
at an unlucky Jew driving his wagon through the street to or
        from Brownsville
or at a Jewish passer-by who had blundered into the neighborhood.
He would, likely as not, have a clod of mud or a couple of stones
        whizzing at his head,
for the boys were not timid
and did not merely send a pebble spinning about your feet as in
        other places.
Into such a neighborhood, then, my parents and grandparents
        had moved,
the only Jews for blocks,
my father deluded by the cheapness of the house and the sunniness
        of the street;
and, perhaps, by the real-estate broker—an old friend.
I could get home from high school just before the grade schools
        were out;
but playing in the street after school,
or even sitting by myself on the stoop of my grandfather's house
reading my lessons,
meant to be baited by boys of all sizes,
from those well on in their teens
to those who seemed just about able to toddle.
Sooner or later, a stone would be shied at me
or a bit of garbage flung into my face.

Long afterwards, I remembered one white-haired Irish child,
a little boy with a red face,
who could hardly have been more than six or seven—
or who was remarkably undersized—

passing and passing again, as I tried sitting on the stoop
before I knew the neighborhood,
and chanting at me with a tireless anger that surprised me:
"Yid! Yid!"
The child's sister, sixteen or so and home from her job just then,
egged him on,
hatred in her thin pallid face
and in the eyes that were too bright,
as if I were somehow to blame for her unhappiness.

But I was not going to stay cooped up in the house
like my grandfather. I had skates and a wagon—
which like the other boys I had made myself—
and would wake at dawn
and play in the empty street for two or three hours—
before anybody else was out except the milkman.
On holidays,
I would go off on long walks
to the parks, libraries, and museums of the city,
and then, with little to be afraid of
along the parkways and avenues by which I went,
had only the blocks of my own neighborhood to fear.
But I left these when it was early
and came back to them after dark.
On sunny days, after school
I went up to the roof
to sit on the tiled ridge, between my grandfather's house and the one
        next to it,
out of sight of street and yard,
and would do my lessons
or read a book from the public library.
Before I was wholly out of the company of the boys of the street,
I heard them tell each other
how dangerous walking through Brownsville was
and boast of doing it.
But the streets of that Jewish ghetto were pleasanter to me
than a walk along any parkway
where, after all, a gang of boys might be after me
at any moment, as they had been once or twice.
In Brownsville I felt completely safe.
I walked along its pavements utterly at ease.
Nobody, I knew, would hurt me or shout a name at me
merely because I was a Jew;

and, as I looked about at the mean buildings and dingy shopwindows,
for it was, mostly, a quarter of poor people,
I could cry aloud with Balaam:
How goodly are thy tents, O Israel!

Yes, it was lucky, I thought, that my grandfather went out seldom:
I had to, indeed I wanted to, go with him.
We were, in fact, bothered only once.
Then the driver of a grocer's wagon drove up to the curb
and, leaning from his seat,
cracked his whip twice above our heads,
but never touched us.
When my grandfather's house had been sold—
it had become decidedly unprofitable:
the flats to rent both empty
and my grandmother more querulous than ever;
and we were all to move away,
my grandparents to Brownsville
and my parents back to the East Side
to have their home near the shop—
before that happy time
the holidays of the Jewish New Year were upon us
and, of course, my grandfather had to go to synagogue.
My uncle, who had come to our home when we lived in Harlem—
in boots and a round hat of Persian lambskin
like a Cossack—said he would go with his father.
I was glad enough to be free of the duty and danger
but uneasy about them.
The first two days of the New Year holidays
went by without any trouble
in spite of my forebodings.
The evening that ends the Day of Atonement
is generally gay;
almost everybody then hurries from synagogue
to break the fast. But that evening
my grandfather and uncle were not yet home,
although it had long been dark and all the stars were out.
Of course, it was a long way from Brownsville,
but they should have been home
no matter how slowly they walked.
I went down to the stoop to wait for them,
unafraid for the moment of the gibes, or worse, of the boys.

At last my grandfather came,
stumbling through the darkness—
alone.
"Where's Uncle?" I asked.
My grandfather did not stop to answer
but the tears ran over the red rims of his eyes
and he hurried upstairs,
swaying from side to side. I was about to follow
when I saw my uncle in the doorway to the street:
without his new hat and the blood running down his face
from a gash on his forehead.
After the wound had been washed and bandaged,
he told us what had happened:
as he and my grandfather were passing a saloon,
before which some of the neighborhood roughs were standing,
a little boy, set on by the gang,
ran up to strike my grandfather with a stick.
Uncle snatched it away.
No sooner had he done so
than some of the gang sprang upon him,
clouted him on the head,
and sent him sprawling into the gutter.
I tried to blame my uncle
for going down the street that he did—
although it was a short cut—
instead of staying on the busier avenue;
and my father blamed him
for taking the stick from the little boy.
Uncle stood near the stove,
his back against the hot-water boiler,
trying to warm himself,
and never said a word.
My grandmother was muttering that this country
was no better than Russia, after all;
and my parents and I felt ashamed,
as if somehow we were to blame,
and we tried to explain that what had happened was unusual,
that only the neighborhood we lived in was like that,
and what a wonderful country this was—
that all our love for it and our praise
was not unmerited.

The house in which we now lived was old—
dark rooms and low ceilings.
Once our maid, who happened to be Hungarian,
reached her hand up into the cupboard for a dish
and touched a dead rat
that had crawled there to die—poisoned, no doubt.
"Disgusting, disgusting," she kept saying in German
and, to my amusement, shuddered whenever she thought of it.
(A pretty blonde,
    too slight to do the housework she had to,
    she had come, unlike the Ukrainian peasant girls that generally worked
            for us,
    from a town instead of a village.)

My parents' place of business was so near
my mother could come home whenever she felt like it
to see how things were going, but she came seldom
for there was always something to do in the shop
that would not wait. I was all of thirteen
and saw no need for any uneasiness on her part.
But it was not wholly unwarranted by that neighborhood:
we were only a block and a half from the Bowery,
where the cheapest lodging-houses, saloons, and eating-places were
and where the men who did the humblest work lived;
these were aristocrats, no doubt,
among the crowd out of work
and the riffraff who stood idly in doorways
and about the pillars of the railway overhead and shuffled along
        the sidewalk.

Once there was a gentle knock at the door.
Just back from school, I opened it
and a man, so tall he stooped as he stood in the doorway—
his shoulders filled it—
put his foot across the threshold.
I could not close the door—and did not try to—
but waited for him to speak or move.
He was silent, his small eyes shining,
and he peered about,
hesitating and thinking what to do next.
The pretty maid had just put a plate of borsht—

which my mother had taught her how to make—
on the table. She moaned
and rushed to the front room,
although she could not get out of the flat that way,
for the front door was locked and my mother had the key.
But perhaps she felt safer near the windows that opened on the street,
three stories below,
and she was out of the visitor's sight.
"What do you want?" I asked.
The stranger—I took him for a Russian peasant,
since there were some in the neighborhood—
did not answer,
but there was such unhappiness in his drawn face
that I felt friendly and unafraid.
"Will you have something to eat?" I asked cheerfully
and pointed to the chair I had been about to take.
We both looked at the table and saw,
beside the plate of borsht and a round loaf of black bread,
the long bread knife.
Without a word, the man seated himself clumsily
and I cut him a thick slab of bread
and then another. After a moment's hesitation,
I left the knife beside the bread to show that I was not afraid.
The man ate steadily and I stood to one side like a waiter.
I filled the plate once more with borsht,
and dumped in plenty of cabbage and potatoes
from the bottom of the pot. As soon as he was through
and his plate empty again, he got up,
glanced at me for a second out of his narrow eyes,
then bowed his head slightly
and warily, softly, without a word,
edged out of the door.
I closed it after him just as quietly,
and silently turned the big brass key in the lock.
I went into the front room to find the maid:
she was on her knees,
muttering her prayers as fast as she could,
and stood up, embarrassed,
as I looked at her and smiled.

   12

I still went to school in Brooklyn,
for the high school I went to was one of the best in the country.

The grammar school I had come from was a dingy yellow building
among the tenements and noisy avenues of the East Side;
but on every side of the high school were blocks of quiet streets,
shaded by maples,
and the building itself, partly covered with ivy,
was a pleasant, if sober, red brick.
It had seemed to me, when I first saw the building,
that I should be happy there.
The dislike of Jews, however, that was in certain streets of Brooklyn
was in the classrooms, too;
and, sometimes, when Jewish pupils forgot about it
or mistook some careless geniality for friendliness,
they suddenly found, like people who live over a geological fault,
how uncertain the ground was.

During the first year of high school,
when the pupils were all beginners together
and had an annex to themselves,
I saw none of this dislike.
One of the bigger boys, it is true,
would always slam into me as we all ran out to lunch
and knock me against the wooden wall around the yard,
but I had no reason to think the fellow did it for any other reason
than that he was taller and older
and was having the fun
any dog might have worrying a rabbit.
I was tempted to tell our classroom teacher about it,
after a particularly good banging,
but I was doubtful if the teacher's jurisdiction went that far
and uncertain how, with that calm Gentile smile of his,
he would take my tale.
I concluded it was better to suffer the daily buffeting
than to stoop to such ignominy.
Once, indeed, in story-book fashion,
I turned on my tormentor and punched as hard as I could.
Unlike the books, however, he laughed
as he warded off my fists—easily enough,
and then proceeded to strike me fast and hard;
so that I realized, as I leaned breathlessly
against the wall
while my tormentor and the others ran on to get their lunch,
that until then the fellow had just been playing
and had been almost kind.
With the rest, Jews and Gentiles,

I was friendly enough
during the brief while we were together
merely as boys and not as pupils.
Winter mornings, those who were almost tardy—
among whom I was generally one,
for I had to come all the way from Manhattan—
would slide and slip across the ice-covered courtyard
in our hurry to reach the classroom before the bell should ring
and, as we did so, we would look at each other in friendliest fashion
and laugh. We spoke to each other confidentially
in the back-room of the delicatessen store—
to which we raced at noon—
where we ate our lunch together while we looked at the owner
who was so fat there was hardly room for him behind the counter.
He would smile and gurgle with pleasure
and murmur our orders and thank us softly
as he pushed the sandwiches over the counter
and gathered our pennies with his small fat hands.
He is going to die soon, we said to each other:
he has fatty degeneration of the heart and cannot last long.
This his helper had told us—a weedy boy with a sour smile,
the owner's bastard. The helper himself had told us he was that
and grinned.
And we boys would watch him look at his father with malice
whenever the fat man in his gentle wheedling voice
spoke to him.

Those who were promoted after the first year
were shifted to the main building. There we Jews
found the climate chillier.
To begin with, the immigration that followed the Russian massacres—
which had brought my parents to this country—
was just then sending its first students to the school
from the new ghettos of Brownsville and Williamsburg.
The school, which had never had more than a few Jews,
suddenly had many—half a class, sometimes, Jewish.
Besides, those who had come in the past
were generally sons of German or Hungarian Jews
who had been in the United States quite a while,
and even before that
had lived in a civilization somewhat like this country's.
The parents of those pupils often had money
and a home in the tree-shaded neighborhood of the school.

But the new boys were, for the most part, children of poor people
who had hardly had time to learn much of the speech and accent of
      the land;
boys with strange and difficult Polish or Russian names,
in ill-fitting clothes and often ill at ease,
who, because of this, were sometimes loud and brash.
So, because I was thin-skinned or too young to be sensible,
I was no longer carefree at school:
the ice on which I walked seemed to me everywhere thin.

13

There was a small settlement-house near where we lived
and I became friendly with two of the boys I met there—
Eugene and Gabriel, children of Hungarian Jews.
The three of us had this in common:
we liked to write
which for us then, still in high school, meant mostly reading.
Eugene's father had a store in which he sold flannel shirts and woolen
      underwear to firemen.
Years before, he had peddled them about the fire-houses of the city.
No doubt, he had then to put up with a good deal of joking,
for he was a small, homely man, and a Jew at that.
When I knew him, he had authority in his voice
and dignity in his bearing,
and was respected by his customers—and tenants,
for he owned several tenements in the neighborhood
and these were kept as clean and orderly as his store.
If the day was sunny, I would usually find Eugene sitting in front of it.
While his father spread the flannel along the counter for the shirts
      he sold,
layer on layer, and cut it according to the patterns,
Eugene and I, outside, would be talking about poetry,
especially the poetry of the new men—new to us—
Francis Thompson, Arthur Symons, and Ernest Dowson.
This was not in our English course,
and Eugene and I felt superior because we read them,
and were proud of ourselves because we, too, were writing verse,
and trying our hands at sonnets
and the French confectionary Austin Dobson—for one—was good at.

Gabriel was older than either of us—
a sarcastic fellow. But he knew much more than I

and was so generous of all he knew
that I listened humbly and did not mind his smiles and quiet gibes.
He had read much verse,
chiefly the Elizabethans and the metaphysical poets,
and their nimble speech delighted him.
His own verse, merely gymnastics of his own quick mind,
was full of sudden twists of thought—
balancing itself on the necessity of rhyme and a strict meter.
He prided himself on how fast he could dash it off
and never kept anything of what he wrote,
except as he happened to remember some of it,
and seldom gave it a second thought.
His parents, unlike Eugene's, were poor
and lived in a dingy house—in a dingy flat.
From the back of it, I could see the yards unevenly paved
and the multitudinous windows of tenements
and many clotheslines, always hung with washing.
Sometimes his mother—or stepmother—a stout sad-faced woman,
would come out of a dark bedroom,
which had neither door nor window and only a hanging in the doorway,
at the sound of our cheerful voices;
or would leave the front room, where she sat at a window watching
          the mean street below,
to look at us and go back without a word.
I would see Gabriel's father, too, at times:
a stout man, shabbily dressed,
who spoke briefly to his wife in a low voice
and never to his son while I was there.
I guessed that he had a pushcart,
or did something even humbler like peddling from a basket;
for his son, in spite of a smile when he spoke of his father's work,
seemed anxious to hide it.

Gabriel showed me where to buy second-hand books,
and on Saturdays we would walk from stall to stall.
It was no use looking at books that cost a quarter or more—
for we seldom had more than a couple of dimes to spend—
but still we managed to buy many a dusty, ill-smelling volume.
We handled many books of sermons and many of verse;
looked at each patiently,
for among the sermons we might find those of Latimer or even Donne—
although we never did—
and we dipped into each book of verse,
for of course we knew that Rossetti or Swinburne had found the Rubaiyat

in just such a pile.
One Saturday, Gabriel bought a copy of the Greek Anthology—
in Greek, for he could read it—
and I found in a single volume all the English poets
from Ben Jonson to Beattie.
It had been bound in brown morocco, but only one board remained,
and the pages had yellow spots.
Still, the small print was clear
and, as the "advertisement" or introduction said,
"all the classical English poets" were there.
Few poems, no matter in how many cantos, were left out,
except those "unsuited to the perusal of youth."
This, no doubt, more than the damaged binding and spotted pages
had condemned it to lie among the cheapest books.
And on this fortunate day, to the envy of Gabriel,
who had taught me to admire Sartain's deep shading and thin lines,
I had also found a book with more than twenty of his engravings.
(Gabriel praised much others held cheap—
only, so he thought, because of their stupidity.)
With our new possessions
we walked slowly down the sunny avenue
to Gabriel's home. As we did so,
a ship, keeping time with us, went smoothly down the river,
hull hidden, but masts and sails showing
above the gutter of each street we crossed.

We had our supper in the large kitchen—
a roll each and coffee. The coffee was mostly chicory with hot milk,
which I did not care for,
but the roll was fresh and hot and the sweet butter on it very good.
Afterwards, as we each sat by a window
and looked out into the bright world—
for it was still daylight—
we set ourselves to writing sonnets on a given theme.
We knew that Keats and Leigh Hunt used to do that.
I had Gabriel choose the theme,
for this was to be a test of my skill in writing verse
as against his. He finished long before I did.
It had become twilight,
but there was still light enough to read what we had written.
Gabriel's sonnet was something fantastic,
which I did not care for; but he said that he liked mine—
and, indeed, I liked it very much.

One evening, when I had not seen Gabriel in years,
and we had become men with serious and unpleasant work to do
        for our living,
I was on a station where the subway ran above ground
in a neighborhood to which I went seldom.
It was late at night
and the train was long in coming.
The cold open air was pleasanter than the foul air of the waiting-room
and I walked about, lost in thought,
and listened to my steps crunching the newly-fallen snow.
It lay an inch thick on the narrow wooden planking
beyond the cement platform. At the very end of the station
I came upon Gabriel, under a bright light:
the slack body and the small head with yellow hair and green eyes.
There was a rather pretty woman with him;
they were talking together familiarly
and yet without any great interest in what each was saying,
as husband and wife at times talk to each other.
He looked at me for a moment coldly
and then shifted his eyes;
and I turned slowly
and stood at a distance waiting for the train.

   14

My father bought a house near Brownsville
and we moved—back to Brooklyn.
I was to have a room of my own
and should have been happy; at least my mother thought so.
But I lay flat on the bed, staring at the blue sky,
and was miserable. My mother stopped bustling at setting the rooms
        to rights
and opened the door to scold me,
and reminded me scornfully of the twilight of the flat we had left,
its rats, and the smells of the street.
I did not trouble to tell her why I had liked it
but got up and went slowly about whatever I had to do.
However, the neighborhood, although not Jewish,
was unlike that other in which we had last lived in Brooklyn,
and more or less friendly.

My two new friends, like Eugene and Gabriel, were Jewish
but they were the children of Polish or Russian Jews.

Both lived in Brownsville,
and Saul often walked home with me from school.
His father had a candy store in the very street where I had been born
fifteen years before. It was now a dingy street—
small wooden houses in which the poorest Jews of Brownsville lived.
The store itself was a cheerless place
in spite of its merchandise: the walls had only cracks for decoration—
bare of any picture or poster,
and the paint that was once bright green,
too bright a green, I suppose,
had long been darkened.
The store was never heated. It had a single gas-jet,
lit only when it was so dark
a customer could hardly see his hand,
to say nothing of the stock.
This was kept in little saucers in three showcases,
before which stood a narrow unpainted stand for the smaller children
to climb upon. The glass of the showcases was dirty and smeared
under the fingers of the children—
the chief, if not the only, customers—
as they meditated their purchases or pointed them out at last
after much prompting and prodding from behind the counter;
trooping in to buy a pennysworth
and, shouting and sharing,
leaving the door wide open or banging it to.

My friend's father could not really have thought to make a living out
        of the place;
with his wife and children to help run it,
he had hoped, no doubt, to eke out
whatever he could earn as a sewing-machine operator.
They lived in back of the store; and I could see Saul's father and mother
        shuffling about,
with lined faces, stooped and somewhat dazed;
I would glance at the greenish black teeth of his pretty sister—
she was eating too much candy, I supposed.
My friend was shorter than I, although somewhat older,
but he, too, like his parents, walked with a stoop.
At no time did he seem ridiculous to me;
not even when his parents bought him a suit for Passover
and the new unwrinkled cloth showed how ill-fitting it was
and that the sleeves were much too long.

After school, Saul and I would sometimes go to a public playground
     in Brownsville.
There boys would play at handball, although the ground was uneven
and covered with pebbles—
no one could tell just how the ball would bounce.
Whenever Saul was there, while others played games,
ran after each other, or swung on the bars and rings,
he persisted in learning how to fall:
work his way up the inclined ladder, higher and higher,
and then drop to the ground.
The small, somewhat clumsy body would fall upon the hard-packed sand,
pick itself up,
and Saul—his body jerking—
would work his way up the ladder again.
The trick, he explained, was to land lightly
and not sting the soles of one's feet.
"But why learn how to fall?" I asked. "What good is it?"
"I don't know," he would answer, smiling foolishly.
"I want to!"
Once, when I was in his home, I stood at the window
looking into the yard:
it was full of old wagons, the shafts high in the air;
along the back fence cats were walking
gracefully,
and now and then one jumped to the ground
landing lightly on its feet.
The father of Saul's friend, Charles, was even poorer than Saul's father.
This friend became, after a fashion, also mine.
I who had all the cake I cared for—
cookies sprinkled thick with chopped almonds
or a dark brown cake, cut into chunks, fragrant with honey—
met in Saul's friend a cheerful lad
content if he had a lump of sugar for dessert.
He lived near the railroad tracks that ran through Brownsville,
next to the lots where rubbish was dumped
and his interest was philosophy, as mine was verse:
he talked—very well it seemed to me—
of Spinoza and Bergson and the others.

We took a pleasant walk together
one Saturday in the spring or autumn, Charles and I;
the weather was mild, the air clear;
the twilight blue,

the stars, at first single,
many.
We walked under the trees along the parkway
that led back to Brownsville
and talked most of Bergson's theory of laughter.

In a day or two I had a note from him:
his father had died suddenly
and could I lend him ten dollars
which he would surely repay in a week?
I did not think he would—
in a week or even in a month,
for I had noticed that boys who asked for a coin, at least from me,
and, unasked, were explicit about repayment
(old hands at borrowing)
seldom repaid the loan as glibly.
But, of course, I got the money from my father
and brought it to Charles as fast as I could.

Charles did not repay it.
He had better things to do
with what little money he could get.
But the small debt troubled him, perhaps,
because he never came to see me again
and when I went to his home
he was uncomfortable.
His mother could not pay the rent,
even for so poor a place as theirs;
and Charles did not let me know
where they moved to.
He had been so uneasy at the sight of me,
when the time he himself had set for repayment was long gone,
that, too young and inexperienced,
I did not know enough to hunt him up or write to him
to say that so trivial a matter
should not come between a poet and a philosopher.

15

I went to my grandfather's to say good-bye:
I was going away to a school out West.
As I came in,
my grandfather turned from the window at which he sat

(sick, skin yellow, eyes bleary—
   but his hair still dark,
   for my grandfather had hardly any grey hair in his beard or on his head—
   he would sit at the window, reading a Hebrew book).
   He rose with difficulty—
   he had been expecting me, it seemed—
   stretched out his hands and blessed me in a loud voice:
   in Hebrew, of course,
   and I did not know what he was saying.
   When he had blessed me,
   my grandfather turned aside and burst into tears.
"It is only for a little while, Grandpa," I said
   in my broken Yiddish. "I'll be back in June."
(By June my grandfather was dead.)
   He did not answer.
   Perhaps my grandfather was in tears for other reasons:
   perhaps, because, in spite of all the learning I had acquired in high school,
   I knew not a word of the sacred text of the Torah
   and was going out into the world
   with none of the accumulated wisdom of my people to guide me,
   with no prayers with which to talk to the God of my people,
   a soul—
   for it is not easy to be a Jew or, perhaps, a man—
   doomed by his ignorance to stumble and blunder.

   16

   I now went to law school in the evening.
   The instruction was by reading cases—
   no lectures that stuffed pap into the mouth of the student;
   and we soon learned, under the incitement of our teachers,
   to question—if questioning was called for—
   the opinion of each case
   and, perhaps, that of our teachers.
   Most of my fellow students were older than I
   and earnest (almost all worked during the day
   in factories or in law offices),
   and their questions had steel in them;
   unlike the students in the morning or afternoon classes,
   mostly just out of high school
   and too timid to speak or, if they did,
   poked feeble questions
   like the sticks that children use as swords.

At first I read more poetry than cases,
but then threw myself zestfully
into the dog fight that each period became
and, to be ready for it,
learned to probe beneath the facts of each case
for the living principle of law
and to trace it, if I could,
to the solid trunk from which it sprang;
confused as it all was to me at first,
I soon saw the law in its elements as a beautiful order
in which benefit balanced obligation
and nothing was without its reason—or reasons.

The law that we studied
was not always the actual law
of judges or statutes
but an ideal—
from which new branches were ever springing
as society became complicated
and the new rights of its individuals clear.
I found it delightful
to climb those green heights,
to bathe in the clear waters of reason,
to use words for their daylight meaning
and not as prisms
playing with the rainbows of connotation:
after the dim lights, the colored phrases, the cloying music,
the hints of what the poets meant
and did not quite say
(for to suggest was to create
and to name was to destroy—
according to the Symbolists, at least),
the plain sunlight of the cases,
the sharp prose,
the forthright speech of the judges;
it was good, too, to stick my mind against the sentences of a judge,
and drag the meaning out of the shell of words.
And when our teacher of contracts,
who was also the dean of the school,
produced a theory of acceptance
(which was not actually the law anywhere),
I was delighted, walking along the streets deep in thought,
to find a flaw in the theory

and boldly produce another, my very own—
to find that I, too, could think like a lawyer.

I soon had no time for writing or reading anything but law
and spent my days in the law library
diligently reading cases and memorizing sentences that seemed meaty;
reading each page as often as I liked
with nothing to jog my elbow or step on my heel;
sifting the facts of each case until I had only the hard essentials;
underlining words and phrases
until I had plotted the judge's reasoning;
and digging for the bedrock of law on which the cases stood—
or did not stand.
The noise of the street was far away—
ten storeys below;
far away, too, the worry and noise of my parents' shop;
before me was all that was left of eager argument and eager parties,
now merely names that might just as well have been,
and in the talk of the law students often were,
single letters of the alphabet:
all the blood—the heartache and the heartening—gone out of the words
and only, as a pattern for thinking,
the cool bones of the judge's reasoning.
And I felt no regret for the glittering words I had played with
and only pleasure to be working with ideas—
of rights and wrongs and their elements
and of justice between men in their intricate affairs.

The last class was over at ten.
I would try to get home before midnight
and had to walk briskly to do it:
a mile or two to the bridge
through streets now mostly empty and still;
over the bridge again,
often meeting with nobody for the whole mile of it,
especially if the wind was cold or when it would snow or rain;
and then the long walk in Brooklyn, five or six miles,
the streets quiet and dark and the neighborhood of my home
quietest of all—
lawns and gardens, a park and empty lots.

Suddenly all delight in my studies was gone—
melted with the snow in the spring.

True enough, the studies of the second year were less interesting
than those of the first:
less probing after principle and more of practice,
less general reasoning and more of statutory requirement,
necessary enough but detailed and dull;
but what bothered me most, unlooked for
and against will and reason,
with the suddenness of a fever,
was the longing to write:
as if all that I had seen and heard and remembered
and, for the most part, felt only slightly,
was not gone, as I had thought,
but stored in a reservoir
that now, filled to the brim, was overrunning—
pouring over on all sides.
(It was, of course, no reservoir, but only a kettleful—
but it had come to a boil.)
And here I was, busied with this tiresome study of the law,
these tiring studies that left me no time
and, if time, no strength
to write. My bulky lawbooks had become, over night,
too heavy to lift and the cases palaver.

17

I had been bothered by a secret weariness
with meter and regular stanzas
grown a little stale. The smooth lines and rhymes
seemed to me affected, a false stress on words and syllables—
fake flowers
in the streets in which I walked.
And yet I found prose
without the burst of song and sudden dancing—
without the intensity which I wanted.
The brand-new verse some Americans were beginning to write—
after the French "free verse," perhaps,
or the irregular rhythms of Walt Whitman,
the English translations of the Hebrew Bible
and, earlier yet, the rough verse of the Anglo-Saxons—
seemed to me, when I first read it,
right:
not cut to patterns, however cleverly,
nor poured into ready molds,

but words and phrases flowing as the thought;
to be read just as common speech
but for stopping at the turn of each line—
and this like a rest in music or a turn in the dance.
(I found it no criticism that to read such verse as prose
was to have a kind of prose,
for that was not to read it as it was written.)
And with the even artificial beat of the old meters,
I gave up the artifice of rhyme:
not only because I had the authority of Milton
and the usage of the Elizabethans in their plays;
I liked a Doric music better.

Now, too I became friendly with one my own age,
whom I had met the summer before
thinking him just another acquaintance.
Al proved to be as helpful as my new reading.
He had come to see me at my home that summer
about to teach in the West where I had studied
five years before
that I might tell him of the place;
I had little to say and he listened
almost indifferently,
smiling half in friendship and half mockingly,
hardly looking at me with his bright blue eyes.
When he was back next summer for his vacation,
with nothing better to do, perhaps,
he came to see me again
but now we had the new verse to talk of.
I showed him what of mine had been taken for publication
in a new magazine for verse only;
but he read my verse as I had never read verse before,
scrutinizing it, phrase by phrase
and word by word, thought and image, thought and sound;
and much, if not all, that had seemed good to me
now had the dead sound of a counterfeit coin
on his marble good sense.
That was the way he had read Shakespeare at college—
without such effect, of course—
and so, except that I gave little thought
to image or sound,
was how I had read my law cases.
But, in spite of my early dislike of journalism

because of its hurried and careless writing,
I used to write verse just as carelessly—
as it flew into my head.
Now doing just what Al did,
I saw that I could use the expensive machinery
that had cost me four years of hard work at law
and which I had thought useless for my writing:
prying sentences open to look at the exact meaning;
weighing words to choose only those that had meat for my purpose
and throwing the rest away as empty shells.
I, too, could scrutinize every word and phrase
as if in a document or the opinion of a judge
and listen, as well, for tones and overtones,
leaving only the pithy, the necessary, the clear and plain.

Al read nothing on his knees,
and delighted in finding out for himself
what made a poem or story tick—
if it did. We began to spend much time together,
our spirits swaggering about,
blaming and praising each other's writing,
as well as that of the rest of the world—
"we poets whose lives begin in gladness."
Perhaps, if all our eager talk had been written down,
some of it would have seemed, afterwards,
as jejune as comments an arrogant self
had written in the margin of books
in those proud days when I read with a pencil.
But not all. We might, for example, talk about the story from the Japanese
that Lafcadio Hearn used. A man is lost in the woods.
It is going to storm. Anxious to ask his way,
he hurries up to what he takes for a peasant,
walking ahead of him in the gathering darkness.
The peasant—or whatever it is he is talking to—
turns
and the traveler sees a face without nose or eyes,
smooth as an egg, and rushes off.
Then, as he runs, stumbling, anxious now only to get away,
he sees again what he takes to be a peasant walking ahead of him.
He runs up, eager for any human companionship
after that earlier sight,
and blurts out what he has just seen;
and the same face turns to him again and asks:

"Was it anything like this?"
I might have said that the story was moving
because it meant that we should meet again
the horrible we thought we had escaped,
or that our secret terrors warn us
of what we shall surely face. Al said:
"Compare this with a German fairy tale.
When the Germans want to make a figure horrible,
a witch, for instance,
they enlarge the eyes, lengthen the nose, the teeth, the nails—
they add, they exaggerate;
but the Japanese make a more horrible figure
because less human:
they take everything away—nose, mouth, and even eyes."

I reread my verse that had been taken for publication
and found much in so few lines to change or strike out
and wrote the magazine about it,
but the editor assured me, of the longer poem,
that it was meant—
by Apollo, no doubt—
to be in quatrains, as first written,
and that the irregularities with which I proposed to remedy the verse
only spoiled it.
However, if changes were in order,
she suggested a number off-hand
and these I could not see at all.
In the meantime, I had sent her more verse,
of which she took another poem
to add to the two to be published,
but would not have one or two I thought the best—
better than any of mine she had taken.
The other magazines, to judge by what they were printing,
were not even worth bothering with, I thought,
with the arrogance of the young;
and for the judgment of the editor who was to print my verse
I had, by this time,
little respect.
Besides, publication in a magazine, pleasant as it would be,
seemed less important than perfection,
at least whatever degree of it I could reach.
And, as I thought about it,
it seemed to me that if I could accustom myself to working at my
        verse daily,

revising until I had a group to my own satisfaction,
and could have group after group printed,
I might in time, say, in a lifetime,
have a few poems—
the quintessence of all I had to say.
But I could not, it seemed to me,
just put my verse away in a drawer until the Messiah should come;
for the impulse to write—in which I had such pleasure—
and above all to revise wholeheartedly,
would be, perhaps would have to be, stimulated
by regular publication.
And again, revision year after year
of what I might have lying about
unpublished,
would become destructive merely,
rubbing out much that by constant review
would seem unnecessary
and had become tiresome.
Publication in a magazine, such as was now promised,
of a couple of poems now and then—
even as I would have them—
hardly seemed worth while.
But, since I did not hope for a publisher
to print my verse soon at his own risk
and I did not have the money to pay for a publisher's imprint—
nor did I relish the pretence—
why, I thought, I should print privately,
that is, pay the printer and make no pretence of having a publisher at all.
There was little notice to be had that way, I knew,
among the crowd of new books;
but, besides the stimulation to write and revise,
I would clear my head and heart
for new work. Yes, the work was the thing.
Large circulation is pleasant, of course,
but I did not find it necessary:
as if one has seen something exciting in the street
he must tell it—
perhaps because man is communicative—
but, after he has told his vision
once or twice,
handed on his knowledge to two or three,
he is free to go about his other business.

Besides, the urgency of war (for the country was now in the First
    World War)
made it seem advisable to arrange my affairs;
and, since my affairs were verse,
to put it, slight though in bulk and value, in order
and leave it printed behind me;
for I doubted that anyone else
would go to that trouble and any expense.
I knew two stories to strengthen me in my resolution—
one I had read and the other my mother told me;
Balzac's story of the painter who kept working at his painting
until when seen last it was only a mass of paint,
except for a beautiful hand
which showed what the painting might have been—
this for the danger of endless revision;
and my mother's story of her father
who became a kind of broker
making his little commissions on sales of cattle or wheat
and beguiled his spirit as he wandered about the countryside
writing verse in Hebrew—
until he suddenly died of influenza far from home.
And when with his bundle of clothes there was brought back a sheaf
    of papers—
his verse, the writing of thirty years—
my grandmother burnt every scrap of it, dearly as she loved him;
for fear that the writing which she could not read
or, if she could, did not understand,
might send her children to jail
should any of it be construed as treasonable against the Czar.
Well, I would leave no writing of mine,
if I could help it,
to the mercy of those who loved me.
I would print
and, though I knew it was an unlikely way to gain name or money
(not that I cared much for either),
I also knew a Chinese proverb
that one who can work ten years without recognition
will be known everywhere,
and the tradition in English verse of private publication
as the "Rubaiyat" was published and "Leaves of Grass."
Later, when I was to have much time and a little money,
I learnt how to print;
indeed, setting type by hand and running a platen-press by foot

is not too hard:
the great wheel turning, the rollers moving down over the sticky
        black platen,
shining arms sliding smoothly into their grooves
and the type closing on the blank paper—
to leave a printed sheet.
I would stop the wheel at each revolution,
unable to feed the press as a printer could
but, slow as I was, I would print four hundred sheets in a couple
        of hours—
more than enough.
A difficulty was room for the heavy press.
I had it in the basement of my parents' house;
when they moved, the press was dismantled,
coated with oil, stored, and finally sold—and lost.

18

During the First World War, I was back in law school
for a course or two,
waiting to be admitted to the corps training there.
The study of law in that time of violence
was a luxury,
and I never tasted the pleasure of it as much.
But I did not have to drill,
or sleep on one of the cots I had seen in the basement of a school
        building
(better than the trenches at that!):
before I was admitted to the corps,
there was talk of an armistice
and soon enough news of it.

As we sat in class, just a handful,
we could hear the factory whistles
and the whistles of the boats on the river.
And then, class over, we stopped on the broad stairs that led from the
        school building
to listen to the motor trucks racing uptown,
blowing their horns for all they were worth.
It was twilight by then,
and the moon was shining in the clear autumn sky.
In spite of all the noise on the avenue, a block away,
the sound came to those of us on the stairs

much diminished—almost the buzz of insects.
A great sabbath had begun.

The man who taught us international law
stood on the steps, too,
still talking to us,
and he spoke cautiously of the nationalism
excited by the President and the Allies against Austria,
sorry that the policy would undo the work of many centuries
to have men forget in a wide empire of law—
based on justice and equity—
the accidental differences of their birth.
But his voice was just another small voice
among all those many voices which were sounding happily,
raucously,
as the lights of the city began to shine.

19

I now set myself to finishing another booklet
and began to write a play in verse—
in the staccato manner the German impressionists were using;
even though I knew it would be at least as unlikely for me to find
        a producer for the play
as a publisher for my other verse,
since audiences—before the radio—had become, for the most part,
spectators of the action rather than listeners.
Even I, when a play by an Elizabethan other than Shakespeare had
        been given,
found it hard to follow the speeches
and the detailed imagery;
but, although prose "pithy as the speech of peasants"—
which Synge and Tolstoi used—
was good,
I was sure, thinking of Shakespeare and Goethe on the stage,
the play was at its best in verse.
And I remembered the ending of the first part of "Faust"
as I had heard it in the German theater in New York;
I was wound up tighter and tighter
until I thought some nerve in me would snap or artery burst
if I did not escape.
Yet I could not move from my seat.
When the play was over,

I thought I understood Aristotle's "purging" by tragedy,
for I walked upon air:
so trivial did all my troubles seem
after what I had just lived through on the stage.

20
Epilogue

The rest is like the manna of the Israelites
which, gathered into their baskets,
made a great heap
but did not outlast the day.

The Fifth Book of the Maccabees

I

Gaza of the Philistines was still a great city: the Arabs of the wilderness traded there for pottery and knives; and caravans from Egypt stopped in Gaza because of its many wells of fresh water and the gardens on every side. But its inhabitants were no longer a warlike people. Even the speech they once spoke had long been forgotten: Nehemiah, three hundred years before, heard the last of it in Ashdod.

The army of Judea pitched their tents on the sand dunes between Gaza and the sea and in the groves of olive trees—under a sky alive with kites and vultures. Above the camp bristling with spears was the blue standard: a lion rampant embroidered upon it and the motto of the Hasmoneans, "Who is like You among the mighty, Lord?"

Then the soldiers of the king of Judea walked the narrow streets and entered the temples of the new gods of Gaza which were the gods of the Greeks and had failed it. And the Jews spoke of Samson who, blinded, did grind in its prison; of how the Israelites had once hidden in caves and holes from the Philistines; and the Jews praised the Lord of Hosts, blessed be His name!

The king of Judea put to death the chief men of the city in their temple of Apollo and razed Gaza—wall and towers, temples and dwellings—he razed it to the ground, and came back to Jerusalem: through crowds waving palm branches and greeting him with the clash of cymbals and shouts of praise. But at the feast in the court of the king's palace, amidst the huzzas, the soldiers heard a sharp dissenting voice—an old man berating the king: "Enough for you, Alexander Jannai, the crown of David, and leave the miter of the high priest! Even if you had the right to wear it, it is not to be worn at a feast like this and by one whose hands have shed much blood!"

The king sat grinding his teeth while men and officers shouted. The captains of the mercenaries—not Jewish at all and eager to show devotion —had hands on hilts, when the king in a loud voice cried: "Peace!" At the word slaves rushed into the courtyard and some began handing about cakes of fresh bread in baskets while others poured the red wine into cups. Still others brought leather bottles of wine and left them on the tables, and many a cruse of oil for the salted herbs, and lumps of figs and dates.

---

* The four books of the Maccabees are, of course, among the writings of the Apocrypha; I have based this "book" in part on the "The Jewish War" and "Antiquities of the Jews" by Josephus. —C. R.

Along the wall of the courtyard
the pomegranate trees were in blossom;
doves murmured in the branches
and, on the barren ground,
dust swirled about the blue wings.
The dancing girls began the dances
of Alexandria and Antioch,
moving hands and fingers, shoulders and body,
but feet hardly at all;
watching them, the soldiers were soon joking
and breaking out into song.

Bearded men in the hall of the palace:
gaping at the good flooring
of heavy cedar boards; at the walls—
four rows of white stone,
the top carved into trees and plants
so skillfully
branches and leaves seemed to move.
"Judea is grain, Galilee straw,
and all beyond—chaff!"

Narrow square forehead, a long curved nose
thick at the nostrils,
thick lips but a well-formed mouth, a strong jaw,
a long black beard, heavy black eyebrows
and keen—but narrow—black eyes:
the king of Judea came in,
a goblet of red wine in his hand,
walking unsteadily
in shoes of soft red leather.

In the courtyard they were singing
the Song of Deborah:
"The river Kishon swept them away,
the ancient river, the river Kishon.
O my soul,
you have trodden down strength!"

2

Walking in the gardens of the king, "Do you really suppose," one of the
women of the court said mockingly, "that God gave the Law to Moses in

the clouds and smoke of a mountain? That the Books of Moses, dreary with genealogies and laws, may be likened for knowledge to Aristotle, for wisdom and beauty of speech to Plato?"

Her nose was small and straight and her eyes blue,
her lips full and her chin round;
a Jewess and yet with her red hair and blue eyes
a very daughter of the Amorites.
The red hair, glistening with gold dust,
was bound in a snood
over which the hair tumbled
in ringlets;
and little golden bells were about her ankles.

She wore a necklace of the coins of Judea, showing spokes of a wheel and a galley at sea: curious symbols for a nation in the hills. But apt enough for the ambition of its king—or for a scattered people. Her companion reached for her hand but she drew it away while her eyes led him on. She looked at him sideways, turning her head ever so slightly and smiling the while; and then, suddenly, looked him full in the face, her own face very earnest, and her wide-open eyes shining with a thousand points of blue light.

"The Pharisees," she said, "teach the Unwritten Law, and yet the Book of Deuteronomy says plainly: 'You shall not add to the word which I command you.'" And she mocked at the Pharisees for a belief in angels: in body like the wind or like the flames of fire! And for the teaching that the dead will live again: "As grass," she said, "will grow on a paved street."

In the moonlight they looked down upon the pavement of flat roofs on the slopes before them: the white houses of Jerusalem crowded together with its narrow winding streets of stairs and steep lanes. "The king and all men of sense," she said, "see the hope of our country in making it rich and strong. Such a country as Parthia would wish for an ally—or Rome."

3

The Feast of Booths is a festival of thanksgiving for what has been gathered from threshing-floor and wine-press; and the people made themselves booths—as they are commanded in the Torah—of the branches of thick trees and of palms and of the willows of the brook: everyone upon the roof of his house or in his court that they might remember how they had lived in booths when the Lord brought Israel out of Egypt. And Jerusalem was crowded with pilgrims who had come with their sacrifices to see Alexander Jannai, the king and high priest, sacrifice for the nation: a crush of joyous people on the stairs of the streets, holding palm leaves and branches of willows and twigs of myrtle as well as citrons—symbols of the fruit of a goodly tree with which to rejoice before the Lord. The king, in his purple robe of high priest with its fringe of golden bells and pomegranates— a bell and a pomegranate, a bell and a pomegranate—his broad girdle embroidered with flowers and threads of gold, wore the high priest's breastplate of twelve precious stones, each cut with the name of a tribe of Israel, and on his linen cap the triple crown with its whorl of golden leaves.

In the days of the prophet Samuel, when he judged the people in Mizpah, the Israelites drew water and poured it out before the Lord for rain. Now, the land of Israel—unlike Egypt—is watered by rain, and on the Feast of Booths after the long summer the Pharisees, many living in the mean quarters of the cities, held much by this libation: their own small cisterns almost dry. Three blasts on the ram's horn greeted the procession bringing water from the fountain of Siloam to the Water Gate; and the worshippers watched the king, as high priest, take the golden flask up to the great altar and turn to the golden basins—one for water and the other for wine. But Alexander Jannai poured the water on the ground and, as some reported, upon his feet: out of contempt, perhaps, for the Pharisees.

The Pharisees pelted the king with citrons. Straightway the king and high priest, grandson of Simon and grandnephew of Judah the Maccabee, sent for his mercenaries—heathen from the mountains of Asia Minor— who had been drawn up beyond the walls of the Temple.

With stony faces and naked swords
they ran into the sacred grounds
cutting down the worshippers.
Bodies of young and old were lying
everywhere:
holiday garments stained with blood
and blood gathering in pools
on the stone flags of the court and flowing into
the gutters
over the scattered palm leaves
and branches of willows
and the twigs of myrtle.

That night there were no lamps, no candles,
in the Women's Court of the Temple—
so many burning
every courtyard in the city used to be alight;
no pious men danced
with burning torches in their hands
singing to the Lord, while the Levites on the steps

played on harps and lutes, sounded their cymbals and trumpets,
answering psalm with psalm; and every heart was glad.
So that it was a saying:
he who did not see this
never saw true rejoicing.

4

The army of the king was scattered in flight. But the Pharisees with
Demetrius of Damascus left him, not to march farther into Judea against
fellow Jews and a Jewish king. Then Pharisees still troublesome in the
cities and countryside were brought to Jerusalem in chains; and Alexan-
der Jannai's workmen set up rows of crosses in a place beyond the city for
the punishment Palestine had learnt from the Macedonian kings of Syria.
(But it was rumored that the king would set the Pharisees free as Joseph
once freed his brothers in Egypt.) Two or three days before the festival of
Passover the Pharisees were brought from their dungeons, befouled and
dreadfully pale, and with them their kin imprisoned also; and all were led
beyond the city into the bright sunshine among the blossoms of the
spring.

The spectators began to weep and sob as the prisoners were halted in
the wood of crosses. One of the Pharisees was heard saying: "How beau-
tiful the world is! I had hardly noticed it." And the man's companion said:
"It is written in the Song of Songs: 'love is as strong as death.' If a man
dies for love of God, thinking with all his might only of the Lord, will he
feel his wounds?"

Stoning, burning, strangling, or the sword: none of "the four deaths"
of Jewish law has the pain of crucifixion. But it was the custom of the Jews
to have the condemned drink of wine and frankincense and go to his
death benumbed. Without more ado, however, the executioners began
hoisting the Pharisees upon the crosses and driving the shrieking nails
through hands and feet; and seized upon wives and children to cut their
throats before the dying men.

Above, in the gardens of the king,
the king and the king's courtiers and their women
sat watching the executions.
Wine and baskets of fruit and cakes
were brought to the tables;
and, as they ate and drank,
they sang the songs of love and the drinking songs
of Alexandria and Damascus.

The sky was bright and blue that day
and at evening a deeper blue
as star after star began to shine.
The guards who were to watch the Pharisees
twisting in their slow death
gathered in a hollow
out of the cold wind.

5

An officer of the Jews besieging Ragab saw in a growing cloud of dust a heavy litter and the horsemen riding slowly on all sides. The queen! He went into the king's tent with steps that fell softly on the carpet. Alexander Jannai lay under a sealskin, bony forehead and black hair wet with sweat, trembling for cold in the heat of noon; his hands on the covering plucking at the fur.

The leather curtains of the litter parted although the heavy wheels had not come to a stop, and the queen stepped out before anyone could help her to the ground. The officers caught a glimpse of her round rouged face, wet with tears, under the long veil flowing in the wind as she went towards the king's tent with a quick firm tread.

It was said, afterwards, that the dying king advised Salome, his queen, to make her peace with the Pharisees. Be this as it may, she sent for her brother, ben-Shatah, who had sat in the Sanhedrin and had answered the king: "The Wisdom that I serve makes me your equal." She sent also for the other leaders of the Pharisees—in exile among the Arabs or in Egypt; and queen and Pharisees ruled the land.

Many quoted the psalm: "Weeping may lodge for a night
but joy comes in the morning."
Yet some said: "Not a palm tree in Judea
to which the horse of a Persian will not be tied
and not a coffin in the land
from which the horse of a Mede
will not be eating straw."

The Pharisees gave Alexander Jannai a burial worthy of a better king. His tomb with its round turret—the roof curving inward to a spire—is in the valley to the east of Jerusalem among the cedars.

6

The pounding of the battering-rams against a corner of the tower, tallest of all—from which the archers guarded the entrance to the Temple—was beginning to show in cracks between the heavy stones. On a Sabbath, under the blows of the ram, the tower crashed. Brass trumpets sounding the attack, the waiting Romans scrambled over the great stones and through the cloud of dust: first, a son of Sulla with a great force behind him. Elsewhere, along the wall, centurions and their men were climbing it on the scaling-ladders.

Pompey stopped to smile at an inscription in Greek beside the gate: "No foreigner may pass. The guilt for his death will be his own!" And entered the court of the Temple, followed by his trumpeter. The priests were going about the Sabbath service as if that Sabbath were like any other. So, during the siege, they had offered the sacrifices twice a day— let rocks and arrows fall where they might. Frantic like the fish that eat men when blood is in the water, the armored Romans turned upon the priests and Levites and killed them. And Pompey went behind the heavy curtain of fine linen, embroidered with blue, purple and scarlet flowers, into the gloom of the Holy of Holies, sword in hand, to see the God of the Jews—and found an empty room.

Then the legions marched away from Jerusalem:
at the head of each
rode a tribune
with red or black plumes on his helmet;
behind each tribune, on foot, the first centurion
with the legion's eagle of silver or bronze on a staff;
stocky soldier trudging behind stocky soldier,
sinewy men
used to hard work, plain living and pain.

Their leather coats, heavy with bands of iron or brass,
over sleeveless woolen shirts;
a greave of bronze on the right leg—
the forward leg in battle—
and feet in heavy sandals;
a heavy square shield of wood plated with iron
hung at each man's left. The badge of his cohort,
a bright wreath or a thunderbolt, perhaps, painted about the boss,
but now, on the march, under a leather cover.

At his right, hanging from a shoulder belt
the short heavy sword, two-edged and pointed,
good for thrusting; his heavy spear—square wooden shaft and its iron
    taken apart—
on the legionary's shoulder; his helmet of iron or leather with bands
    of brass
hanging on his breast; and his other belongings in bundles:
woolen cloak, a pan for baking, a handmill, perhaps, and his ration of
    grain for a number of days,
saw, spade, and ax, a sickle, cord, and baskets,
all tied to the long forked stick on his shoulder, too—
the stick soldiers jokingly called "my mule."

The legion's horses and mules followed it
with the heavy tents of leather and the scaling-ladders,
and mule after mule laden with sacks of grain;
then cattle and sheep in droves and the carts of the merchants.
After the legions came Spanish soldiers in jerkins of leather
with small round targets instead of heavy shields;
barefoot Numidians carrying darts;
men from the Balearic Islands with slings;
and archers from Crete and Syria without shields or helmets
but with heavy sleeves of leather;
and last lumbered the engines
that had broken down the great tower of the Temple
and the walls of many cities and great fortresses.

Now with this legion, now with that,
Pompey rode among the young noblemen
who had come from Rome to study the art of war.
His lictor, scribe, and servants followed him,
and his trumpeter
and a standard-bearer
with Pompey's white standard
and his name on it in red.

"The river Kishon swept them away,
the ancient river, the river Kishon.
O my soul,
you have trodden down strength!"

JEWS IN BABYLONIA

Jews in Babylonia*

I

I

Plough, sow and reap,
thresh and winnow
in the season of the wind;
a woman is grinding wheat
or baking bread.
In the third watch of the night
the child sucks from the breast of its mother
and the woman talks with her husband.

Plough, sow and reap,
bind the sheaves, thresh and winnow;
shear the sheep,
wash the wool,
comb it and weave it.

Wheat and barley,
straw and stubble;
the cock crows, the horse neighs, and the ass brays;
an ox is grazing in a meadow or straying on the road
or rubbing itself against a wall
(a black ox for its hide,
a red one for its flesh,
and a white one for ploughing);

plough, sow, cut, bind, thresh, winnow, and set up a stack.

2

A cow to plough with
and an ass to drive;
a goat for milking
and an ewe for shearing.
A hen for laying eggs
and a date tree for its fruit;
a bed on which to sit
and a table at which to eat.

---

* Collages based for the most part on translations from the Talmud.

3

Plane the wood
into boards;
chisel the stones;
beat the wool and bleach it,
spin it and weave it.

A beast with its load
and a bit in its mouth
and a bell on its neck;
an ass with its bundle of wood
and a camel with a load of flax and an iron nose-ring
or a horse with bells between its eyes;
the horn gores,
the hoof kicks,
the teeth bite.

4

The bread has become moldy
and the dates blown down by the wind;
the iron has slipped from the helve.
The wool was to be dyed red
but the dyer dyed it black.

The dead woman has forgotten her comb
and tube of eye-paint;
the dead cobbler has forgotten his knife,
the dead butcher his chopper,
and the dead carpenter his adze.

A goat can be driven off with a shout.
But where is the man to shout?
The bricks pile up, the laths are trimmed,
and the beams are ready. Where is the builder?

To be buried in a linen shroud
or in a matting of reeds—
but where are the dead of the Flood
and where the dead of Nebuchadnezzar?

1

Palm trees in a valley
and reeds beside the bed of a stream:
a caravan camped in the valley, surrounded by camels,
saddles, saddle cushions and saddle bags.
The dried leaves of a palm for fuel
or, tied together, to sit on.

A walled town with Jews:
houses with balconies on courtyards
and a porter's lodge at each gate;
a market square with stalls and shutters,
the synagogue and bath-house.

Flowing rivers and gushing springs,
the tide of the sea,
and water dripping from the roof.

2

The old man may have forgotten most of what he knew
but even the fragments of the broken Tables of the Law
were kept—out of respect—in the Ark.

3

As when a girl with smooth shining yellow hair
comes into a room where three young men are hard at work
and all three look up smiling joyfully.

4

When her father walked from his house to the House of Study,
his servants spread woolen cloths before his feet,
and the poor who followed rolled them up and took them away;
now his daughter is picking barley grains in the dung of Arab cattle,
looking for barley grains among the hoofs of the horses.

5

A purple cloak and a white horse with a red bridle
and the black walls of the charcoal-burner;
clothing of cloth, of leather, or of sacking;
eating coarse bread instead of fine,
drinking new wine instead of old,
and sleeping on straw instead of in a soft bed,
but, rejoicing at your lot,
you are rich.

6

If the ship you are traveling on is wrecked,
a plank may come floating your way;
and on it you may ride wave after wave
until you walk again on dry land.

III

1

The rock is hard
but iron splits it;
iron is hard
but fire softens it;
fire is strong
but water quenches it—
and the clouds carry the water away
and the wind scatters them.

2

The hyena will turn into a bat
and a bat into a thorn.

3

The dog eats the lamb and a cat the hens,
and lions fill their dens with prey.

4

The blood of his wounds
and the tears of her eyes.

The Angel of Death in time of war
does not distinguish
between the righteous and the wicked.

5

If you cannot look at the sun—
only one of God's ministers—
how can you see God Himself?

IV

1

Clap hands and slap your thighs;
adding indulgence to indulgence, sin to sin,
the thread of the spider becomes a rope.

2

Only bones and nut shells left on the table.
Degenerate son;
vinegar, son of wine!

3

They praise each other;
like whores
painting one another.

V

I kill and I quicken;
I wound and I heal;
I speak out of the whirlwind
and a thorn bush.
When the earth was still a waste

without grass or tree, bird and beast,
I was; and when the earth will be a waste again
without bird or beast or man—
I am.

The sun shines
and the rain falls;
all are equal before Me—
man and beast alike:

those treading the winepress or bringing in sheaves;
the merchants and their porters
and those coming into town to sell from wicker baskets;
the rich man feeling for his purse
and he who sits before a scroll of the Law
written with a fine reed-pen and by a skilled penman;
the shepherd with his wallet
and the blind man with his staff—
with a torch at night
not to see but to be seen;
the dryer of figs; the quarryman and the man who smoothes and
        polishes the stones;
the night watchman, the watchman of a cucumber bed,
and the man guarding his fruit against birds
or his gourds against wild beasts,
clapping his hands or stamping his foot;
the ass-driver and the camel-driver,
those with boots muddied by clay;
and those who walk between thorns and thistles, thorns and briers;

the bull and bullock, calf, ram and lamb, kid or goat;
cat and marten, and the squeaking mice,
the cackling hens, doves hopping about,
and the fowl scratching on a dung-heap;
the ravens screaming and screeching,
falcon or hawk,
the wolf, the lion, bear, leopard, panther and the snake,
the flies, the gnats and worms—
even the worms eating away at the scrolls of the Law—
and the mites of grapes,
the locusts, serpents and scorpions:
all are equal before Me;

all the creatures that live in the sea
and those that live upon the dry land,
and the creatures that live in the air
and those that live in fire.

LAST POEMS

THE GOOD OLD DAYS: RECITATIVE*
HISTORICAL EPISODES

I
New England (1637?)†

She worked as a maid
but now wanted to go to her old master
in another settlement.
The way to it was through woods and swamp—
days away—
and how was she to get there?
He was willing to go with her
for fifteen shillings
and they left together.

He was back in two days.
"How is it that you are back so soon?" a neighbor asked.
"And why is there blood upon your hat
and on your clothing?"
"From a pigeon that I killed."
"And how did you get that scratch on the left side of your nose?"
"From a bramble."
"So broad a scratch?"
"To tell the truth: from my gun."
"But you fire your gun from the right."

Half or so a year afterwards,
her body was found by an Indian in a swamp,
miles from where the man she had gone with said he had left her;
the flesh rotted off
and all her clothing in a heap beside her.

---

* In editing the following episodes I thought of myself as a kind of archaeologist. I did not
invent the episodes but neither did the original writers. I brushed off the words I thought
unnecessary, now and then substituted words I thought more effective than the original
wording, and added whatever rhythm I could by way of verse.   —C. R.
† From *Winthrop's Journal*, 1637 (in *American History: Source Readings*, edited by Neil Har-
ris, David J. Rothman, Stephan Thernstrom).

II
*Deerfield (1703)**

Before the break of day the minister was awakened
by the sound of hatchets
breaking open the door and windows.
He ran towards the door:
about twenty Indians with painted faces
were coming into the house
howling.

Three Indians took hold of him,
and bound him as he stood in his night-shirt,
and began to rifle the house going into every room.
As he lay, bound and helpless, he thought of his wife and children—
his wife had given birth only a few weeks before—
and he remembered the passage in Isaiah:
"I shall go to the gates of the grave
deprived of the rest of my years . . ."

The Indians had taken two of his children to the door
and killed them,
as well as the Negro woman
who helped take care of them;
keeping him bound with the cord about one arm,
they let him put on his clothes with the other;
and let his wife dress herself, too,
as well as their children left alive.

When the sun was an hour high
all were led out of the house
for the journey of three hundred miles to Quebec—
snow up to their knees.
Many of the houses were now on fire;
and, as they left the town,
he saw his house and barn burning.

At first the minister was not allowed to speak to any of his fellow captives
as they marched,
but on the second day he had another Indian to watch him
and was allowed to speak with his wife when he overtook her

---

* From John Williams, *The Redeemed Captive Returning to Zion* (in *American History: Source Readings*, edited by Neil Harris, *et al.*).

and could walk with her and help her along.
She told him that she was losing her strength
and they must expect to part
and she hoped that God would keep him alive and their children still
        among the living—
but not a word of complaint
saying that it was the will of God.

When they came to a small river
the captives had to wade it;
the water knee-deep
and the current swift.
After that they had to climb a hill,
almost a mountain,
and the minister's strength was almost gone when he came to the top;
but he was allowed to sit down
and even unburdened of his pack.

He begged the Indian in charge of him
to let him go down and help his wife
but the man would not let him;
and he asked each of the captives as they passed
about her;
and heard at last that in going through the river
she fell
and plunged headfirst into the water;
and, after that, at the foot of the hill
the Indian who held her captive
killed her
with one stroke of his hatchet
and left the body
as meat for the fowls and beasts.

    III
    Incident in Mexico (1835)*

The two had gone through unsettled country
where no water was to be had for the horses they were riding
and suddenly
they came upon a stream
flowing over a bed of yellow sand.

---

* From *A Winter in the West*, by Charles Fenno Hoffman (in *The American Scene: 1600–1860*, edited by William J. Chute).

The horses sprang forward
to drink
and the riders dismounted,
holding the reins loosely in their hands,
while the horses stepped down from the bank
into the clear water.
But one of the riders
saw the forefeet of his horse
sink quickly—too quickly—into the stream's bottom of sand
and jerked the horse away.

The other horse, eager to drink, went on
and sank to his shoulders in the sand.
As the horse tried to get out,
lifting his chest high,
the sand drew his haunches into the sand.
The horse gave a shrill cry,
tossing his head;
his mane fluttered for a moment on the water
and then the sand closed over him.

IV
Slave Sale: New Orleans*

To begin with, the slaves had to wash themselves well,
and the men who had beards had to shave them off;
the men were then given a new suit each,
cheap but clean, and a hat, shirt, and shoes;
and the women were each given a frock of calico
and a handkerchief to tie about their heads.
They were then led by the man selling them into a large room;
the men placed on one side, the women at the other;
the tallest at the head of each row
and then the next in size
and so on to the shortest.

Many called to look at the slaves for sale
and the seller kept talking about their qualities;
made them hold up their heads and walk about briskly;
and those who might buy had them open their mouths

---

* From *Twelve Years a Slave* (1853), by Solomon Northrup (in *A Documentary History of the Negro People in the United States*, edited by Herbert Aptheker).

to look at their teeth,
and felt their arms and bodies,
just as they might a horse for sale;
and asked each what they could do.
Sometimes a man or woman would be taken to a small house in the yard,
to be stripped and looked at carefully:
if they had the scars of whips on their backs
that would show they had been troublesome.

During the day a number of sales were made;
and a planter from Baton Rouge bought Eliza's little son.
Before that the boy had to jump and run across the floor
to show his activity.
But all the time the trade was going on,
his mother was crying and wringing her hands
and kept begging the man who was thinking of buying the boy
not to buy him unless he bought her, too,
and her little daughter:
and Eliza kept saying that if he did she would be "the most faithful
            slave that ever lived."
But the man from Baton Rouge said he could not afford to buy her,
and then she began to cry aloud in her grief.

The man selling the slaves turned on her, his whip lifted,
and told her to stop her noise:
if she would not stop her "sniveling"
he would take her into the yard
and give her a hundred lashes.
She tried to wipe away her tears
but could not
and said she wanted to be with her children
and kept begging the man selling the slaves and the man from
            Baton Rouge—
who by that time had bought her son—
not to separate the three of them, mother, son, and daughter;
and over and over again kept saying how faithful and obedient she
            would be
and how hard she would work day and night.

But the man from Baton Rouge
said again he could not buy mother and son, let alone the three,
and that only the boy must go with him.
Then Eliza ran to her son, hugged him and kissed him

again and again
and her tears kept falling on his face.
The man selling the slaves kept cursing her
and called her a blubbering, howling wench
and ordered her back to her place in line
and to behave herself
or he would give her something really to cry about.

2
EXODUS 3:13

Day after day in the wilderness,
year after year,
until you see a bush burning.
Yes, but you have to climb a mountain
to speak with God.

3
CITY

The blind man with a white cane
to guard him from walking into a building
or tripping on a curb—
but will it keep him from a pool of rain
on the sidewalk?

4
CITY

Listen!
The police-car's siren
and that's a fire-engine.
Our city, too, has its native birds.

5
CITY LAWN

Young trees in a circle
with bright new leaves—
swaying gently;
three stiff tulips
with petals still yellow;

a pigeon,
a sparrow,
and scraps of white paper.

6

Reading some of the German poets of the last century;
sad, yes, but sweet and gentle.
Just then a knock on the door
and I opened it:
Hitler!

7

Now that you are seventy-five, Basil Bunting,
permit me to write a little about your biography—
the little I know.
Just before the Second World War
you came to Los Angeles
because you thought that living there was cheaper than in New York;
and when I asked you what you thought of doing for a living
you said that you could translate from the Persian—
or was it Arabic?
I remember that now
when I read the poems of yours that Pound used in his anthology—
about the farmers going to Canada.
In Los Angeles, they had no use for your knowledge of Persian—
        or Arabic,
but the English found it useful enough during the Second World War.

8

WALKING IN NEW YORK

I

Fifth Avenue has many visitors
and many of these have cameras:
they take pictures of themselves, of course,
or of buildings,
and even of trees in Central Park.

But I have yet to see anyone
taking a photograph of the old woman

who stands on the sidewalk
wearing the blanket in which she has slept on a bench:
her stockings fallen
and showing her naked legs
streaked with black dirt;
her grey hair disheveled
and her face also streaked with smudges.

II

The tramp with torn shoes
and clothing dirty and wrinkled—
dirty hands and face—
takes a comb out of his pocket
and carefully combs his hair.

III
Mother Nature

It has been raining at night
but the park is beautiful
this spring morning.
Except, I suppose, for the worm that a robin has just pulled
from a patch of damp earth
and is dividing into quarters
with the bird's sharp bill.

IV
Machine Age

A dozen pigeons on a roof
idling away the day.
But above them, part of the weathervane,
working away in the sun and wind,
head lifted,
the gilt rooster.

9

A tree in the courtyard blossomed early this spring
with large purple and white flowers
but the weather turning cold
and a cold wind blowing day after day

many of the petals have fallen
and the rest are withered and streaked with brown.

The warm sun is shining again
and a bird chirping away in the branches;
but what is its song?
A prayer for the dead flowers?

10

JUST BEFORE THE SUN GOES DOWN

I

Of all that I have written
you say: "How much was poorly said."
But look!
The oak has many acorns
that a single oak might live.

II

Young men and women in a ballet
on the platform:
how romantic!
And a young man is climbing a shaky ladder
to photograph it:
this is realism.

III

Sometimes, as I cross a street,
a pack of automobiles comes speeding towards me.
But, of course, I am much better off
than the traveler in a forest—long ago—
whom a pack of wolves pursue.

IV

After forgetting this and that—
even what has just been said or done—
and watching the old men and women
in the house where I live
walking with sticks, crutches, or a sort of cradle about them,

even wheeled in chairs,
I have concluded
that I must have my own mental crutch—
a notebook.

V
Free Verse

Not like flowers in the city
in neat rows or in circles
but like dandelions
scattered on a lawn.

VI
Machine Age

Even the patient carried through the traffic
to a hospital
is silent,
and the ambulance screams for him.

APPENDIX: OBITER DICTA

CHRONOLOGY

NOTES

INDEX OF TITLES AND FIRST LINES

First, there is the *need*; then, the *way*, the *name*, the *formula*.

When I was at school, I read verse for my own pleasure and wrote a little, but when I grew older, twenty-one or so, I grew tired of regular meters and stanzas: they had become a little stale; the smooth lines and the rhymes I used to read with pleasure now seemed affected, a false stress on words and syllables. And yet I found prose unsatisfactory, too: without the burst of song and the sudden dancing, without the intensity that I wanted. I wanted to be brief and emphatic, as it seemed to me I could be best in verse.

The brand-new verse some American poets were beginning to write, Ezra Pound and H.D. (Hilda Doolittle) for example, with sources in the French free verse other poets had been writing, as well as in the irregular rhythms of Walt Whitman, perhaps in the King James translation of the Hebrew Bible, and perhaps too in the rough rhythm of Anglo-Saxon verse, seemed to me, when I first read it, just right: not cut to patterns, however cleverly, nor poured into ready molds, but words and phrases flowing as the thought; to be read just like common speech but for stopping at the end of each line—and this like a rest in music or a turn in the dance. (I found it no criticism that to read such verse as prose was to have a kind of prose, for that was not to read it as it was written.) And with the regular beat of the old meters, I gave up the artifice of rhyme—except now and then; not only because I had the authority of Milton for this and the usage of the Elizabethans in the plays, but because I liked a Doric music better.

So much for method; now, as for matter. By the term "objectivist," I suppose a writer may be meant who does not write directly about his feelings but about what he sees and hears; who is restricted almost to the testimony of a witness in a court of law; and who expresses his feelings indirectly by the selection of his subject matter and, if he writes in verse, by its music. I have tried to write like that. If the formula was fresh and new to some of us, it was not new.

In a recent paperback, *A Study of Goethe,* by Barker Fairley, among several references to "objectivism" I find the following:

> [After 1789, when Goethe had come back from Italy,] more and more, as he was never weary of saying, he deprecated the concern of poets and writers with their own feelings and insisted that it was their business to observe the character of the world about them, a point of view which comes out with amusing dryness in his dealings with the poet-improviser O. L. B. Wolff of Hamburg, who visited him in 1826. Recognizing that Wolff suffered like everyone else from subjectivity, the common complaint of the times as Goethe came to believe, he set him a

small task with a view to correcting it. "Describe your return to Hamburg," Goethe said to him, which Wolff promptly set about doing according to his lights. But what was the result? Not a description of Hamburg, but, as Goethe complained to Eckermann . . . the sentiments of a son returning to his parents, relatives, and friends, so that his effort, devoid, as it was, of any local touches, might equally well have been called a return to Merseburg or a return to Jena. Yet Hamburg, he [that is, Goethe] added feelingly, was such an interesting place, with a character all its own. Nevertheless Goethe saw a real future for the man if only he could learn the lesson of objectivity, and learn it quickly. . . . This he [Goethe] considered indispensable, not only for Wolff, but for poets everywhere. If a poet is only able to express his own meagre feelings, he went on to say, he is not a poet at all: he must make the world as his own and express that. . . . "All that is wrong with our young poets today," he said [in 1824] . . . "is that their feelings are not important and yet they cannot get away from them."

"Did he in this instance," Fairley goes on to say, "conform to his own standard or is it nearer to truth to say that he practiced one thing and preached another?" Fairley adds: "Thus, whatever he may say or suggest to the contrary, it was not by following the advice he gave to others, it was not by suppressing his feelings and writing with his eye on the object, that he retained his stature as a poet, though he did this successfully for a time, but rather by continuing to vent his feelings as before and writing lyrically as he had done in his youth."

However, in *selecting the objects* we write about and the *music* we use—in verse—we certainly, it seems to me, express our feelings; in other words, effective writing in verse is *always* an expression of the writer's feelings, but it may be direct or indirect; and, if indirect, it may be called—by way of distinction from a direct expression of feeling—"objective." This, of course, does not go as far as a sentence I read in a pamphlet on Japanese art, translated from the French, but I think it faces in that direction. The sentence reads: "For *Zen*, in the search for illumination, that is to say, immediate contact with the essence of the universe . . . puts the strongest emphasis on personal effort *and forgetfulness of self*." (The italics are mine.)

To sum up, then, the way I have tried to write, as distinguished from the technical aspects of verse: I believe in clarity of meaning and therefore in precision; I believe in intensity and therefore in writing concisely; and, finally, I believe in writing about the object itself, and I let the reader, or listener, draw his own conclusions and make his own comparisons and analogies. They are sometimes better than the writer himself intended and profounder. I remember a Hindu saying: a work of art has many faces.

I have just mentioned "reader" or "listener" in the alternative. It is not an idle distinction, now that we have the radio and television. I remember in Bellamy's book about the future, which had a vogue about the beginning of this century, I think, one of the characters *heard* a novel played on a disk instead of *reading* it; and the listener was back in those days when few if any could read and verse was generally meant to be heard.

Now, in reading aloud to an audience, as I am about to do, brevity, instead of a merit, may well be a defect: one who reads to himself may read as slowly as he pleases and reread as often as he likes; but, for the listener who continues to listen, whatever he has just heard is gone—for the time being; just as a movement seen in a dance or a phrase heard in music. Those who read or recited to listeners came to depend, to some extent, on repetition of thought, as we find it in the Bible, or repetition of phrases, as in the refrain of ballads. In any event, it seems to me, the technique of those who write verse for radio and television will differ from those who write for the printed page—as I have done.

I have a few notes to add to the above:

I do not believe writers are *merely* influenced by others—nor, for that matter, [are they] followers of any political doctrine. There must be a fertile soil to begin with for ideas to grow and flourish. For example, an American historian has said, correctly I think, that the American Revolution began when the first Englishmen left for the wilderness of America.

*

I had—and have—three rules in writing prose or verse: first and above all to be clear, because communication is the purpose of writing (as of speaking); then, to write in rhythm, because that adds to the meaning, as well as the beauty, of speech; and finally to be concise, because that adds to the beauty, as well as the effectiveness, of speech. As for clarity, this seems no longer fashionable in some contemporary writing: the cryptic, I suppose, is. (Perhaps this is an extension—or a legacy—of the Symbolist doctrine: to suggest is to create; to name is to destroy.)

*

Clarity, precision, order, but the answer is intensity: with intensity we have compression, rhythm, maybe rhyme, maybe alliteration. The words move out of prose into verse as the speech becomes passionate and musical instead of flat.

*

Incidentally, I read somewhere that among the ancient Greeks there was an intermediary between song and straight prose—I suppose a prose that is chanted. A good deal of the Bible is read like that in the Orthodox service in synagogue.

*

A Japanese student in America, on being asked the difference between prose and poetry, said: "Poetry consists of gists and piths" (note by Ezra Pound in his *ABC of Reading*). I would add "half the meaning [of poetry] is in the music," to quote R. H. Blyth, an Englishman who lives in Japan and has written extensively on the *haiku*. Well, if not "half," a good deal of it.

*

Pound himself has said in his book mentioned above: "Music begins to atrophy when it departs too far from the dance, and poetry begins to atrophy when it gets too far from music."

*

Mentioning Pound, you all know, of course, the rules for the "free verse" the Imagists wrote—although as T. S. Eliot has said, There is no *free* verse: no verse is free: "to use . . . no word that does not contribute to the presentation . . . as regards rhythm, to compose in the sequence of the musical phrase, not in the sequence of a metronome." I have always thought of these rules or "don'ts" in connection with Pound—who certainly publicized them—but it seems that they were formulated by F. S. Flint and first published in *Poetry* of Chicago, in the March 1913 issue, a year or so after the magazine was founded. Anyway, I must have read them there then. The use of "the language of common speech," according to William Pratt's *The Imagist Poem*, is a legacy from Whitman. But I should say Wordsworth.

*

In a letter to Harriet Monroe, then editor of *Poetry*, dated 1915, Pound said, "Objectivity and again objectivity . . . no Tennysonianisms of speech; nothing—nothing that you couldn't, in some circumstance, in the stress of some emotion, actually say. Every literaryism, every book word . . . Language is made out of concrete things. General expressions in non-concrete terms are a laziness; they are talk, not art, not creation." I take this from *The Letters of Ezra Pound 1907–1941*, edited by D. D. Paige. But the subject matter of this quotation, if not the letter itself, must have appeared in

Poetry, for, as you all know, Pound was the "foreign correspondent" of the magazine. However, in a note, dated 1937, in the Paige book, Pound credits Ford Madox Ford with "hammering this point of view into him."

Incidentally, in comparing Pound's own ideas in his verse with his magnificent translations, I agree with the distinction drawn by R. P. Blackmur in his *Form and Value in Modern Poetry*, when he says of Pound (p. 111): "If the uses of language include expression, communication, and the clear exhibition of ideas, Mr. Pound is everywhere a master of his medium *so long as the matter in hand is not his own, [that is] is translation or paraphrase*." (Italics mine.)

*

With respect to the treatment of subject matter in verse and the use of the term "objectivist" and "objectivism," let me again refer to the rules with respect to testimony in a court of law. Evidence to be admissible in a trial cannot state conclusions of fact: it must state the facts themselves. For example, a witness in an action for negligence cannot say: the man injured was negligent in crossing the street. He must limit himself to a description of how the man crossed: did he stop before crossing? Did he look? Did he listen? The conclusions of fact are for the jury—and, let us add in our case, for the reader.

I have quoted Goethe, but let me add to this the following, which I came across in a book called *Poems of the Late T'ang*, translated, with an introduction, by A. C. Graham. At the very beginning, Mr. Graham quotes a Chinese poet of the eleventh century: "Poetry presents *the thing* in order to convey *the feeling*. It should be *precise* about the thing and *reticent* about the feeling. . . ." Further on, in commenting on the poetry of Li Ho, who lived from 791 to 817, Mr. Graham says: "A rigour in seeking the objective correlative of emotion is a strong point of most Chinese poetry of all periods." (The phrase "the objective correlative," as you know, is T. S. Eliot's.)

*

With respect to direct speech without metaphor or simile:* I found the following in a review of two translations of Sappho, in the *New York Review of Books* (March 3, 1966), not without interest:

> At her most intense she writes the kind of poetry that Stevens dreamed of, a poetry that "Without evasion by a single

---

* Incidentally, I remember how annoyed my instructor in the law of equity was with the expression common in the law cases, the plaintiff must come into equity "with clean hands." He objected to "with clean hands" because it was a metaphor.

metaphor" sees "the very thing itself and nothing else." English poetry is, in this special sense, incurably "evasive" and requires a richer medium to achieve equally powerful effects.

*

Let me add three more quotations, or a summary of quotations, that may not be without interest:

English verse is, of course as you know, based on stress and not, as in Latin, for example, on quantity—that is, whether a syllable is long or short. But I submit that quantity, although secondary, is not negligible in English verse—particularly "free verse." Nor for that matter is stress in Latin. For example, the *Aeneid*, as I remember it, though the beginning of each line is based simply on quantity, at the end of the line the metrical accent and the accent of ordinary pronunciation coincide so that the effect of the line is like the rise and fall of a wave.

Now to the reference I have in mind. Bright and Miller in their book on versification (Miller was my teacher at the University of Missouri) point out that the favorite foot in English versification, as you also all know, is the iamb: that is, an unstressed syllable followed by a stressed syllable. The opposite, a stressed syllable followed by an unstressed syllable (that is, a trochee), or a stressed syllable followed by two unstressed syllables (that is, a dactyl), is comparatively rare in English. Their explanation, as I remember it, is: almost all English words are accented on the first syllable or, where there are several syllables, on one of the first syllables,* but where that is also the stress of meter as well as of pronunciation the result is a monotony that the poets have instinctively avoided.

Now as to the way verse, regular and free, is usually printed, and incidentally of the necessity of a brief stop, perhaps very brief, at the end of each line, let me read this letter from T. S. Eliot, dated September 27, 1928, and reprinted in the London *Times Literary Supplement* of February 25, 1965:

> Sir,— In your interesting leading article of September 13 your reviewer makes one point which seems to me of some importance, and which may easily be overlooked. He quotes the well-known passage from North's Plutarch (Coriolanus's speech to Aufidius), and follows it with the equally famous version of Shakespeare, which he prints as prose. He observes that the

---

* For example: in the line "The quality of mercy is not strained," the accent of "mercy" and the primary accent of "quality" is on the first syllables but the verse stress is on the second syllable of each foot. This may be called "counterpoint."

version of Shakespeare is "a far better piece of prose than the original".

I make precisely the opposite observation. The prose of North is fine prose, the verse of Shakespeare is great poetry. And printed as prose, the verse of Shakespeare seems to me to be bad prose. As prose, it is difficult to grasp; as prose, it is badly constructed. North's I find much superior—as prose.

What I think your reviewer, like many other people, has overlooked is this: that verse, whatever else it may or may not be, is itself a system of *punctuation*: the usual marks of punctuation themselves are differently employed. If your reviewer were right, the method ought to be reversible; so that some passages of great prose could be converted into fine verse; and I do not believe he can find an example.

The editor in 1965 comments in part as follows:

Mr. Eliot drew attention to one radical feature of verse which he felt was commonly overlooked: that arrangement into lines immediately gives the writer scope for different effects of punctuation, which means in fact different pauses and stresses, and that these are an essential element in the effect verse has on us. But this is not all that verse arrangement does. Just as pausing for so long at commas is a habit we only learn from experience of hearing people read prose, and pausing for so long at line-breaks is a habit we fall into either from hearing people read verse or by extension of our prose-reading habits, so our tendency to look for an underlying "beat" or rhythm in words arranged in verse form is a convention learnt from experience. It is because there exists this convention that any words arranged in verse form will at once set the trained reader of poetry searching for a rhythm in them—that is to say, seeing if there is not some detectable degree of regularity in the fall of the stresses, and then reading the whole poem with slightly greater emphasis on the natural stresses which coincide with the stresses of the underlying beat. This convention is, with the "punctuating" convention, one of the pair of devices that enable a poet to get effects of varying speed and emphasis more vigorous and more subtle than the prose-writer has at his command. Of course other sound effects may play their part in poetry, assonances and alliterations and rhymes, as part of the whole dramatic gesture of the poem. But it is the two we have mentioned that are newly brought into play when a piece of existing prose is reshaped into verse.

Now, on the general subject of writing verse, let me quote a Russian, Stanislavski of the Russian Art Theater, as relayed to me by a friend: "Art is love—plus technique" and "The way to the universal is through the national." I think the second may be encouraging to those of us who write about the United States and the neighborhoods we know and through which we are not—to use another Russian expression—simply "fellow travelers."

*

Finally, I should like to compare a poem by William Carlos Williams, a poem that may be called "Objectivist," from his *Pictures from Brueghel*, with one by Auden, which I am sure you all know, on the same theme, to show, not that Auden is better than Williams (this is hardly fair, for I think that Williams has written better poems than the one I am about to read), but merely that no formula should be treated with reverence—not even an "Objectivist" one.

Landscape with the Fall of Icarus

According to Brueghel
when Icarus fell
it was spring

a farmer was ploughing
his field
the whole pageantry

of the year was
awake tingling
with itself

sweating in the sun
that melted
the wings' wax

unsignificantly
off the coast
there was

a splash quite unnoticed
this was
Icarus drowning

Musée des Beaux Arts

About suffering they were never wrong,
The Old Masters: how well they understood
Its human position; how it takes place
While someone else is eating or opening a window or just walking
    dully along;
How, when the aged are reverently, passionately waiting
For the miraculous birth, there always must be
Children who did not specially want it to happen, skating
On a pond at the edge of the wood:
They never forgot
That even the dreadful martyrdom must run its course
Anyhow in a corner, some untidy spot
Where the dogs go on with their doggy life and the torturer's horse
Scratches its innocent behind on a tree.
In Brueghel's *Icarus*, for instance: how everything turns away
Quite leisurely from the disaster; the ploughman may
Have heard the splash, the forsaken cry,
But for him it was not an important failure; the sun shone
As it had to on the white legs disappearing into the green
Water; and the expensive delicate ship that must have seen
Something amazing, a boy falling out of the sky,
Had somewhere to get to and sailed calmly on.

1894

Charles Reznikoff born August 30, in semi-rural Brownsville, Brooklyn, the first of three children of Nathan Reznikoff (b. 1869) and Sarah Yetta Wolvovsky (b. 1867), Russian Jews who had fled the pogroms that followed the assassination of Alexander II in 1881. (Nathan, the former proprietor of a small butcher's shop in the village of Znamenka, sold his business to buy passage to America; his cousin Sarah Yetta gave up her sewing business to follow him. Upon arriving in New York City, they shared a workshop on the Lower East Side, where they sewed ladies' wrappers on commission; later they married, moved to Brooklyn, and eventually started a hat-making business with Sarah's brother Israel). Sarah calls her son Yehezqel (Ezekiel), after her late father, but at her American physician's pragmatic advice he is registered at birth as "Charles." The name *Reznikoff* is the Russian form of *Reznik*, a Slavic word for "butcher."

1896–1901

Brother, Paul, a future hematologist and professor of medicine, born 1896; the brothers, close as children, will drift apart as adults. Young Charles witnesses the arrival in New York City of his paternal grandparents and several other Russian relatives.

1901–1906

Sister, Lillian, born 1901; she will become a talented pianist and music teacher. Family moves to upper west side of Manhattan, near the Hudson River, then downtown to Fourth Street, near the East River. Charles attends grammar school in "a dingy yellow building/among the tenements and noisy avenues of the East Side." While not a competitive student, he is a precocious one, graduating from the eighth grade when he is eleven, three years ahead of his class. During these years, he first hears a family story that impresses him deeply: his grandfather Ezekiel Wolvovsky (1839–1887), for whom he was named, had been a poet, but his verses— written in Hebrew—had been lost. He had made his living as a peddler and had died among strangers on one of his trips far from home. When his clothes and other possessions were returned to his widow, she found among them the manuscript of poems in a language she could not understand. Fearing that the words might contain subversive sentiments that would endanger the entire family, she destroyed the manuscript.

1906–1910

Family moves back to Brooklyn, a mile from Reznikoff's birthplace in Brownsville. Reznikoff attends Boys' High School, then one of the best public high schools in the country, from which he graduates in 1910, aged fifteen. Reads extensively in poetry and writes first poems. Begins physical and spiritual discipline of walking, sometimes up to twenty miles a day. He will continue "going to and fro and and walking up and down" the New York cityscape until the last years of his life; for him it is a passion second only to writing. Grandfather Simon Reznikoff dies, 1910.

1910–1911

Spends academic year at the journalism school of the University of Missouri, Columbia. "I found out that journalism is more concerned with news than with writing, and that I—to use the old adage—was more concerned with dog bites man than with man bites dog." Takes compulsory ROTC course and contributes light verse to the college newspaper and literary annual.

1911–1912

Returns to parents' house (1752 Union Street, Brooklyn) to contemplate future. "I wanted to stay home, just stay home and write, but my parents, naturally, insisted that some education might be helpful." Briefly considers pursuing a Ph.D. in history at Columbia; meanwhile, works as a salesman for the Artistic Millinery Company, his parents' hat-manufacturing business. "And then one day, passing N.Y.U. Law School, I remembered that Heine had studied law and Goethe had studied law, so that seemed fine. They only had two hours a day of studying, and then the rest of the day I'd be free. So I applied and was admitted. I was just eighteen then."

1912–1915

Studies for three years at New York University Law School, where he acquires the invaluable critical habit of "prying sentences open to look at the exact meaning" and, when writing, "weighing words to choose only those that had meat for my purpose / and throwing the rest away as empty shells." Graduates second in his class.

1916

Admitted to the bar of the State of New York and takes first cases—including one from a cousin, which he loses. Meets Albert Lewin (b. 1894), a like-minded graduate of Harvard's master's program in English, and the two become fast friends, trading poems and making reading assignments for each other. Lewin reads all of Reznikoff's poetry and quickly becomes his unofficial editor and most trusted critic.

1917

Realizing that his interest in the law is chiefly scholarly, abandons private practice and takes graduate courses in law at Columbia University. Begins to submit poems to magazines, including Harriet Monroe's *Poetry*, founded in Chicago in 1912. Miss Monroe accepts three poems for publication, but does not print them immediately.

1918

In early spring, reports to draft board and, due to poor eyesight, is marked for limited military duties. Remembering the fate of his Grandfather Ezekiel, resolves to publish a pamphlet of his best poems before assuming a military clerkship and perhaps "ending up in France, hell, or heaven." Asks Harriet Monroe for permission to print the three items she has accepted, knowing that this means forgoing publication in *Poetry*. Sends manuscript of twenty-three poems to Lewin, now a professor of English at the University of Missouri, Columbia, for criticism. In June, privately publishes first book, a paperbound chapbook called *Rhythms*. Enters officers' training camp at Columbia University in preparation for joining the American Expeditionary Force to France, but on November 11, "before I could sleep downstairs in the basement and march around the campus," the war ends. Decides to resume work with parents' hat company as a shipping clerk and part-time salesman.

1919

Publishes second paperbound chapbook, *Rhythms II*, a collection of twenty-five new poems.

1920

Samuel Roth, the proprietor of The Poetry Bookshop, 49 West Eighth Street, New York, brings out Reznikoff's *Poems*, a paperbound omnibus comprising revised versions of the poems in *Rhythms* and *Rhythms II* and a third group of thirty-nine more recent poems.

1921

Declines Roth's offer to bring out *Uriel Acosta: A Play & A Fourth Group of Verse*, and publishes book himself.

1922

Privately publishes *Chatterton, The Black Death & Meriwether Lewis*, a collection of three verse plays. This and his previous self-published books are sold exclusively through The Sunwise Turn, an avant-garde bookshop and art gallery run by Mary Mowbray-Clarke at 53 West Forty-fourth Street, New York City.

1923

The Sunwise Turn arranges for design, printing, and sale of *Coral & Captive Israel: Two Plays*; Reznikoff pays the printing bill. Reznikoff leaves his parents' business and is given a monthly stipend of $25. Takes a series of odd jobs to supplement this, including selling advertising space for *The Menorah Journal*, a bi-monthly magazine of Jewish American art and opinion founded in 1915. Over the next four decades, Reznikoff will contribute dozens of poems to *The Menorah Journal*—as well as plays, stories, essays, and reviews—until the magazine ceases publication in 1962.

1924

Albert Lewin, working as a reader in Samuel Goldwyn's New York office, moves to California to join Metro-Goldwyn-Mayer's script department.

1925

Reznikoff moves into his Uncle Simon Reznikoff's house (1379 Union Street, Brooklyn).

1927

In March, writes to Albert Lewin: "I bought a press (worked by a treadle) in January and had it set up in our basement. I have printed (the blackest ink on glaring white paper) almost 32 pages of [my collected works,] a book of verse and plays (to run about 200 pages). I just blunder along." In the end, Reznikoff breaks his book into two hardcover volumes: printing of *Five Groups of Verse*, dedicated to Lewin, is completed in May (80 pages, 375 copies); printing of *Nine Plays* is completed in November

(122 pages, 400 copies). Begins courtship of Marie Syrkin (b. 1899), the daughter of Nachman Syrkin, the founder of Labor Zionism. A poet and journalist involved in Zionist causes, she works as a teacher of English at the Textile High School, in Lower Manhattan. She is separated but not divorced from Aaron Bodansky, whom she met when he was a bio-chemistry instructor at Cornell, and with whom she shares custody of their three-year-old son, David.

1929

Privately publishes miscellany, *By the Waters of Manhattan*, in an edition of 200 copies. Contents include "By the Waters of Manhattan" (a group of autobiographical short stories reprinted from *The Menorah Journal*), "Early History of a Seamstress" (a memoir by Sarah Reznikoff, as told to her son), and "Editing and Glosses" (two narrative poems, "Israel" and "King David," based on Old Testament sources). Though conceived as an annual publication, this miscellany will have no sequel. At one of the almost-weekly dinners of the *Menorah* group, Reznikoff meets the poet and crit-ic Louis Zukofsky, ten years his junior and an ardent admirer of his work.

1930

Marie Syrkin travels to Reno for a divorce. On May 27, she and Reznikoff marry in New York, and the newlyweds take an apartment in Riverdale, the Bronx. The Artistic Millinery warehouse burns, ending the Reznikoffs' hat-making business and, consequently, Charles's $25-a-month stipend. The three Reznikoff children decide to help their parents pay off their debts, requiring Charles to seek full-time employment. Finds work at the American Law Book Company, Brooklyn, as a writer for *Corpus Juris*, a legal encyclopedia that, when completed in 1935, will run to seventy-one volumes. *By the Waters of Manhattan*, a novel based on the *Menorah Journal* stories and his mother's oral history, is sold to Charles Boni for his inno-vative series of inexpensive "PaperBooks"; Boni pays $1,000 for the rights and Louis Untermeyer writes an introduction. Lionel Trilling, reviewing the book in *The Menorah Journal*, says that "Mr. Reznikoff's work is remarkable and original in American literature, because he brings to a 'realistic' theme a prose style that, without any of the postures of the 'styl-ist,' is of the greatest delicacy and distinction. But more important . . . he has written the first story of the Jewish immigrant that is not false." Through Zukofsky, Reznikoff meets the poet George Oppen and his wife, Mary, recently arrived in New York from San Francisco. At the suggestion of Ezra Pound, Zukofsky is invited by Harriet Monroe to guest-edit an issue of *Poetry* dedicated to new American poetry.

1931

The Zukofsky issue of *Poetry*, published in February, includes poems by Reznikoff, Marianne Moore, George Oppen, Ezra Pound, Carl Rakosi, William Carlos Williams, and others; it also includes Zukofsky's critical essay "Sincerity and Objectification: With Special Reference to the Work of Charles Reznikoff." In his introduction to the issue, Zukofsky coins the term "Objectivist" to describe both Reznikoff's work and the aesthetic that underpins all the poems he has collected here. The Objectivist poet, he says, strives to see things *objectively*—not symbolically, allegorically, or subjectively—and to embody this sincere act of seeing in a poem, using only necessary words. Albert Lewin, now Irving Thalberg's personal assistant at MGM, invites Reznikoff to visit him and his wife in California. In April, takes leave of absence from *Corpus Juris* and embarks on cross-country bus trip, making stops along the way to sell hats for his parents' business. Returns to New York in late June.

1932

Sister, Lillian, marries her first cousin, the dentist Charles H. Wolfe (born Wolvovsky); the couple moves into the house at 1379 Union Street, Brooklyn. Mary and George Oppen, now living in Le Beausset, France, found an avant-garde press, To Publishers, with Zukofsky in New York as editor. Among their first titles is *An "Objectivist" Anthology*, an expanded edition of Zukofsky's Objectivist issue of *Poetry*. The American warehouse for To Publishers is Lillian's basement.

1933

The Oppens return from France and with Zukofsky and Reznikoff found the Objectivist Press to publish their own work and "that of other writers whose work they think ought to be read." Reznikoff works on long prose work, *Testimony*, which grows out of his work on *Corpus Juris*. While reading court cases from every year in the nation's history and from every state in the union, Reznikoff could sometimes see in the facts of a case details of the time and place, and it occurs to him "that out of such material [a history of the nation] could be written up, not from the standpoint of the individual, as in diaries, nor merely from the angle of the unusual, as in newspapers, but from *every* standpoint—as many standpoints as were provided by the witnesses themselves." These witnesses, Kenneth Burke would later write, "be they plaintiff or defendant, interested or disinterested witness, slave or slave-owner, brutal sea captain or recorder of his brutality," speak to us directly, and Reznikoff contrives, by selection of testimony and "by a few hundred 'factual' words, to stir our feelings and our memories. . . . These bare recitals, devoid of 'psychology,' send us questing through our stock of psychoanalytic lore as no introspective accounts could do" and artfully "inspire our sympathies."

1934

In the spring, the Objectivist Press publishes its first list: *William Carlos Williams: Collected Poems 1921–1931*, with a preface by Wallace Stevens; *Discrete Series*, by George Oppen, with a foreword by Ezra Pound; and *Testimony*, by Reznikoff, with an introduction by Kenneth Burke. The fall list includes two new volumes by Reznikoff: *Jerusalem the Golden*, a collection of short poems (dedicated to Marie), and *In Memoriam: 1933*, a long poem first published in the Fall 1934 issue of *The Menorah Journal*. Marie is a founder and a guiding spirit of *The Jewish Frontier*, a Labor Zionist journal edited by Hayim Greenberg, to which she will contribute many essays throughout the rest of her life.

1935

The American Law Book Company changes hands, and the new management, finding Reznikoff an unproductive perfectionist, dismisses him with only two weeks' pay. Does freelance editorial work but finds it difficult to pay his share of the household expenses.

1936

Separate Way, a collection of poems, is the final book published by the Objectivist Press. Privately publishes *Early History of a Sewing-Machine Operator*, the story of Nathan Reznikoff as told to Charles Reznikoff.

1937

Mother dies 12 February; she is memorialized in Reznikoff's poem "Kaddish," which *The Menorah Journal* publishes in the fall.

1937–1939

In March 1937, Albert Lewin, now a very successful producer with Paramount Pictures, learns of Reznikoff's financial troubles and offers him a job in Hollywood as a researcher and script-reader at $75 a week. Reznikoff lives sometimes in the Lewins' house in Santa Monica, sometimes in the inexpensive Hotel Carmel quite nearby, sometimes in an efficiency apartment; Marie visits him during her summer vacations. In abundant leisure time, writes poems, makes notes for a prose work about Hollywood, and plans novel about Jews massacred in Europe during the Crusades. In June 1939, Lewin leaves Paramount and Reznikoff loses his sinecure. Returns to New York, and he and Marie live at 364 West Eighteenth Street, Manhattan.

1941

Privately publishes *Going To and Fro and Walking Up and Down*, dedicated "To the memory of Sarah Yetta Reznikoff, my mother." This collection reprints "Kaddish"; it also includes four items based on law cases that revisit the materials and aesthetic strategies of *Testimony* (1934), but this time in verse, not prose.

1942

Father, Nathan Reznikoff, dies.

1944

The Lionhearted: A Story about the Jews of Medieval England is published by the Jewish Publication Society of America, Philadelphia. Marie's first book, *Your School, Your Children: A Teacher Looks at What's Wrong with Our Schools*, is published by L. B. Fisher, New York.

1947

Blessed Is the Match: The Story of Jewish Resistance, by Marie Syrkin, is published by the Jewish Publication Society.

1948

After death of founding editor Hayim Greenberg, Marie assumes editorship of *The Jewish Frontier*.

1950

Sister, Lillian Reznikoff Wolfe, dies April 11; Reznikoff writes "In Memoriam: L.R.W." In September, Marie takes position as assistant professor of English and the humanities at Brandeis, in Waltham, Massachusetts; she continues to edit *The Jewish Frontier* from her university office. For the next sixteen years, Reznikoff will live alone in the apartment on Eighteenth

Street, with Marie returning only for short stays. It is probably during this year that he returns to his notes for a Hollywood book and begins writing *The Manner "Music,"* an autobiographical novel that will be found among his papers after his death. *The Jews of Charleston*, a history of the Jewish community of Charleston, South Carolina, written by Reznikoff with Uriah Engelmann, is published by the Jewish Publication Society.

1951

"The Beginnings of the Family Fortune," a memoir of his mother and father, published in *Commentary* (November). Reznikoff's translation of *Stories and Fantasies from the Jewish Past*, a collection of ten tales by Emil Bernard Cohn, published by the Jewish Publication Society.

1952–1954

Commissioned by the Jewish Publication Society to write a history of the Jews of Cleveland. Reznikoff's extensive and meticulous research does not develop into a publishable narrative, and he reluctantly abandons the project.

1955

"The Fifth Book of the Maccabees" published in *Commentary* (August). When the managing editor of *The Jewish Frontier* leaves the magazine, Reznikoff takes his place in the New York office. Marie will later remember that Reznikoff "would prepare the copy I chose with meticulous care and, because I would not let him revise, with basic indifference. He proofread the material . . . with precision. His galleys and dummies were works of art, with carefully ruled red and black lines to guide the typesetter. At the printers he was a favorite; they forgave his slowness in their marvel at the aesthetic results achieved." Reznikoff will continue his duties at the magazine until 1962. The first issue of *Midstream*, the journal of the Theodore Herzl Foundation, appears in the fall, with contributions by Reznikoff and Marie; Marie will join the editorial board, and Reznikoff will contribute poetry regularly throughout the rest of his life.

1956

Reznikoff's translation of *Three Years in America, 1859–1862*, by Israel Joseph Benjamin, published in two volumes by the Jewish Publication Society. Benjamin was a German-Jewish journalist and a tart observer of social and political life in the U.S. in the years leading up to the Civil War.

1957

Louis Marshall, Champion of Liberty: Selected Papers and Addresses, edited by Reznikoff, published in two volumes by the Jewish Publication Society. Marshall (1856–1929) was a New York-based Constitutional lawyer who worked to secure religious, political, and cultural freedom for all American minority groups.

1959

Privately publishes his first collection in eighteen years, *Inscriptions: 1944–1956,* dedicated "with love to Marie." It is probably in this year that Reznikoff plans his great four-volume poem *Testimony: The United States,* a social, economic, cultural, and legal history of the United States and its people, 1885–1915.

1962

By the Waters of Manhattan: Selected Verse, with an introduction by C. P. Snow, published jointly by New Directions (James Laughlin) and the *San Francisco Review* (June Oppen Degnan, sister of George Oppen). Reznikoff dedicates the book to Marie; Al Lewin attends publication party at the Gotham Book Mart.

1963

By the Waters of Manhattan is awarded the Kovner Poetry Prize of the Jewish Book Council of America. Reznikoff privately publishes *Family Chronicle,* a prose work comprising revised versions of "Early History of a Seamstress," "Early History of a Sewing-Machine Operator," and "The Beginnings of the Family Fortune" (now called "Needle Trade").

1965

Testimony: The United States 1885–1890: Recitative published jointly by New Directions and the *San Francisco Review.*

1966

Marie, elected an executive of the World Zionist Organization, retires from Brandeis and returns to New York City. She and Reznikoff take apartment on the twenty-fourth floor of Lincoln Towers, 180 West End Avenue.

1968

Dropped by New Directions due to poor sales. Privately publishes *Testimony: The United States 1891–1900: Recitative* in an edition of 200 copies.

1969

Privately publishes *By the Well of Living and Seeing & The Fifth Book of the Maccabees*, dedicated "To the memory of Albert Lewin," who died in May 1968. At invitation of editor Milton Hindus, contributes entries on Ezra Pound and Louis Zukofsky to *The Encyclopædia Judaica*. *Family Chronicle* published in London by Norton Bailey with The Human Constitution, Ltd. "Jews in Babylonia" published in *Midstream* (August–September). Begins working in earnest on third and fourth volumes of *Testimony*, devoted to the years 1901–1910 and 1911–1915.

1970

At request of the editor of the reference work *Contemporary Poets*, describes his poetry in thirty-five words: "'Objectivist'; images clear but the meaning not stated but suggested by the objective details and the music of the verse; words pithy and plain; without the artifice of regular meters; themes, chiefly Jewish, American, urban."

1971

Marie steps down from editorship of *The Jewish Frontier*. In May Reznikoff receives the Morton Dauwen Zabel Award and $2,500 from the American Institute of Arts and Letters; the citation reads: "To Charles Reznikoff, born by the waters of Manhattan. Mr. Reznikoff was educated for the law but has instead dedicated his life to giving sworn testimony in the court of poetry against the swaggering injustices of our culture and on behalf of its meek wonders."

1971–1973

At Marie's urging, applies the technique of *Testimony* to the records of the Nuremberg trials and the Eichmann trials. The result is his last major poem, *Holocaust*.

1973–1976

In early 1973, at the invitation of Andrew Crozier, poet and proprietor of the Ferry Press, London, revises his privately printed *Testimony 1891–1900* and combines it with the manuscript of *Testimony 1901–1910*. The Ferry Press announces *Testimony: The United States 1891–1910* for spring 1975, but in November 1974 Crozier pronounces the book too costly to print and publication is canceled. (*Testimony 1901–1910* remains unpublished, and the final volume, *Testimony 1911–1915*, remains unfinished in draft form.) In late 1973, John Martin, founder and publisher of Black Sparrow Press, enters into an agreement with Reznikoff to publish his complete poetry. The series begins with *By the Well of Living and Seeing: New and Selected Poems 1918–1973* (1974) and continues with *Holocaust* (1975) and *The Complete Poems of Charles Reznikoff 1918–1975* (two volumes, 1976 and 1977); all these volumes are edited by Black Sparrow's house editor, Seamus Cooney, in close collaboration with Reznikoff. (New editions of *Testimony: The United States 1885–1890* [1978] and *Testimony: The United States 1891–1900* [incorporating Reznikoff's revisions for the Ferry Press edition, 1979], are published posthumously. Martin also publishes the novel *The Manner "Music,"* with an introduction by Robert Creeley [1976]; *Charles Reznikoff: A Critical Essay,* by Milton Hindus [1977]; and *Selected Letters of Charles Reznikoff 1917–1976,* edited by Hindus [1997].)

1976

On afternoon of January 21, says to Marie, with uncharacteristic serenity: "I have never made money but I have done everything that I most wanted to do." Suffers massive heart attack later that day, and dies at St. Vincent's Hospital, New York, just before dawn on January 22. As stipulated in his will, there are no speeches at his funeral and he is buried in a plain pine coffin in the Reznikoff family plot, Old Mount Carmel Cemetery, Brooklyn. Marie chooses a simple granite slab for a tombstone, on which she has engraved the words "Charles Reznikoff, Maker, 1894–1976" and a favorite line from one of his poems: ". . . and the day's brightness dwindles into stars."

Readers seeking further biographical information are referred to the following books and periodicals, from which facts for this chronology have been drawn: Charles Reznikoff: A Critical Essay, *by Milton Hindus (Santa Barbara: Black Sparrow Press, 1977);* Charles Reznikoff: Man and Poet, *edited by Milton Hindus (Orono, Me.: National Poetry Foundation & The University of Maine, 1984);* Sagetrieb *13:1–2, edited by Burton N. Hatlen (Orono, Me.: National Poetry Foundation, Spring–Fall 1994);* Selected Letters of Charles Reznikoff *1917–1976, edited by Milton Hindus (Santa Rosa: Black Sparrow Press, 1997), and* A Menorah for Athena: Charles Reznikoff and the Jewish Dilemmas of Objectivist Poetry, *by Stephen Fredman (Chicago: University of Chicago Press, 2001).*

NOTES

The following notes fall into four categories: bibliographical references, order of poems in various editions, textual variants, and omitted poems. In the textual variants, minor changes in spelling and punctuation have not been recorded. When variants in a poem or a stanza are many, the entire text has been reprinted for ease of reading. Capitalization in all quotations has been made to conform with Reznikoff's later practice, which is also followed in the body of this book.

Rhythms, Reznikoff's first book, was published by the author in Brooklyn, New York, in 1918. It contained twenty-three unnumbered poems. When he reprinted the group in *Poems* (1920), Reznikoff rearranged the order, dropped five poems, and revised thirteen others. He again revised and rearranged the group for *Five Groups of Verse* (1927), restoring one of the omitted poems. This third version is the one reproduced here.

Order of Poems

The following tables show how the original ordering of the poems in *Rhythms* was changed in *Poems* (1920) and again in *Five Groups of Verse* (1927). Numbers have been assigned to the unnumbered poems in the first two books. An asterisk indicates a text revised from the printing immediately preceding.

1918	1920	1927	1927	1920	1918
1	1*	1	1	1*	1
2	13*	10	2	2*	3
3	2*	2	3	6*	8
4	16*	16	4	5*	11
5	10*	15	5*	7*	13
6	8	17	6*	15*	15
7	—	—	7*	14*	14
8	6*	3*	8	3	17
9	—	—	9*	4*	18
10	9	18	10	13*	2
11	5*	4	11	11*	21
12	—	—	12*	—	20
13	7*	5	13	17	23
14	14*	7*	14*	12*	22
15	15*	6*	15	10*	5
16	—	—	16	16*	4
17	3	8	17	8	6
18	4*	9*	18	9	10
19	18*	19*	19*	18*	19
20	—	12*	—	—	7
21	11*	11	—	—	9
22	12*	14*	—	—	12
23	17	13	—	—	16

Textual Variants

1. 1918: The last stanza begins with two lines omitted in 1920 and later: *the wandering body / break into dust;*

2. 1918: First line omitted in 1920 and later: *In this room once belonging to me*

3. 1918: A two-paragraph prose poem, as follows:

   Think not to shut me up in yourself: I'll drain your beauty, then fling aside the cup.

   So one day tired of the sky and host of stars I'll thrust the tinsel by.

4. 1918: Title: *"The Suicide"*

5. 1918: Line 1: line break after *spread*

6. 1918: Two stanzas, as follows:

   They dug her grave so deep
   no voice can creep
   to her.

   She can feel no stir
   of joy when her girl sings,
   and quietly she sleeps
   when her girl weeps.

   1920: No stanza breaks.

7. 1918: Text as follows:

   The tragedies men move in are mostly played
   behind stone walls, shut doors, and curtained windows.
   The hero of the fifth act, Death, frequents
   dark chambers, rooms with blinds drawn; for he knows
   that he is terrible, but only sad
   along the highway underneath the sky.
   On Brooklyn Bridge I saw a man drop dead.
   It meant no more than if he were a sparrow;
   for tower on tower behind the bridge arose
   the buildings on Manhattan, tall white towers
   agleam with lights; below, the wide blue bay
   stretched out to meet the high blue sky and the first white star.

   1920: As 1927 except line 4: *to meet bay and sky.*

9. 1918: Line 1: *The pale-faced shop-girls leave*
   No stanza breaks.

   1920: As 1927 except no break after line 4.

10. 1918: Text as follows:

> *Hair and faces glossy with sweat in August*
> *at night through narrow streets glaring with lights*
> *people move as if in funeral processions.*
> *They stand on stoops weeds in a stagnant pool,*
> *they sit at windows waiting for a wind that never comes.*
> *Only the sun, again, like the lidless eye of God.*
>
> *No one else in the street—but a great wind blowing,*
> *the store-lamps dimmed behind the thickly frosted panes,*
> *the stars like the sun broken and scattered into a million bits.*
> *To-morrow long clouds shutting out the day*
> *and maybe snow or thick rain dropping heavily.*

11. 1918: Stanza 2 begins with two lines omitted in 1920 and later: *Among the stones / I came upon his bones*:

12. 1918: Line 3: *white sands*;
    Line 4: *And each tree stands a*
    Line 7: *fleet of ships at*

    1920: Poem omitted.

14. 1918: Title: *"On One Whom the Germans Shot"*
    Line 1: *are spilled and*
    Line 1a: *Gaudier-Brzeska,*

    1920: As 1927 except line 1a retained.

15. 1918: Line 3: *understanding's like*
    Line 4: *through a mist*

16. 1918: Title: *"Her Secret Thoughts Were Fingers"*
    Subtitle (giving source): *Spoon River Anthology*

19. 1918: Line 1: *My work done, / I sit at the window at ease*
    Lines 3–4: *shines / with sunlight. From*

    1920: As 1927, but stanza break between lines 2 and 3.

Omitted Poems

1918: [7]

> *Look triumphantly*
> *with your face's beauty*
> *on others, not on me.*
> *I see*
> *in your green eyes two leaves*
> *of the forbidden tree.*

1918: [9]

I lost my godhead and became a beast.
Circe, you fed him with a feast
of kisses. Now, take care, for see
what claws have grown on me.

1918: [12]

Queen Esther said to herself What is there to fear? We move in our
orbits like the stars.
But in the night looking at the black fields and river she could not
help thinking of Vashti's white cheeks hollowed like shells.

1918: [16]

Come away,
the clod in the mound
will hear no sound
and the coffined stone
no moan.
Come away.

Rhythms II was published by the author in Brooklyn, New York, in 1919. It contained twenty-five unnumbered poems. For *Poems* (1920), Reznikoff rearranged the sequence, combined two poems into one, and revised ten others. For *Five Groups of Verse* (1927), he again rearranged the order, revised two poems, and dropped two. As a final revision, in *By the Waters of Manhattan: Selected Verse* (1962), one poem had its title deleted. The present text follows the 1927 version with that one deletion.

Order of Poems

The following tables show how the original ordering of the poems in *Rhythms II* was changed in *Poems* (1920) and again in *Five Groups of Verse* (1927). Numbers have been assigned to the unnumbered poems in the first two books. An asterisk indicates a text revised from the printing immediately preceding.

1919	1920	1927	1927	1920	1919
1	2	4	1	1	11
2	3	12	2	8*	7
3	4	6	3	13*	8
4	5	10	4	2	1
5	6*	9	5[1962*]	9	6
6	9	5[1962*]	6	4	3
7	8*	2	7	11*	23
8	13*	3	8	10*	21
9	7*	15	9	6*	5
10	15	14	10	5	4
11	1	1	11*	12	20
12	19	–	12	3	2
13	17*	18	13	14*	18
14 } 15	21*	20*	14	15	10
			15	7*	9
16	20	–	16	16*	24
17	22	19	17	18*	25
18	14*	13	18	17*	13
19	24	22	19	22	17
20	12	11*	20*	21*	14 & 15
21	10*	8	21	23	22
22	23	21	22	24	19
23	11*	7	–	19	12
24	16*	16	–	20	16
25	18*	17			

Textual Variants

2.   1919:   Stanza break after line 2.

3.   1919:   Line 1: line break after *knocked,*
             No stanza break after line 4.

5.   1919, 1920, 1927: Title: *"In the Ghetto"*

7.   1919:   Line 3: *rags she cleans*

8.   1919:   Text as follows:

> *In the shop she, her mother and grandmother.*
> *Women at windows in still streets*
>
> *or reading, the glow on their resting hands.*

9.   1919:   No stanza break.

11. 1919, 1920: Line 1: *who taught patiently*

12. 1919:   Line 2: *between set teeth*

13. 1919:   Title: *"Central Park: Winter"*

15. 1919:   Text as follows:

PESTILENCE

> *Streamers of crepe idling before doors.*
>
> *Now the huge moon*
> *at the end of the street like a house afire.*

16. 1919:   Lines 1–1a: *Mice whisk over the unswept floor, / shadows;*

17. 1919:   Lines 2–2a: *toast, / lettuce leaves and a spoonful of mayonnaise.*
             Line 3: *the painted women*

20. 1919:   Two poems, as follows:

[12]

> *She moved effortless,*
> *a swan on a still lake*
> *hardly beating the water with golden feet.*
>
> *Straight brow and nose,*
> *curved lips and chin.*

Sorrow before her
was gone like noise from a street,
snow falling.

[13]

I remember her all in white
in a house under great trees,
shaded and still in summer;

a white curtain turning in her open window
and a swan dipping a white neck in the trees' shadow.

1920:   One poem, as follows:

Like a curtain turning in an open window.

Like a swan effortless
on a lake shaded and still in summer,
dipping a white neck in the trees' shadow,
hardly beating the water with golden feet.

Sorrow before her
was gone like noise from a street,
snow falling.

Omitted Poems

1919:   [10], 1920: [19]

Delicately rouged,
you turn your face
and your widened eyes,
a child seemingly.

1919:   [14], 1920: [20]

The water broke on the slope of her hips
and foamed about her.
The slender moon stood in the blue heavens.

Poems was published by Samuel Roth at the New York Poetry Book Shop, 49 West Eighth Street, in 1920. It contained unnumbered revised versions of the contents of the two earlier books and thirty-nine new poems. Of the new poems, thirty-two were unnumbered and the others were grouped under the collective titles "Nightmares" and "Four of Us." For *Five Groups of Verse* (1927), Reznikoff dropped about a fifth of the new poems and revised most of the others. The present text follows that revision, except for one poem further revised for *By the Waters of Manhattan: Selected Verse* (1962).

Order of Poems

The following tables show how the original ordering of the new work in *Poems* was changed in *Five Groups of Verse* (1927). The poems in the 1920 book have been assigned consecutive numbers; nos. 33–35 appeared under the collective title "Nightmares," and nos. 36–39 under the title "Four of Us." An asterisk indicates a revised text.

1920	1927	1927	1920
1	1	1	1
2	7	2*	3
3	2*	3*	6
4	14	4*	7
5	6*	5*	8
6	3*	6*	5
7	4*	7	2
8	5*	8	29
9	9*	9*	9
10	24*	10*	36
11	29	11* [1962*]	37
12 ⎱		12*	38
13 ⎰	23*	13*	39
14	30*	14	4
15	16*	15*	16
16	15*	16*	15
17	27*	17	25
18	–	18	27
19	–	19	28
20	28*	20	24
21	21*	21*	21
22	22*	22*	22

1920	1927	1927	1920
23	–	23*	12 & 13
24	20	24*	10
25	17	25*	31
26	–	26*	35
27	18	27*	17
28	19	28*	20
29	8	29	11
30	–	30*	14
31	25*	–	18
32	–	–	19
33	–	–	23
34	–	–	26
35	26*	–	30
36	10*	–	32
37	11*	–	33
38	12*	–	34
39	13*		

Textual Variants

2. 1920: Line 1: *men or boys*
   Line 3: *But this*

3. 1920: Two lines as a stanza preceding line 1:

   Blocking hats with a boy helper
   he tells of the sluts he visits.

   Line 1: *Girls outshout*

4. 1920: Line 1: *The fruit pedlar . . . shop loft to shop loft*
   Line 2: *on the stone stairs*
   Line 3: *and lifting the apple basket on to his knees breathes*

5. 1920: Line 2: *or was it seconds in dozens?*

6. 1920: Line 1: *built dull-red factories*
   Line 2: *in the dull-green depths.*

9. 1920: Line 2: *the brown baked apple*
   Line 3: *sucks the taste, eating*

10–13. 1920: Printed as a group under the collective title *"Four of Us."*

10. 1920: Text as follows:

Four of Us

I

Sleepless, breathing the black air, he heard footsteps along the street
and then click, the street-lamp was out,
darkness jumped like a black cat upon his chest.

Dawn, the window became grey,
the bed-clothes were lit up and his sleeping wife's head
as if the darkness had gathered and melted into that heap of loose hair.

Soon her eyes would open, disks of light blue, strange in a Jewess,
he would turn away; for the eyes would look curiously the way they had
*   been looking for months,*
How are you getting on? Still not doing well?
And her left hand would raise itself slowly and pull on the lobe of her
*   left ear;*
and her eyes shine with a slight pity the way a woman looks at a mouse
*   in a trap's cage;*

no longer the calm look with which she had greeted him
when he was chief clerk at the silk store in the Russian town,
the town he carried about like picture postal-cards in a vest pocket,
edges and colors fast being frayed away.

He had been a clerk thirty years and the firm had grown
and like the moon the chief clerk at his home
shone with the light of the store, the large sun.
Relatives in America would send him money to dole out
to poorer relatives not to be trusted with sums.

Day, the noise of splashing water, somebody washing,
his children in underwear thudding about with bare feet,
pulling on clothes in a hurry and bending over to lace up shoes.
Soon the door would close, again and again, all would be gone,
the three elder to shops, the younger ones to school.

For these he had come to America that they might study and the boys be
*   free from army service;*
he wanted to lift and spread them as he had been doing, boughs of himself
*   the trunk.*
Now they were going to work and could study only at night,
snipping bits for years, perhaps ten or more, to make their patched
*   learning*
and pooling wages to pay for themselves and him and his wife.

He would have liked to gather them into his arms and feed them learning
as easily as a baby sucks milk from a woman's breast.
He could only offer to carry them food from the kitchen
or run downstairs to the grocer's for pickles or a bottle of ketchup,

something to make life pleasanter, tastier;
to try to stick hairs in the stiff hide of life and make it a fur to wrap
    them snug.

If only his business were not a flower-pot into which he had spilled
    his money
day by day carefully and now was spilling borrowings,
and nothing came up from the black earth.

His friends had told him that knowing silk and not knowing the
    land's speech,
he should buy a few pieces of silk from a mill-agent or jobber
and job among stores on the East Side.

Thirty years clerk in a store where business was done leisurely,
discussed over glasses of tea in a back-office,
and now to walk the streets and meet men hasty and abrupt.
Without rooms that keep out the waves of wind,
many days toes and fingers sore with cold
between tenements and barrels heaped with ashes or garbage.

Once he had gone beyond the known streets,
no Jewish signs nor were the houses as tall,
another poverty drizzled upon them.
Three young men were loafing in front of an empty store.
They smiled as he passed. Something pasty struck his cheek.
He looked at what had fallen off wet and blackened by gutter-water.
He looked back at the laughing three, one was ready to throw something
    else.

He would never do well. The stores bought directly from places he bought
    at and as cheaply,
those who had no credit with others he could not trust.
He had made sales to stores whose owner's credit
was not bad but not above worry, sales at a trifling profit,
perhaps more than average, but he would have to sell much more than
    he did.

Younger relatives now excused themselves after a few words
and hurried into the noise of their shops to some matter of their own.
Men who sold him goods were vexed at his small purchases.

The day was the first warm day of spring.
The sunlight fell in large living oblongs on the wooden floor;
he opened a window, the air blew in warm and fragrant
as if a gardener were mowing grass below.

But this sunlight showed where his shoes' leather had cracked and gaped,
his faded trousers, the bottoms frayed with walking,
showed his clothes like a symbol of himself.

He had no money. Borrow again?
Not from his kin and his children had such need of theirs.

*In winter when rain drummed on stone and glass marches at night and
     sullen war*
or when the streets were heaped with snow turning black
his own music was sung and his own despair imaged.

*But now in spring he was forgotten easily like the thought of somebody
     else's sorrow.*
The flagged yards and the fire-escapes were glinting with sunlight
*and the tall fences dirtied by rain with their rows of nails on top,
     bleeding rust.*
*Women were opening windows and shaking clothes joyously into
     the yards,*
*his own wife had gone to the grocer or butcher, his children were at work
     or school,*
only he was useless like an old pot left in the kitchen for a while.

He pulled down the window-shade and laid himself near the stove.
He liked the floor's hardness.
*The pour of gas sickened him, he was half-minded to pull the rubber tube
     out of his mouth,*
but he felt weak and dizzy, too weak to move his hand.

11. 1920: Line 1: *by the top-floor window*
           Line 2: *and looked over the tenement into the sky*
           Line 3: *where the new moon was like a girl alone on a roof thinking.*
           Line 5: *tears at the sore within her*
           Line 6: *smile, her eyes clear.*
           Line 7: stanza break precedes Line 7a: *She who once slim and gentle
           would soon be clumsy, talking harshly.*
           Line 8: printed as a separate stanza.

     1927: As 1962 but retains the extra stanza of lines 7 and 7a.
           Line 7a: *she who, slim and gentle once, would soon become clumsy, talking
           harshly.*

12. 1920: Line 1: *pitch-dark. The gas had been turned off by the company.* Stanza
           break follows.
           Line 1a: *A candle-light before him, hot wax dripping over his fingers,*
           Line 2: *his old room*
           Line 2a: *his sister removing the furniture had emptied desk and bookcase
           in a heap.*
           Line 3: *through books and papers.*
           Line 7: *ought to have known the*
           Line 9: *died down.*
           Line 10: *the white paper into*
           Line 11a: *There was no need to read them first, he knew the contents word
           by word.*
           Line 14: *for an instant before*

Line 15: *sick with its one window opening on the parlour.*
Line 16a: *He walked into his den again. The white box?*
Line 17: *gauze. Moths flew out like dust.*

13. 1920: Line 1: *From her bed she . . . the snow-flakes crossing*
Line 9a: *over the plains*
Line 10: *between fields*

15. 1920: Line 1: *The slender tree stands alone*
Line 2: two lines, as follows: *between the roofs of the far town / and the wood far away like a low hill.*
Line 3: *In the vast open*

16. 1920: No title. Text as follows:

The city breaks in houses to the sea, uneasy with waves,
and the lonely sun clashes like brass cymbals.
In the streets truck-horses, muscles sliding under the steaming hides,
pound the sparks flying about their hoofs;
and fires, those gorgeous beasts, squirm in the furnaces
under the looms weaving us.

At evening by cellars cold with air of rivers at night,
we, whose lives are only a few words,
watch the young moon leaning over the baby at her breast
and the stars small to our littleness.

21. 1920: Line 1: *again low words*
Lines 2a–2b: an additional stanza:

The rays of the orderly street-lamps, drops of light in the darkness,
keep pointing to us.

22. 1920: Line 2a: *and sat around, dark spaces about a sun.*
Line 5: *Within and about*

23. 1920: Two separate poems, as follows:

[12]

Hour after hour in easy-chairs on the porch rocking,
hearing the wind in shade trees along the street
and looking into the yard's green growth.

At times a storm comes up and the dust is blown in long curves along
*   the street,*
over the carts driven slowly, drivers and horses nodding.

Afterwards the still clouds; children too young to be at school come out
*   to play*
with little shrill voices.

Thoughts are taken up and put aside, nothing cut into, nothing is done,
but pleasant meetings of friend with friend, short walks,
daily food and the long sleep at nights.

[13]

Years are thrown away as if I were immortal,
by day selling and looking pleasant
and the nights spent in talking
shining words, sometimes, like fireflies in the darkness,
lighting and going out and after all no light.

I think at times of some of the plans I had.

24. 1920: Line 1: *street with head*

25. 1920: No title and an additional line, as follows:

   Trees shrugging their shoulders in the wind and the ceaseless weaving of
   the uneven water.

26. 1920: No title but printed as the third of three poems under the collective
   title *"Nightmares."* (For the other two, see the "Omitted Poems" that
   follow.) Text as follows:

   The street is white and cold under the huge moon,
   the trees' shadows lie in black pools on the lawns.

27. 1920: No title. Text as follows:

   Trees standing far off in winter
   against a polished blue sky
   with boughs blown about like brown hair;

   the stiff lines of the twigs
   blurred by the April buds;

   or branches crowded with leaves
   and a wind turning
   their dark green light.

28. 1920: Line 1: *moon's rim and*

30. 1920: Order of stanzas reversed.

   Omitted Poems

   1920: [18]

   On the shaken water
   of the shining sea

we lay like seaweed
carelessly.

Afterwards running
with outstretched hands
we chase each other
across the sands.

1920: [19]

I look at her through spectacles
and remember women
whom I saw for a while
walking on and away.

1920: [23]

Steam-shovel, in the hollow where yard and poplars were,
going home we would look at the rows of poplars.

1920: [26]

She woke at a child crying
and turned to the empty cradle,
forgetting.

1920: [30]

Under the heavens furrowed with clouds
a man behind his stumbling plough.

1920: [32]

The rain fell and stopped but the clouds stayed
over the warehouses lonely at night.

A man in the street mumbling to himself,
screeched.
Then walked on mumbling to himself
between the warehouses.

1920: [33] and [34]

NIGHTMARES

I

The elevated railroad made the street darker than others
and it had no stores.

Walking there after midnight I saw an old man coming.

We passed and I walked a long way and suddenly turned,
he stood where I had left him, looking after me.

I turned a corner and hid in a doorway, waiting to see if he would follow.
I waited long and then I saw his deformed shadow coming slowly.

I felt for the door-knob. The door was locked.
I bit my clenched fingers to keep from screaming.

    II

Up a street that a railway overhead made a tunnel
he pushed through the shuffling men to a lame beggar with a girl
      of twelve
and hit the beggar's back. The girl stared, the men shuffled by.

The beggar and the girl hurried on; with a long step, laughing, he was
      up to them
and kept hitting the turning beggar.

Her hair fell over the girl's face and she stuck her chin out trying to drag
      the beggar away
and the beggar kept raising his hands, head turning, twisting feet and
      body along
in a knot which is being unravelled,
questioning the face of the laughing man
and the incurious faces of the men shuffling by.

Seeing an ice-cream cart he called the girl away from the beggar.
She gorged on a bar of frozen rainbow
and he placed the pennies on the wet top of the cart, laughing.

Uriel Acosta: A Play & A Fourth Group of Verse was published by the author in New York in 1921. More than half of the book consisted of the verse play *Uriel Acosta*; the rest consisted of new poems, the first twenty-four of them unnumbered and the remaining twenty-seven numbered under the collective title "Jews." For *Five Groups of Verse* (1927) Reznikoff rearranged the order (though leaving the "Jews" sequence largely intact), dropped two poems, and revised all but three of the others. The present text follows that of *Five Groups of Verse*.

Order of Poems

The following tables show how the order of the poems in *Uriel Acosta & A Fourth Group of Verse* was changed in *Five Groups of Verse* (1927). An asterisk indicates a revised text.

1921	1927	1927	1921
1	19*	1*	4
2	40*	2*	5
3	47*	3*	6
4	1*	4*	9
5	2*	5*	10
6	3*	6	12
7	—	7*	8
8	7*	8	16
9	4*	9*	15
10	5*	10*	19
11	—	11*	13 & 14
12	6	12*	17
13	11*	13*	18
14		14*	20
15 }	9*	15*	21
16 }	8	16*	23
17	12*	17*	22
18	13*	18*	24
19	10*	19*	1
20	14*	20*	25
21	15*	21*	26
22	17*	22*	27
23	16*	23*	28

1921	1927	1927	1921
24	18*	25*	29
25	20*	25*	30
26	21*	26*	31
27	22*	27*	32
28	23*	28*	33
29	24*	29*	34
30	25*	30*	35
31	26*	31*	36
32	27*	32*	37
33	28*	33*	38
34	29*	34*	39
35	30*	35*	40
36	31*	36*	41
37	32*	37*	42
38	33*	38	43
39	34*	39*	44
40	35*	40*	2
41	36*	41*	45
42	37*	42*	46
43	38	43*	47
44	39*	44*	48
45	41*	45*	49
46	42*	46*	50
47	43*	47*	3
48	44*	48*	51
49	45*	–	7
50	46*	–	11
51	48*		

Textual Variants

1. 1921: Title: *"Sunday Walks"*
Line 1: *Over stones* line break after *dust*; remainder printed as new line.
Line 2: printed as two lines with break after *gloom,*
Line 3: *slime. Beyond, thickets of*
Line 4: *tree stretched up, dead.*
Line 5: *A dead duck lay, head*
Line 6: *tide was out . . . pool lay on the*
Line 7: *Someone had thrown*
Line 8: *of tin cans rusted;*
Line 9: *rust, crept in*
Line 10: *clouds showed like*

2. 1921: Line 3: *as finger knuckles, seated upon the*
   Line 9: *away so many*

3. 1921: No title.
   Line 4: *fish mouldy*

4. 1921: Line 1: *Under grey cloud*
   Line 3: *their shadows of smoke*

5. 1921: No title.
   Line 1: *Between factory chimneys grease*
   Line 2: *In the drizzle tugs drag their guts of smoke.*

7. 1921: Line 8: *white tops of*
   Line 9: *into whiffs of spray*
   Line 17: *were towns*
   Line 23: *flew in the wind over the lake.*

9. 1921: Before line 1 a deleted line: *In the restaurant panelled with mirrors, the old woman faces her daughter.*

10. 1921: Line 1: *and the knights*
    Line 2: line break after *open,*
    Line 2a: *pulling their guts*

11(I). 1921: Line 1: *night." "Good night." Another day gone.*
    Line 4: *about? Then supper and chat, chat.*

11(II). 1921: Line 2: *Why am I taking trouble to please him? I talk. I turn*

12. 1921: Line 1: *than wind*

13. 1921: Line 1: *In spring sparrows*
    Stanza break after line 1.

14. 1921: Line 1: *trees stand in*

15. 1921: Line 2: *Here on the . . . girl rakes the fallen leaves*

16. 1921: Deleted first line: *Do you remember that summer when we were in the country*
    Line 1: *and we*
    Line 2: *beyond?*
    Line 3: printed as continuation of line 2.
    Line 5: *yellow daisies and golden-rod*
    Line 6a: *and we walked about in the blaze over our heads and hands.*

17. 1921: Line 1: *dinner on Sunday afternoon we*
    Line 2: *into the . . . the marsh along the bay*
    Line 3: *blue cloudless sky*
    Line 4: *would watch the base-ball players; in the noisy,*

Line 5: *Afterwards, in the evening, glad and at ease, we walked back to the city, stretching out rows*
Line 6: *lamp after lamp lighting as the . . . way, or women*

18. 1921: Line 1: *I woke. Swiftly*
Line 4: *Hidden from me in*

19. 1921: Text as follows:

> *He showed me the album. "But this?" I asked.*
> *I knew his sister, her face somewhat the picture's but none of that delicacy.*
> *"My mother before her marriage." Coming in, I had met*
> *a round-shouldered woman with a shrivelled face.*
> *His father at the table with friends still out-shouted the wheels,*
> *though the day's work was done and the shop closed until morning.*
> *Afterwards I left and went through their candy store with one show-case*
> *of candy,*
> *in little heaps in little saucers, ever so many for a penny.*
> *A single gas-jet flared in the empty store. They kept no lights in the*
> *window. I stepped into the night.*

20–48. Twenty-seven of the twenty-nine poems that follow were numbered and printed in 1921 under the collective title "Jews." The exceptions are numbers 40 and 47 below.

20. 1921: Line 1: *before supper.*
Line 2: *the curtains.*
Line 3: *It had been snowing, the street under the black sky was bluish white.*
Line 6: combined with line 5 as *The boys were after him.*
Line 7a: *The room was cold. They put ashes on the fire before going to bed.*
Line 11: *He stopped, standing knee-deep*
Line 14: *snow. Houses and streets were still.*

21. 1921: The following stanza precedes line 1:

> *His grandfather was a wisp of a man with a little beard.*
> *He led grandfather home through Seventh Street Park.*
> *A knot of men were larking with a girl. They pushed a man into*
> *grandfather.*
> *He fell and rolled, covered with dust, to the railing.*

Line 2: *Only on holy days he went out of the house to synagogue.*
Line 4: *happened, only on* No stanza break between lines 5 and 6.
Line 6: *Kippur his uncle*
Line 6a: *And the boy stayed home, relieved.*
Stanza break between lines 6a and 7.

22. 1921: Lines 3–4: printed as one line.
Lines 9–10: printed as one line.
Line 11: *In March*

Line 13: *large and color*
Line 16: *tree was still and the branches, only the end twigs moved a little.*
Line 17: *thought, "Trees are symmetrical—and whatever grows and lives*
—in shape—and in change during the years.
Line 17a: *So my own life is symmetrical and the lives of men."*
Lines 18–19: printed as one line.

23. 1921: Line 3: *Under bushes*
Line 4: *lakes and air,*
Lines 3–4: printed as one line.
Line 5: *on the earth.*
Line 6: *and there spread, and there holes, globules hanging in disorder. He*
thought, "The symmetry in growth and life on earth, our sense of order,
Line 7: *Is uncontrolling in the universe of these wheels."*

24. 1921: Line 1: *and children to make a home.*
Line 3: *teach him for an hour, night after night.*
Stanza break after line 3.
Lines 6–7 *printed as one line.*
Stanza break after line 8.
Line 12: *High school would*
Stanza break after line 17.
Line 19: *throat, with his*
Line 21: *back the chair*
Stanza break after line 22.
Line 22a: *She came back late. She asked the women on the stoop if her*
mother was home.
Line 22b: *Where have you been?" "In the library, Ma." She told her*
mother nothing.

25. 1921: Line 1: *From where he lay in the sun the trees*
Line 2: *a dull white*
Lines 6–7: printed as one line.
Line 7a: *She came, almost skipping, over the turf; and went her way and*
was gone.

26. 1921: Lines 6ff: two stanzas, as follows:

He might go to her house at last. They were all up, preparing breakfast.
The smell of coffee filled the screened porch.
Her glance bid him welcome. She always spoke little and then low.
Such restraint was in her speech
and in the curving of her body and hands
as she went about her tasks.

The sunlight edged a way upon the porch
and when she walked through it, her yellow hair and the white flesh of
her hands shone.

27. 1921: Line 2: *his paper sliced . . . table in back*   .
Stanza breaks after lines 2, 5, and 7.
Line 9: *knew she*

28. 1921: Line 1: *mother, almost a dwarf, stepped*
Line 2: *stopped to a*
Stanza break after line 2.
Line 4: *houses were set*
Line 5: *take skates*
Line 10: *Webber's coat. Webber*
Stanza break after line 10.
Line 18: *ask fellas about*
Stanza break after line 18.
Line 25: line break after *test?* Remainder combined with line 26.
Stanza break after line 28.
Line 31: *go walking.*

29. 1921: Line 1: *closing, windows*
Line 2: *At last, only a light left here and there of other book-keepers still working.*
Lines 3a–3c:

> *He could see his father seating himself upon the window-sill and*
>   *jumping off.*
> *They found his body on the flags of the yard behind the tenement in*
>   *which they lived.*
> *Since he had been unable to find work and keep at least himself,*
> *his note read, he did not want to be a burden to his wife and son.*

Stanza break after line 3c.
Line 4: *He had worked enough for that night. He went*
Line 5: *about a chasm. Suppose he*
Line 6: *Who was to . . . down, head first?*
Lines 6a–6b:

> *But the shop windows had been left open. He slowly went to the first*
>   *window with his back toward it.*
> *He must think just of going downstairs and not think beyond the bannister.*

30. 1921: Line 1: *She entered high school and found charm in Latin and*
Line 5: *student in one*
Line 6: *reading evenings, but*
Line 7: *books he knew* Line break after *living.* Remainder combined with line 8.
Line 8: *you'll be old*
Line 9a: *When her daughter was born, she began to plan for her education.*

31. 1921: Line 1: *The boy next . . . and sit listening*
Line 3: *evening she spoke*
Line 7: *father would speak kindly*
Line 8: *began asking for*
Line 11: *taken this notion*
Line 13: *When they were out walking, Gabriel*
Line 17: *saved fifty dollars from*
Line 18: *cotton jobbers and*

Line 20: *as if blown up.*
Line 22: *reached his father's home*

32. 1921: Lines 1–1a:

> He came home late that night and was afraid to go through the grocery store,
> where his father was still talking to customers. He went through the tenement hallway into the room, back of the store, where they ate and slept.

Line 3: *stood looking up at him*
Line 6: *basement store. It*
Line 9: *around to neighbors.*
Lines 11–12: printed as one line: "*Well.*" "*But I hear from relatives you're trying to borrow money?*" "*Yes.*" *His father paused. "I hope you get it.*"

33. 1921: Line 1: *He remembered how passing the shop after high school, he had looked up at the sign and gone on, glad*
Line 2: *saw his parents' hair grey and heard*
Line 5: *into; but I have always let you have your own way.*"
No stanza break after line 5.
Line 6: *went selling . . . read* Arrival

34. 1921: Line 2: *through public school*
Line 3: *father engaged her to his . . . face, was short and a little fat.*
Line 4: *hates me, he hates me!*"
Line 4a: *The marriage was elaborate. Her father was well-to-do and she was the only daughter.*
Line 5: *bought her husband a*
Lines 5–6: printed as one line: *bought her husband a . . . had saved up money.*
Line 7: *buy at once, he*
Line 8: *men's smell when . . . ditching. He cheated*
Line 10: *refused him money. He came home.*
Line 11: *The two older*

35. 1921: Line 1: *came to his . . . clouds bunk together.*"
Line 2: *He recited at parties when he was older well-known rants. They*
Line 3: *he made the acquaintance of . . . lawyer. There were rumors of partnerships.*
Line 6: *work, behind a counter, among*
Line 8: *but now he*
Line 9: line break after *making.*

36. 1921: Line 1: *Walking was too slow, he ran softly on the balls of his feet. In a*
Stanza break after line 2.
Line 3: *was sitting up*
Stanza break after line 4.
Line 5: *He sat moodily. He thought*

Line 6: *He thought of noting*
Line 7: *her eyes to-night.*

37. 1921: Line 1: printed as two lines: *man / and on*
Line 3: *Once she saw his mouth jerk, and*
Line 5: *but said nothing.*
Line 7: *awake at night*
Line 8: *Next morning she went down to his store but it*
Line 9: printed as two lines: *searched. / For*
Line 10: *prosperous and he had left it, bank . . . all, untouched.*
Line 12: printed as two lines: *city. / One*
Line 13: printed as two lines: *children. / She*

39. 1921: Line 5: first sentence printed with line 4: *not help laughing. / Sure*
Line 6: *he roomed and boarded in the home of a . . . had kept herself through high school, giving lessons, and was now in*
Line 8: *arm to cure. He sat silently*
Stanza deleted, lines 9a–9c:

The doctor warned him not to go back to work as a smith.
He tried to learn how to make wire-frames in a cousin's shop,
but his fingers were stiff.

Lines 11–12: line break after *discovered him / and searched for . . . cores in the gutter to throw . . . they walked past, as if intent*
Lines 13a–13b:

Finally, he would just walk through the street once or twice of an evening.
*   Once he thought he saw her. His heart bounded as if struck.*
He stood still to steady himself; but the girl, coming nearer, he saw it was not she.

40. 1921: Line 1: *mother came and sat beside him. "What are you reading? Read*
Line 2: *"But you . . . Ma. What's the use?" "Read me a little. What do you care?"*
Line 6: *He read to her and she listened*
Line 7: *sheets she*
Line 8: *And from*

41. 1921: Line 3: *had been scrimping from day to day all*
Line 4: *When his uncle died, he left*
Line 6: *but within a year he*

42. 1921: Line 3: *near the railroad tracks and the*
Stanza break after line 3.
Line 4: *father had been sick for years; but he was . . . merchandise."*
Line 5: *of. He gave up his studies and taught in a school on the East Side.*
Line 6: *three, and others . . . most came*
Line 8: *and evening, daily; Sunday he slept all morning and afterwards took a walk.*
No stanza break after line 8.

Line 10: *forty. It had been book and books when a boy, he had to win prizes and a scholarship to keep going. And now so many years in the school.*
Line 11: *whom he would care to*
Line 12: *up his work to what else . . . turn? He felt afraid to break the routine which he had grown used to.*

43. 1921: Line 3: *There's a Chinese restaurant upstairs. Water came through the ceiling and damaged silk. The water*
Line 4: *kinds of engineers; they*

44. 1921: Text as follows:

> *Her daughters were well married; their husbands earned enough and*
> *   more each year. Both could afford maids; she always found their*
> *   children clean and happy.*
> *Her husband's business was good and they had as much as two elderly*
> *   people needed. They went to theatre oftener than they used to. She*
> *   was planning to buy new furniture.*
>
> *Her younger daughter died in childbirth. Her son-in-law married again.*
> *   Coming to see the children, she could not help crying for her dead*
> *   daughter.*
> *Her son-in-law had to ask her not to call.*
>
> *Now when she woke it was broad day. Her husband had gone to the store*
> *   long before.*
> *She wrapped her head and shoulders in a shawl, knitting her thoughts.*
> *She got up at last and poured herself some brandy. The room was cold.*
> *When she went out she took a brandy flask in her bag to nip in lavatories.*
> *Her older daughter's husband forbade her the house. She was noisy about*
> *   her dead daughter when drunk. And there were the children and the*
> *   neighbors.*
>
> *Her older daughter died in childbirth.*
> *Her son-in-law married again. The new wife took the older children from*
> *   school and sent them to work.*
> *They became coarse, their house was full of quarrelling.*
>
> *Their grandmother was now in an asylum. Her husband came to see her.*
> *   Once he saw the lunatic children playing in the yard.*
> *"Why do you cry?" she asked. He pointed. "You cry for them but not for*
> *   me."*
> *Afterwards she told her husband, "I am sharpening a knife to kill my*
> *   grandchildren; but not you, you must pay for my board here."*

45. 1921: Line 2: *Once the stores were burned*
Line 4: *sign on his*
Line 7: *do with Mendel?" . . . Siberia." "Do you think it would be right for me to place a Jew*
Line 9: *grandchildren took them into the streets to sell.*
Lines 10–11: printed as one line: *money. His son, the*

46. 1921: Text as follows:

> His daughter belonged to a club. The club studied modern literature and
>   met, once a month, in each other's house.
> When his daughter's turn came she told him that the club would come.
>   That evening they were to discuss Maeterlinck; but the old man
>   thought that they were coming to meet him.
> They were seated at last in the parlor. Embarrassed, she asked them not
>   to begin; her father wanted to speak to them.
> The members whispered to each other, "Who is her father?"
> "I thank you, young men and women," he said, "for the honor of your
>   visit. I suppose you would like to hear me recite some of my poems."
>   He began to chant.

47. 1921: No title.
Line 1: *The neighbors*
Line 2: *because her figure was*
Line 2a: *and, it was said, her husband had been a shoemaker before
becoming a doctor.*
Line 4: *newcomers*
Line 5: *afterwards, and these to others, and*
Line 10: *conductor came and raised*
Line 15: *became so hot*
Line 16: *station. The*
Line 18: *drink, ah good! If*

48. 1921: Line 1: *beside the bench*
Line 3: *begin. Though it was early the sunny . . . walked near the houses.*
Line 4: *finish and then he*
Stanza break after line 4.
Line 5: *with a black*
Stanza break after line 6.
Line 9: *work at the*

Omitted Poems

1921: [7]

OFFICE HELP

Morning after morning the sun shone.

*She kept making her entries
until the street
filled with twilight.*

1921: [11]

*In the even curves of gutters and even curves of gutters
the irregular slope of the park's barren hill.*

Five Groups of Verse was published by the author in 1927 from 5 West Fourth Street, New York, and dedicated "to Albert Lewin in token of his help." The colophon reads: "I set the type by hand and did the press work. 375 copies were printed and the type distributed; this is Number _____. C. R." In addition to the revised versions of the poems from the four earlier books of verse, the collection contained a fifth group of twenty numbered poems. These are printed here, with one revision made for *By the Waters of Manhattan: Selected Verse* (1962).

Textual Variant

20. 1927: between stanzas 2 and 3 the following stanza omitted in 1962:

> *The altar blazes. I bring*
> *my thoughts to heap upon it.*
> *The smoke of my breath*
> *is an offering.*

ISRAEL AND KING DAVID

In 1929 Reznikoff published what was intended to be the first of an annual series, though it had no successor. *By the Waters of Manhattan: An Annual* consisted of autobiographical short stories (later revised as part of *By the Waters of Manhattan*, a novel [1930]), family memoirs in prose (later revised as part of *Family Chronicle* [1963]) and, under the heading "Editing and Glosses," two verse narratives based on Old Testament sources. The present texts of the latter, "Israel" and "King David," are those of the first edition.

Jerusalem the Golden was published by the Objectivist Press, 10 West Thirty-sixth Street, New York, in 1934. The Press consisted of Reznikoff, George Oppen, and Louis Zukofsky. It was an outgrowth of Zukofsky's editorial work for the "Objectivist" number of *Poetry* (February 1931) and for his book *An "Objectivist" Anthology*, published in France in 1932 by George and Mary Oppen under the imprint "To Publishers." The Press's mission statement, written by Reznikoff and printed on the back panel of *Jerusalem*'s dust wrapper, reads:

> The Objectivist Press is an organization of writers who are publishing their own work and that of other writers whose work they think ought to be read.

The wrapper also lists an Advisory Board consisting of Ezra Pound and William Carlos Williams, with Zukofsky as "Sec'y." Already in 1934 the Press had published Williams's *Collected Poems*, with a preface by Wallace Stevens, Oppen's *Discrete Series*, with a foreword by Pound, and Reznikoff's prose work *Testimony*, with an introduction by Kenneth Burke.

Jerusalem the Golden bears the following dedication and epigraph:

To Marie

Sunt bona, sunt quaedam mediocra, sunt mala plura
Quae legis hic: aliter non fit, Avite, liber.
(Martial, Lib. I:XVI)

(Loosely translated, Martial's Latin reads: "Some of what you read here is good, some is mediocre, but most is bad: a book, Avitus, cannot be made any other way.") The acknowledgment thanks "the editors of *Contempo*, *Pagany*, *Poetry*, and *The Menorah Journal* for permission to reprint whatever they have used." The present text is that of the first edition, with a few revisions made for *By the Waters of Manhattan* (1962).

Textual Variants

3. 1934: Line 8: *look longingly at moon*

8. 1934: Poem opens with the following stanza:

> *This morning the dawn*
> *did not redden the white wooden frame of the window;*
> *the rain drops hang in a row*
> *from the rail of the fire-escape.*

22. 1934: Poem ends with following three lines:

> *In front of the pigeon house the white pigeons*
> *are preening themselves; in the yard*
> *white chickens with bright red combs bustle about.*

28. 1934: Title: *"Idyll"*

46. 1934: Poem opens with the following stanza:

> *The squads, platoons, and regiments*
> *of lighted windows,*
> *ephemeral under the evening star-*

Line 1: *feast*

70. 1934: Poem opens with the following stanza:

> *The green water of the lake brimming over*
> *in silence,*
> *quietly in motion.*

In Memoriam: 1933

Like *Jerusalem the Golden*, *In Memoriam: 1933* was published by the Objectivist Press in 1934. The contents were reprinted from the Fall 1934 issue of *The Menorah Journal*. Most of the last poem and three brief extracts from the others were reprinted in *By the Waters of Manhattan: Selected Verse* (1962), with the speakers' names omitted. The present text follows the first edition, corrected at a couple of points from the 1962 printing.

Textual Variants

7. 1934:   Paragraph 2, line 7: *leaders of the phalanx, of legions*
            Line 8: *masters of chariots, of the long*

Separate Way

Separate Way was published by the Objectivist Press in 1936. Acknowledgment was made to "the editors of *Jewish Frontier* and *The Menorah Journal* for permission to reprint whatever they have used." The poems were titled but not numbered consecutively, as they are here following the example of the selections printed in *By the Waters of Manhattan* (1962), which also made a few other small revisions.

Textual Variants

1. 1934:   Part IV, line 1: *How pleasant is the wind, or the sun.*
            Line 1a: *to those behind windows;*
            Line 2: *and the silence*

2. 1934:   Title: *"Malicious Women Greet You"*

3. 1934:   Title: *"Insignificance"*

    1962:   Part II not reprinted.

8. 1962:   Stanzas 4 and 5 not reprinted.

Going To and Fro and Walking Up and Down was published by the author in New York in 1941. It was dedicated "to the memory of Sarah Yetta Reznikoff, my mother, who was born in what was then the city of Elizavetgrad, Russia, the daughter of Ezekiel and Hannah Wolvovsky, and who died in New York City, sixty-eight years of age, February 12, 1937."

The five poem-sequences, unnumbered in the original edition, are here assigned arabic numerals for ease of reference in the Notes. In *By the Waters of Manhattan: Selected Poems* (1962), the author reprinted seventeen of the thirty-five poems of "Autobiography: New York," but omitted the sequence title and numbered the selections consecutively with the others from the book. Choosing from "Autobiography: Hollywood," however, he retained the sequence title and numbered the poems as subsections, as was done in the first edition. I have here followed the style of the first edition for both sequences. A few other small revisions were made in preparing the 1962 selection and have been incorporated here.

Textual Variants

1 (V).1941: Stanza 2 ends *tell of it;* and continues with these lines deleted in 1962:

> *and he whipped the people with whips,*
> *as his son boasted,*
> *until they were ready to cry out, To your tents, Israel!*
> *What share have we in Judah*
> *or the house of Jesse?*

2 (VI). 1941: Title: *"Parkway in Winter"*

2 (X). 1941: Line 3: *in the list of captains* ("David's" added by the author in preparation for the 1962 selection, but the poem was not included there.)

2 (XIII). 1941: Title: *"The Taoist"*

2 (XVIII). 1941: Line 3: *must be an*
Lines 4 and 5 printed as one line, with additional word: *but, look! on this wall quite a primitive drawing.*

3 (I). 1962: prints the second two stanzas only.

3 (XII and XIII). 1941: printed with additional lines as one poem, as follows:

Rainy Season

It has been raining for three days.
The faces of the giants
on the bill-boards
still smile,
but the gilt has been washed from the sky:
we see the iron world.

The gutters are gurgling and the water is over the curbs,
lapping the pavement, even the walls; the gulls are flying—
flying to the dark mountains before another storm.
The cormorants are leaving
the ridges of the sea—
the cold wind and black fog and the noise of the sea.

28. 1934: Title: *"Idyll"*

3 (XXVI). The last four lines appear as a separate untitled poem in 1962.

4. 1941: Footnote: *"The Sinking," "The Job," and "The Immigrants" are based on cases in the law reports.*

4 (I). 1941: Title: *"The Sinking"*

4 (II). 1941: Title: *"The Job"*

4 (III). 1941: Title: *"The Immigrants"*

4 (IV). 1941: erroneously numbered III.

5. 1941: Footnote: *A portion of the daily ritual of the synagogue, specially recited by orphan mourners. Oxford Dict.*

5 (VII and VIII). 1941: printed as one poem: *silenced—* / *my*

Inscriptions: 1944–1956 was published by the author in New York in 1959 and dedicated "with love to Marie." The acknowledgment reads, "I am indebted to the editors of *Commentary, Jewish Frontier, The Menorah Journal,* and *Midstream* for permission to reprint the verse they published. —C.R."

Reznikoff reprinted all but five poems and two sections in *By the Waters of Manhattan: Selected Verse* (1962). (The poems omitted are those here numbered 6, 13(III), 27, 29, 46(III), 52, and 53.) Even so soon after first publication he revised extensively. The present text follows the 1962 versions, with details of the changes given below.

In the first edition the poems were arranged in seven untitled groups, numbered within groups. Here, following the example of the nearly complete 1962 selection, they have been renumbered consecutively.

Order of Poems

In the first edition of *Inscriptions: 1944–1956,* the poems were arranged in untitled groups, each group headed with a roman numeral. Here, as in the 1962 selection, they have been renumbered consecutively. The following table shows the original groupings.

$$I = 1$$
$$II, 1–11 = 2–12$$
$$III, 1 – 3 = 13–15$$
$$IV, 1 – 7 = 16–22$$
$$V, 1–18 = 23–40$$
$$VI, 1 – 7 = 41–47$$
$$VII, 1 – 6 = 48–53$$

Textual Variants

8. 1959: Line 2: *with the useless slag*

14. 1959: Additional stanza following stanza two:

> *The bitterness of parting and the honey of your kiss;*
> *would that, after my death, I could still hear*
> *the sound of the golden bells upon your skirts!*

15. 1959: Poem unnumbered.
    Line 5: *came to cry*
    Line 13: *the angel cried*
    Line 60 (seventh line of last stanza): stanza break, and last stanza beginning with the following lines:

"Though seed and ship and food are lost
earth and sea and dish remain;
but the story of Israel is not so:
we who received the Law perish,
and Your Law remains—in all its glory.

"If the farmer's seed does not receive God's rain will it live?
Forgive the sins of Your people and remember those who served You;
do not regard the foolishness of the ungodly,
but rather those who in spite of tortures kept Your covenant;
do not think of those who have done evil,
but rather of those who acknowledged their awe of You;
and do not will to destroy those who were like cattle,
but look at those who stood in the splendor of Your Law;
and be not angry at those who behaved like beasts,
but love those who have always had faith in Your righteousness.

16. 1959: Between the last two stanzas the following stanza:

Today this creditor is at your office;
tomorrow this one in your home;
until the final creditor of all
places his bony hands upon your breast.
Faster!
Dig your heels into the dust!

Final stanza as follows:

How good to stop
and look out upon eternity a while.
And daily—at Shahris, Minha, Maariv,
in the morning, afternoon, and evening—
be at ease in Zion.

32. A holograph revision in the author's working copy deleted the title of this poem and inserted "Saint" as the speaker of stanza one and "Bird" as the speaker of stanza two. This revision was subsequently canceled.

39. 1959: Line 3: *make my way home alone* (Deleting "home" in his working copy, the author noted in the margin, "printer's error. C.R.")

46. 1959: Title: *"Notes on the Jewish Holidays"*

By the Well of Living and Seeing & The Fifth Book of the Maccabees was published by the author in New York in 1969 as a paperbound book in an edition of 200 copies. It is dedicated "to the memory of ALBERT LEWIN (d. 1968)," and in the author's working copy, with corrections in his hand, Reznikoff has added the words "in gratitude."

The poems in "By the Well of Living and Seeing" (as distinct from the accompanying work, "The Fifth Book of the Maccabees") are in three groups or sequences, the first two untitled and comprising thirty-five and thirty-three poems respectively, the third titled "Early History of a Writer" and comprising twenty poems. The first group was revised in 1973 and expanded to fifty-three poems; this revision was first published in *By the Well of Living and Seeing: New and Selected Poems 1918–1973* (1974). The present text follows the 1974 printing and incorporates changes and corrections made by Reznikoff in his working copy.

Order of Poems

The following table shows how the order of the poems in the first edition was changed when the original sequence of thirty-five was expanded to fifty-three. Asterisk indicates revision.

1969	1973	1973	1969
1	1	1	1
2	2	2	2
3	3	3	3
4	4	4	4
5	5	5	5
6	6*	6*	6
7	13	7	—
8	12	8*	12
9	15	9	—
10	17*	10	—
11	22	11	29
12	8*	12	8
13	16	13	7
14	25	14	—
15	28	15	9
16	32	16	13
17	33	17*	10
18	—	18	—
19	—	19	—

1969	1973	1973	1969
20	34	20	–
21	39	21	–
22	41*	22	11
23	–	23	–
24	42	24	–
25	43	25	14
26	45*	26	–
27	48	27	–
28	–	28	15
29	11	29	–
30	44*	30	–
31	50	31	–
32	45*	32	16
33	49*	33	17
34	51	34	20
35	53	35	–
		36	–
		37	–
		38	–
		39	21
		40	–
		41*	22
		42	24
		43	25
		44*	30
		45*	32 & 26
		4	–
		4	–
		48	27
		49*	33
		50	31
		51	34
		52	–
		53	35

Textual Variants

I (6). 1969: Lines 2–3: *feathers / of the jay; and its*

I (8). 1969: Lines 2–3 combined as one line.
Lines 4–5 combined as one line.

I (17). 1969: Stanza 3, lines 5–6: *glazed; / and I see that it is not a*

I (41). 1969: Title: *"Biblical Lesson"*
Stanza 2, line 3: *from Beth-El by a lion.*

I (44). 1969: Title: *"The Critic"*

I (45). 1969: Stanzas 3 and 4 printed without titles as separate poems.

I (49). 1969: Lines 3–4 combined as one line.

II (3). 1969: Stanza 1, line 2: *Insignificant-looking, rather homely*
Stanza 2, lines 4–5: *post-office, / and I picked*

II (13). 1969: Stanza 1, lines 1–2: *store—/the odds*
Line 3: *Negro was looking*
Line 4: *me said gently*
Line 6: *cup had a*
Line 7: *which was not*
Line 9: *cup covered*
Line 9a: *"This picture is part of a legend," said the Negro.*
Line 10: *if you examine the*
Line 14: *were in a*
Line 15: *I could see him*
Stanza 2, preceding line 1: *When I went out,*
Line 1: *he held the*
Line 2: *and was saying*
Line 14: *he lifted two*
Line 16: *you," said the*
Line 17: *and he added by*
Stanza 3, line 2: *he was building*

II (18). 1969: Line 4: *and gentle face*

II (19). 1969: Line 14: *which means "life."*

III (2). 1969: Between lines 11 and 12 a stanza break.
Line 13: *of such a wonder*

III (6). 1969: Stanza 5, line 7: *promised not to speak.*
Last stanza, line 6: *He said he would-somewhat unwillingly—*
Line 7: *and when we met to go he excused himself,*

III (8). 1969: Stanza 1, line 4: *stiff as a*
Lines 10 and 11: *Jews used to call him, / because*

III (10). 1969: Stanza 5, lines 8–9: *chiefly Irish; / laborers and clerks who . . . houses and flats*
Stanza 8, line 1: *my grandfather's house*

III (17). 1969: Stanza 1, line 8: *song and the sudden*
Line 53: *of a counterfeit /*

III (19). 1969: Line 19: *or artery would burst*

Omitted Poems

1969: [1(18)]

> The two women in the cafeteria seated over their coffee
> a long time; the busboy has taken away the empty cups
> and still they sit there, silent, lost in thought.
> Finally, as they are ready to leave,
> the younger says to the elder: "When I had a husband
> I used to sing and dance; but a 'boy friend'—
> it was poison!" "Yes," says the elder, rising,
> "Don't do it again!" And then she leans over to whisper,
> "Unless he is rich."

1969: [1(19)]

> The petty officer of a ship, ruddy cheeks and casklike chest and belly,
> walking near the waterfront—a man of sixty;
> and next to him, hanging on his arm, a woman of the streets,
> clearly his own age in spite of rouge and lipstick,
> bright colored dress and hat;
> and leaning towards him she asks, "Do you like geraniums?"

1969: [1(23)]

LESSON IN ARCHAEOLOGY

> The writing on clay
> baked in the fire of the palace
> has outlasted
> the writing baked in the sun.

1969: [1(28)]

> "And the Lord sent
> fiery serpents . . ."
> Numbers 21:6

> The prodding of "get me" and "give me"
> and the hiss of "do this!"

"The Fifth Book of the Maccabees" first appeared in *Commentary,* August 1955. It was reprinted in *By the Well of Living and Seeing & The Fifth Book of the Maccabees* (1969). The text has been corrected from the author's working copy.

4.   1969:   Verse stanza 1, line 2: *king and his courtiers*

5.   1969:   Prose paragraph 2, sentence 2: *glimpse of a round*

6.   1969:   Verse stanza 4, line 5: *came the Spanish*
Line 7: indented as though a continuation of line 6.

JEWS IN BABYLONIA

"Jews in Babylonia" first appeared in *Midstream,* August–September 1969. It was reprinted in *By the Well of Living and Seeing: New and Selected Poems 1918–1973* (1974). There were no revisions.

LAST POEMS

This section, which contains unpublished and uncollected poems and fragments found among Charles Reznikoff's papers after his death, first appeared in *Poems 1937–1975: Volume 2 of The Complete Poems of Charles Reznikoff*, published by Black Sparrow Press in 1977. It includes both finished poems, some of which first appeared in magazines, and unrevised texts, in particular a group to which the author had tentatively assigned the title "Just Before the Sun Goes Down."

Sources and Textual Notes

1. From a corrected typescript.

2–4. From a corrected typescript, marked "used *Event* 3 / 1 / '73"; titles of 3 and 4 supplied in holograph. (*Event* is a Canadian magazine.)

6. From a typescript dated April 7, 1973.

7. From Reznikoff's copy of his response to Jonathan Williams's invitation to contribute a poem to a collection planned to celebrate Basil Bunting's seventy-fifth birthday. Reznikoff's accompanying letter is dated August 21, 1974.

8. From a corrected typescript with a title page giving not only "Walking in New York" but also "Rhythms III" as a title, perhaps for a proposed larger group. "Walking in New York" is marked "sent to Malanga"; it appeared in a group of poems edited by Gerard Malanga in *Transatlantic Review* No. 52, Autumn 1975.

9. From a canceled clean typescript, accompanying a corrected typescript-and-holograph draft. The draft bears the titles "Walking To and Fro" (canceled) and "Spring in New York."

10. From a corrected typescript entitled "Additions (1975) unrevised" and carrying in holograph the note "?title 'Just before the sun goes down.'" Three of the poems carry notes for revisions, as follows:

10 (I). Beside line 2: *omit "you say"* (?)
Beside line 5: *(tree)*?

10 (II). Beside line 4: *(high and shaky)*

10 (IV). Above line 4: *(he lives?)*
Above line 7: *(the elderly man has?)*
Above line 8: *he* and *his*

"Obiter Dicta" was first published, under the title "First, there is the need," as *Sparrow* No. 52 (January 1977), one of a series of seventy-two monthly pamphlets issued by Black Sparrow Press from October 1972 through September 1978. My editor's note to that number read, in part: "This [untitled] manuscript was found among the papers of Charles Reznikoff at his death in 1976. It is evidently the text—'something I've written down'—that he reads from briefly at a couple of points in his interview with L. S. Dembo during a visit to the University of Wisconsin in May 1968. (See *Contemporary Literature*, 10:2 [Spring 1969], pp. 193–202)." This interview is now more easily found in *Charles Reznikoff: Man and Poet*, edited by Milton Hindus (Orono, Me.: The National Poetry Foundation & The University of Maine, 1984), pp. 97–107. "Clearly intended for oral delivery, it may have been prepared as a talk"—or as the poet's prefatory comments to a reading from his work—"to be given during that visit. We publish it here as a worthy addition to the small body of comment Reznikoff has left us on his craft."

The third paragraph of this piece is adapted from—or perhaps provided the basis for—the opening stanza of section 17 of the poem "Early History of a Writer," published in 1969 (see pp. 327–328 of the present volume).

When Reznikoff refers to "Bright and Miller," he refers to *The Elements of Versification*, by James Wilson Bright and Raymond Durbin Miller (Boston: Ginn & Co., 1910).

"Landscape with the Fall of Icarus," by William Carlos Williams, was first collected in Williams's *Pictures from Brueghel* (1962). Copyright © 1962 by William Carlos Williams. Reprinted by permission of New Directions Publishing Corporation.

"Musée des Beaux Arts," by W. H. Auden, was first collected in Auden's *Another Time* (1940). Copyright © 1940 by W. H. Auden. Copyright © 1976, 1991 by the Estate of W. H. Auden. Reprinted by permission of Random House, Inc.

Entries in italics refer to poems found complete in the Notes

Born in Dublin, Seamus Cooney was educated in various Christian Brothers schools and earned his B.A. at University College, Dublin. After teaching French at St. Patrick's College, Armagh, he came to the United States to continue his education at Indiana University and at the University of California, Berkeley. While teaching at Loyola University, Los Angeles, he met the publisher John Martin, for whom he would work as house editor of Black Sparrow Press from 1969 to 2003. In addition to overseeing a uniform edition of the works of Charles Reznikoff, Mr. Cooney edited and annotated such Black Sparrow volumes as *Men Without Art*, by Wyndham Lewis, *Notes on "Aaron's Rod,"* by Henry Miller, *John Fante: Selected Letters 1932–1981*, and three collections of letters by Charles Bukowski. Formerly a professor of English at Western Michigan University, he is now a bookseller, doing business online as Celery City Books. He lives with his wife, Chotiros Permpikul, in Portage, Michigan.